Insane Emperors, Sunken Cities, and Earthquake Machines

More Frequently Asked Questions about the Ancient Greeks and Romans

Garrett Ryan

Prometheus Books

Guilford, Connecticut

PB Prometheus Books

An imprint of Globe Pequot, the trade division of
The Rowman & Littlefield Publishing Group, Inc.
4501 Forbes Blvd., Ste. 200
Lanham, MD 20706
www.rowman.com

Distributed by NATIONAL BOOK NETWORK

British Library Cataloguing in Publication Information Available

Library of Congress Cataloging-in-Publication Data

Names: Ryan, Garrett, 1986– author.
Title: Insane emperors, sunken cities, and earthquake machines : more
  frequently asked questions about the ancient Greeks and Romans /
  Garrett Ryan.
Other titles: More frequently asked questions about the ancient Greeks and
  Romans
Description: Lanham, MD : Prometheus, [2023] | Includes bibliographical
  references and index. | Summary: "In a series of short and humorous essays,
  Insane Emperors, Sunken Cities, and Earthquake Machines features more
  answers to questions that ancient historian Garrett Ryan is frequently asked
  in the classroom, in online forums, and on his popular YouTube channel
  Told in Stone"—Provided by publisher.
Identifiers: LCCN 2023005818 (print) | LCCN 2023005819 (ebook) |
  ISBN 9781633888937 (paperback) | ISBN 9781633888944 (epub)
Subjects: LCSH: Civilization, Classical—Miscellanea.
Classification: LCC DE71 .R94 2023 (print) | LCC DE71 (ebook) |
  DDC 938—dc23/eng/20230215
LC record available at https://lccn.loc.gov/2023005818
LC ebook record available at https://lccn.loc.gov/2023005819

Contents

Part III. What Happened?

Part IV. What's Left?

Preface

$\mathcal{L}$ike its predecessor—*Naked Statues, Fat Gladiators, and War Elephants*—this book answers questions about the ancient Greeks and Romans. If you've read *Naked Statues*, the organization of this book will be familiar. If you haven't read *Naked Statues*—and don't worry if you haven't, though I heartily recommend it—the format is simple: a series of short chapters, each answering a question about the classical world.

The topics of those questions range from aspects of daily life (e.g., "Did they drink beer?") to beliefs ("Did they practice Buddhism?"), technologies ("Did they come close to an industrial revolution?"), famous events ("How deadly was the eruption that destroyed Pompeii?"), and modern legacies ("Why are ancient cities buried?").

Whatever the topic, I've done my best to make each answer accessible and concise. As you read, I encourage you to glance at the footnotes, which parade a cavalcade of intriguing facts that didn't quite fit into the main narrative.* All primary sources are cited at the book's end.[1]

---

* For example: despite its unassuming paperback cover, this book has distinguished predecessors. Nineteen centuries ago, Plutarch wrote a treatise called *Roman Questions*, in which he considered (among many other things) why Roman ladies kissed all their relatives on the lips. During the reign of Marcus Aurelius, a Roman scholar produced a book of trivia that began by tackling that eternal question: "How tall was Hercules?" More recently (relatively speaking), the Renaissance humanist Politian composed his *Miscellanea*, two collections of brief but brilliant essays on classical topics.

I

DID THEY?

Did the Ancient Greeks and Romans Wear Swimsuits?

$\mathcal{I}$magine a valley in the hills above Rome, overhung with clouds. Among the mossy stones and fragrant rhododendrons is a pool, fed by trickling springs. Rain speckles the surface. At one end of the pool, an iron grate rusts among the rushes. A slender stream of water slips through. For fifty miles it descends, until the sculpted mortar and rock-bottomed settling pools of the aqueduct give way to labyrinths of lead pipes. Then a gilded ceiling, half-hidden by steam, shimmers into being; and mosaics twinkle on distant walls as the water cascades to the marble pools of the Baths of Caracalla.

With their soaring vaults, gigantic windows,* and dazzling arrays of saunas and pools, the Baths of Caracalla were an imperially sponsored love song to a time-honored bathing culture. Although Homer's heroes had indulged in the occasional hot bath, the first public bathing facilities appeared in Greek cities during the Classical period. Most of these early baths consisted of little more than a room with rows of tubs in which bathers could sit as attendants poured water over them. Roman baths were more ambitious. Almost from the beginning, they featured suites of hot, warm, and cold rooms, centered on communal pools and warmed by furnaces that funneled

---

* The caldarium of the Baths of Caracalla was a rotunda 115 feet in diameter and an estimated 140 feet tall—as high, and nearly as wide, as the Pantheon. The glass windows in the rotunda's south wall were larger than those of any medieval cathedral. On a clear day, when sunlight reflected from the tiled walls and bronze ceiling, scattering rainbows through clouds of steam, the effect must have been breathtaking.

A cutaway drawing of the Baths of Diocletian. *Wikimedia Commons*

heated air beneath their floors.* Even a simple establishment often included an exercise yard and massage tables. Grand imperial foundations like the Baths of Caracalla combined all the amenities of health club and cultural center: lecture halls and food stalls, fountains and libraries, peristyles and pools, garnished by gardens and studded with statuary.[1]

Roman baths were open every day, usually from early afternoon to sunset. Although the first hours might be reserved for the sick and elderly—doctors had to remind patients with open wounds to avoid the pools—the general public streamed in as soon as the opening bell was rung, oil flasks and towels in hand. Extravagant bathers (such as Emperor Commodus, who reportedly laved himself seven or eight times a day) entered with a retinue of slaves, who would attend to their master's whims as he wallowed in the pools. At imperial baths, subsidized by the state, entry was free; elsewhere, it cost a small coin, paid to an attendant stationed by the door.[2]

---

* The furnaces that circulated hot air through the Baths of Caracalla consumed an estimated ten tons of firewood daily.

Bathers might begin by sampling the cheap wines, sausages, and sex sold by vendors scattered around the precinct. Their appetites satisfied, they made their way to the changing rooms, where they removed their clothes and placed them on shelves. Since the attendants responsible for preventing theft tended to be a bit larcenous themselves, wealthy men often stationed a slave or two to watch their belongings. Bathers rubbed themselves with olive oil before continuing to the exercise yard to lift weights, play handball,* wrestle, or box. Having worked up a healthy sweat, they might indulge in a massage or spell at the sauna, where oil and perspiration were scraped from their skin with the curved bronze instrument known as a strigil. Then, at last, they entered the water.† Most bathers began in the caldarium, which contained one or more waist-deep hot tubs. Next came the tepidarium, with its basins of lukewarm water. Finally, the frigidarium, which—depending on the size of the bath—might hold anything from small basins to an Olympic-size swimming pool of unheated water.[3]

Outside the baths, Romans typically bathed nude. Cicero once accused a woman of buying a villa on the Tiber so that she could watch naked men swimming. Nudity, however, was taboo in public places, and indoor bathing was initially no exception; Cato the Elder thought it disgraceful for even close relatives to be unclothed in the same room. An additional complication was the fact that, in some facilities, men and women bathed together. Though far from universal—most cities had separate baths,‡ or at least designated bathing hours, for men and women—this custom was widespread enough to be repeatedly banned by imperial edict, and persistent enough

---

* One of the most popular ball games played at the baths was *harpastum*, a rugby-like team sport that involved passing a small, hard ball back and forth while evading the opposing team's blocking maneuvers. Another favorite was *trigon*, in which three players stood in a triangle, tossing balls with one hand and catching them with the other. The player who missed the fewest throws won.

† A wealthy Roman magnate, having heard that the salty water of the Dead Sea allowed swimmers to bob on the surface, had a shipload imported at vast expense to fill a pool in his private bath.

‡ While visiting a small town south of Rome, an aristocratic lady decided that she wanted to use the men's baths (evidently superior to the female facilities), and ordered an official to evict all the local men while she performed her ablutions.

for Justinian to declare a woman's presence in a male bath adequate grounds for divorce. It may have also encouraged at least a scattering of bathers to don swimsuits.[4]

The Roman poet Martial mentions that some women wore garments in the baths (his own girlfriend, to his profound frustration, was one of them). He also observes that slaves could be seen at the baths in leather girdles—the ancient equivalent of a Speedo. A third-century emperor was remembered for his habit of frequenting baths in a special bathing costume, complete with a sweeping scarlet cloak.* We may even have artistic evidence for bathing costumes in the form of a mosaic that represents a group of young women in bikini-like outfits. None of this, however, suggests that more than a modest minority of Romans sported swimsuits. Abundant literary references leave little doubt that most bathed in the buff.[5]

Imagine swimming, unencumbered by clothes, in a vast marble pool filled with cold water. Skin flushed, you emerge into autumn sunlight and wrap yourself in a towel warmed by the floor. You pad back to the changing room, the heat of the tiles soaking through your sandals, and are relieved to find your tunic still on its shelf. Then you walk out through the gardens, where the leaves of the plane trees are starting to turn, past the fountains that play by the marble pools of the Baths of Caracalla.

---

* A lead curse tablet found at Bath, England, calls down divine retribution on the thief of a (presumably less majestic) bathing tunic.

· 2 ·

Did They Drink Beer?

$\mathcal{M}$any ancient cultures had beer gods. The Sumerians worshipped Ninkasi, who personally prepared the brews quaffed by her fellow deities. Aegir, Norse god of the sea, was famed for his golden brewing kettle and self-filling ale horns. The Lithuanians revered a god of beer, a goddess of beer, and an entirely distinct god of beer fermentation. But the Romans, like the Greeks before them, had no god of beer.* Nor did they want one. For the Greeks and Romans, beer—or, as the Greeks sometimes called it, "barley wine"†—was uncouth, unsavory, and unsuitable for civilized lips. Beer, in a word, was barbaric, guzzled by those who had not yet tasted the fruits of civilization. It brought out the worst in a people: the Pannonians, for example, were said to be angry and murderous, not least because they had nothing better than beer to drink.[1]

A few classical authors admitted that, under certain circumstances, beer could actually taste rather good. Xenophon, for example, observed that Armenian beer—which was customarily sipped through long reed straws—was delicious, once you had acquired

---

* Although Dionysus/Bacchus was sometimes imagined as the god of all intoxicating substances, up to and including beer, he was always associated most closely with wine. One author, noting that Dionysus had given wine only to the Greeks, speculated that beer-drinking peoples had angered the god and been deprived of his blessings.

† The most common Greek word for beer was *zythos* ("frothy"). The Romans used *zythum* for certain varieties of beer, but their usual term was *cervesia*, which survives as the Spanish *cerveza* and Portuguese *cerveja*. The English word "beer" is probably derived from the Latin *bibere*, "to drink."

the taste. More typical, however, was the opinion of the Roman historian Tacitus, who likened German beer to spoiled wine. Beer was also considered unhealthy. Aristotle claimed that those who drank too much of it would fall on their backs stupefied. The physician Dioscorides analyzed the medical properties of two varieties of beer. One, he declared, induced flatulence. The other brought on bad humors and headaches.* The attitude of the Greco-Roman elite toward beer is neatly summarized by an epigram of the emperor Julian, which opines that wine has the fragrance of nectar, while beer reeks like a goat.[2]

In the face of such cultural hostility, it might be assumed that the Greeks and Romans never drank beer. That may have been the case in Classical Greece. The Romans, however, drank a lot of beer. Many Romans, in fact, drank little else. Although wine was always prevalent in Italy, Greece, and other regions climatically suited to viticulture, beer was the beverage of choice for millions, from the Scottish moors to the wastes of Upper Egypt.[†]

To Roman eyes, Gaul—roughly modern France—was the stereotypical beer-drinking land. Although southern Gaul had long been dotted with vineyards, Gauls continued to brew for centuries after the Roman conquest, quaffing beer from mighty aurochs horns at feasts, or at taverns from clay cups marked "fill me with beer!" The beer-drinking culture of Egypt was equally potent. Although wine was produced in Egypt from a very early date, beer was the favorite drink of all classes, to the point that the hieroglyph for "beverage" was a picture of a beer jar. Many varieties were brewed, from the "dark beer" and "sweet beer" served in taverns to the "beer of eternity" stockpiled in tombs. The Roman conquest of Egypt had little effect on beer consumption: centuries later, Galen could still call salt fish and beer "the Alexandrian diet."[3]

---

* If nothing else, beer foam was reportedly good for the skin. Pliny the Elder claims that Gallic women smeared their faces with the stuff.

† After beer, the most popular alternative to wine was probably mead. Though apparently only used in religious rituals and as a medicine by the Greeks, it was widely consumed in some of the Roman Empire's frontier regions, and appears to have been swilled at the court of Attila the Hun. Cider and perry were consumed wherever apples and pears were grown. The steppe nomads beyond the Roman frontier preferred fermented horse milk.

On the other side of the empire, the arrival of Roman soldiers in northern Britain actually boosted local beer production.* An official stationed at a fort along Hadrian's Wall asked a colleague to order more beer for the troops from local brewers—some of whom were likely retired soldiers. If so, they may have honed their craft while still serving in the ranks, since Roman forts often had their own breweries. Whoever brewed it, Roman beer tasted quite different from its modern counterparts. Though usually made, as now, from barley and brewed in the familiar way, Roman beer tended to be sour, and often had to be sweetened with honey or fruits. It wasn't always filtered; and even when it was, the product was much cloudier and grainier than modern beer. Finally, since hops were not added,† it tended to spoil quickly.[4]

To judge from Diocletian's Edict on Maximum Prices, beer was remarkably cheap, costing only a quarter of what was charged for even the least expensive wine. It was also remarkably common. Associations of brewers are attested both in Egypt and on the German frontier, and breweries were attached to some of the grandest Roman villas in the Rhineland. But beer never lost its bad reputation: one late Roman emperor was mocked as a "beer drinker." Thanks to its low cultural status, beer was gradually displaced by wine in many parts of the empire. Gallic beer was an early casualty. Even before the coming of Rome, Gallic elites had begun to import massive quantities of Italian wine, sold at such exorbitant prices that a slave was sometimes exchanged for a single jar. During the imperial era, as grapevines enveloped the countryside, wine became the preferred beverage in most parts of Gaul. An even more dramatic transformation took place in Egypt, where cheap local wine virtually replaced beer over the course of the fourth century.[5]

In western Europe, at least, beer may have been saved by the collapse of the Roman Empire. The Germanic invaders brought with

---

* The tombstone of one Roman veteran proclaims: "While I lived, I drank freely; drink, you who still live!"

† Hops grow wild in central Europe, but they only began to be added to beer during the Middle Ages. Although the first hop gardens appeared in the eighth century, it took nearly a millennium for hops to fully displace the preservative herbs used in most medieval beers.

them a robust beer-drinking culture, which substantially enhanced beer's social standing. A Roman physician working for one of the new barbarian kings found it within himself to actually praise beer as both delicious and nutritious. The empire had fallen; but beer would live on.[6]

• 3 •

Did They Use Drugs?

The tomb had been looted long ago—a deep crater in the grassy mound made that obvious. But since it was due to be bulldozed for the construction of a new power line, archaeologist Andrei Belinski and his team spent nearly a month digging to the ancient kurgan's base. To their surprise, they discovered a stone-lined hollow overlooked by the looters, which contained golden armbands and cups, a heavy golden ring, and two spectacular golden vessels. The outer faces of the vessels swirled with scenes of dueling warriors and mythic beasts. Their insides were coated with a mysterious black residue. A sample was sent for analysis at a nearby lab, which promptly reported that the residue was opium, with traces of marijuana.

The tomb that Belinksi's team uncovered had been constructed by the Scythians, nomadic horsemen who roved the grasslands north of the Black Sea. The ancient Greeks knew the Scythians—the vessels, in fact, may have been produced by Greek craftsmen—and they also knew about the Scythians' fondness for ritually purifying themselves in sweat lodges, where they threw heaps of hemp on hot stones,* producing clouds of marijuana smoke that made them sing and dance as though drunk.[1]

In the classical world, most drug use was medical. Although a number of plants with psychoactive effects were known, such as henbane and mandrake, the most potent and prominent was the opium

---

* A number of Scythian burial mounds in Siberia were found to contain bronze vessels filled with stones and hemp seeds, apparently left smoking when the tomb was sealed.

11

poppy, which was grown throughout the Mediterranean. Poppy seeds were eaten as food and pressed to make oil. But it was the narcotic milk extracted from immature seed pods that gave the opium poppy its critical role in ancient medicine as a painkiller and relaxant. In the *Odyssey*, for example, Helen slips what is almost certainly opium into the drinks of banqueting heroes to help them forget their sorrows. For years, Marcus Aurelius drank a cup of opiated wine every night to help himself sleep.* Mixed with honey or pressed into pills, opium was used to ease everything from skin infections to coughs. Although ancient doctors did not understand that opium was addictive, they were well aware that overdoses could be fatal. At least a few terminally ill Romans, knowing this, ended their lives with the drug.[2]

Like the opium poppy, the hemp plant had many applications in the classical world. The most commercially important of these involved the fibers of the male hemp plant's stem, which were woven into durable clothing, shoes, and ropes. The psychoactive resin of the female plant baffled and intrigued classical physicians. One ancient doctor observed that those who ate hempseed experienced confusion and a sensation of warmth. Others noted that hempseed dampened the sex drive and left the body dehydrated. On the plus side, it was good for earaches. Although there is no textual evidence for medical use of the much more potent leaves and buds, the recent discovery of cannabis resin in the tomb of a Roman woman who died in childbirth suggests that the pains of labor were sometimes eased with hashish.[3]

The Greeks and Romans may have occasionally used psychoactive substances to heighten the effects of religious rituals. In this, they were anticipated by the Minoans, who worshipped the so-called poppy goddess, a female deity with a trancelike expression and diadem of poppy heads. The largest known statue of the goddess

---

* Marcus Aurelius took his opium in theriac, a panacea that was supposed to counteract poisons, calm indigestion, banish sciatica, and lend a hearty boost to the sex drive. This marvelous concoction had dozens of ingredients. A few (such as myrrh) may have had positive effects; others (like viper flesh) cannot have done convalescing digestive systems any favors.

A terra-cotta figurine of the Minoan "poppy goddess," now in the Heraklion Archaeological Museum. *Wikimedia Commons*

was found near a tubular vase used to inhale opium smoke.* The evidence for ritual drug use in the classical world is more ambiguous. The Greeks associated the opium poppy with the fertility goddess Demeter, who is often shown holding bundles of grain and poppy heads. As far as we can tell, however, these poppies were emblems of abundance, not allusions to opium's narcotic power.

It has sometimes been claimed that opium smoke played a role in the incubation rituals of the healing god Asclepius, or that vision-inducing mushrooms were mixed into the wine at Dionysian rites. Though possible, neither of these theories is backed by firm evidence. It has also been suggested that one of the most famous Greek rituals, the Eleusinian Mysteries, involved a hallucinogenic beverage. During an all-night vigil before the climactic ceremony, initiates drank a blend of water, barley flour, and pennyroyal. The ergot fungus, which grows on barley, can have effects similar to those of LSD. If the barley in the initiates' drinks was contaminated with ergot, they could indeed have experienced awe-inspiring visions. The theory is intriguing—but again, definitive proof is lacking.

The scope of recreational drug use is equally unclear. One Roman author mentions a plant that caused uncontrollable laughter when added to wine. Another author notes that fried hempseed was sometimes served as a dessert, and that those who ate large quantities experienced a warm and intoxicating sensation. Neither suggests, however, that consumption of these substances was common. In short, although the Greeks and Romans were aware of the narcotic properties of opium and cannabis, wine—occasionally spiked with psychoactive herbs like mandrake—seems to have almost always been their intoxicant of choice.[4]

The absence of evidence, of course, is not necessarily evidence of absence. Although our textual sources suggest that drug use was limited in the classical world, those sources may be blinkered by the perspectives of their authors. So unless or until more information comes to light, the scope of ancient drug use must remain a mystery.

---

* A similar tubular vase was found at a late Bronze Age site in Cyprus, alongside an ivory cylinder apparently used as an opium pipe.

Did They Have Dentists?

𝒯he invasion of Greece had begun. The Persian ships were drawn up on the beach at Marathon, and soldiers in their myriads massed ashore. In their midst was Hippias, former tyrant of Athens, come to reclaim his city. The night before, he had dreamed that he was destined to be buried in his motherland.* But as he stood on a sandy bank, he coughed, and one of his teeth fell out. After searching for it in vain, Hippias lamented: "We shall never conquer this land; for this tooth has been buried here in my place!"[1]

By the time he landed at Marathon, Hippias was well into his eighties, more than old enough to be excused a vagrant tooth. But he was far from the only classical personage with a less-than-brilliant smile. Augustus, for example, had a mouth full of rotten stumps. And when he was still in his late twenties, Nero had to have a tooth pulled, presumably because of a serious cavity. Despite such practical experience, the Greeks and Romans never understood the root causes of tooth decay.† As a result, they tended to regard dental care as a matter

---

* To be more precise, Hippias had dreamed of having sex with his mother, and chose to regard this as a good omen (on the theory that Athens was his mother city). Remarkably, the only extant classical manual of dream interpretation contains a detailed discussion of how to parse dreams involving intercourse with one's mother.

† In ancient Mesopotamia, cavities were thought to be caused by "worms"—invisible parasites with an insatiable thirst for human blood. This idea survived into the Roman era, when it was cited by Scribonius Largus (who recommended expelling the wretched creatures with henbane). One work in the Aristotelian corpus ponders why sweet figs seem to cause cavities, but stops short of associating sugar with tooth decay. Galen, for his part, blamed corrosive humors.

of cosmetics, not hygiene. The standard, and often sole, implement employed to clean teeth was a toothpick. From the slivers of mastic wood plied by humble hands to the silver and gold models flourished by kings,* toothpicks were correspondingly ubiquitous, and were even given as gifts.[2]

Toothpicks were paired with tooth powders, which were rubbed over the teeth and gums with an enthusiastic finger. Roman authors listed dozens of recipes. In addition to abrasive agents like pumice, pulverized bone, powdered glass, and crushed shell, various concoctions included such ingredients as sheep sweat and the ash of a wolf's head. Some powders would certainly have whitened smiles, though only those few that incorporated herbs and spices beneficial for the teeth and gums would have made any positive contribution to dental health.[†] Nor did they combat halitosis. Bad breath was a chronic condition, despite such antidotes as honey-soaked wool, cremated mouse, and unmixed wine. "Among all animals," one Roman author observed, "man is most prone to bad breath, from bad food, from bad teeth, and especially from old age." Toothache seems to have been almost equally prevalent, not least because the remedies prescribed— which included the burnt heads of mad dogs, grains of sand from the horns of snails, and boiled frogs—would have done little more than distract sufferers.[3]

Although doctors were already extracting teeth and wiring shattered jaws in Classical Greece, most of our knowledge about ancient dentistry comes from Roman sources. Broken teeth were filed down and infected gums were lanced; but in most cases, a dentist's task consisted of nothing more or less than pulling teeth. Extractions were not undertaken lightly: medical handbooks emphasized the risks of a careless operation, which ranged from a dislocated jaw to death. Yet teeth were pulled, frequently enough that "tooth doctors" were a

---

* Agathocles, tyrant of Syracuse, was reportedly assassinated with a poisoned toothpick. Though not fatal, using a vulture quill to pick one's teeth brought on rancid breath. A porcupine quill, by contrast, was thought to be good for the gums.

† The Romans believed—or at least liked to claim—that certain Spanish tribes rinsed their teeth with human urine (aged for the purpose in cisterns). Since all our references are secondhand or satirical, however, it's more likely that we're dealing with rumor and prejudice than with any historical practice.

Copy of a denture found in an Etruscan tomb. *Science Museum, London*

familiar presence in Roman cities. The process differed from today's primarily in the absence of anesthesia: the gum was pulled back, the tooth was loosened by being worked back and forth, and the extraction was performed with a stylus or forceps.* A drain in the Roman Forum yielded eighty-six teeth—all with deep cavities—which had apparently washed out from a dentist's shop. Impressively, not a single tooth had been broken during the procedure.[4]

With the possible exception of a Hellenistic mummy found with a linen-packed tooth, there is no evidence for cavity fillings. Ancient dentists, however, were perfectly capable of strengthening teeth with gold wire; an early Roman law specifically exempted such fastenings from a general prohibition on burying gold with a body. Though never common, artificial teeth—usually in the form of

---

* Those who feared the forceps could visit certain springs or eat a hearty dose of pulverized earthworm to make their teeth fall out. But hope need not be lost along with those teeth: Pliny the Elder reports that the teeth of a certain Greek centenarian grew back in extreme old age.

dental bridges—are well attested. By the Roman imperial era, dentures* were made of everything from ivory to boxwood.[5]

The effectiveness of ancient dental care can best be judged from the skeletons recovered at Pompeii and Herculaneum. Only about a third of the adult skeletons found in the boat sheds at Herculaneum were missing teeth,† and relatively few had cavities. One middle-aged man, however, had lost no fewer than seven teeth, and was suffering from four serious cavities and four abscesses, one so deep that it drained into his sinuses. A young girl wearing expensive jewelry already had five cavities—probably because her family was wealthy enough to give her plenty of snacks smothered in sugary honey.‡ The leisure class was, however, spared the sort of wear visible in the mouth of a young fisherman, whose teeth were badly worn on one side from biting nets.[6]

Rich or poor, the Greeks and Romans ate a great deal of bread, which often contained tiny flakes of tooth-corroding stone from the milling process. And since toothpicks and tooth powders, though effective at removing food scraps and burnishing smiles, were not very good at thorough cleaning, the bases of their teeth were almost invariably caked with plaque. Despite all these problems, ancient teeth were better than one might expect, largely because, in the absence of processed sugar, oral bacteria were less aggressive than they are today. Cavities still occurred, but the pervasive blackened teeth and hollow cheeks of early modern Europe were nearly as distant from the classical experience as they are from ours.

---

* In one epigram, a Roman poet has a personified batch of tooth powder scold an elderly lady for cleaning her dentures, telling her to save the powder for people with real teeth.

† The boat sheds at Herculaneum—a row of low stone arches facing the harbor—sheltered about three hundred people on the night Vesuvius erupted. The volcano entombed them there.

‡ A dialogue from a third-century textbook, describing a Roman child's normal routine, admonishes him to clean his teeth every morning.

Did They Have Tattoos?

In ancient Greek and Latin, the word for "tattoo" was *stigma*.* Like its English equivalent, *stigma* had connotations of infamy and disgrace, a reflection of the classical association of tattoos with slaves, criminals, and barbarians.

The tattooed barbarians known best to the Greeks were the Thracians, who lived north and east of Macedon. Thracian women—especially those of aristocratic birth—tattooed their arms and legs with silhouettes of animals and patterned lines. Mystified Greek authors speculated that the practice somehow commemorated the death of the mythical bard Orpheus, who had been torn to pieces by Thracian maenads. The Scythians, another tattooed people, roamed the vast arc of steppes beyond the Thracians. The bodies of their chieftains, found frozen in the Siberian permafrost, display a dazzling array of designs, from rearing stallions to fantastic beasts. On the other side of the world known to the Greeks, the mummies of Egyptian women exhibit tattooed dots and lines. Roman authors remarked on the Egyptian custom of tattooing children.† In Syria, worshippers tattooed their wrists with marks of devotion to the gods—a custom so widespread that the author of Leviticus forbade the Israelites from tattooing themselves.[1]

---

* *Stigma* originally meant "dot" or "mark." One distinguished grammarian came to be known as *Stigmatias*, because he specialized in punctuating the works of Homer.

† The Greek author Xenophon encountered a tribe on the coast of the Black Sea that tattooed children with elaborate floral designs.

A Thracian maenad with tattooed arms attacking Orpheus, on a red-figure vase now in the Munich Antikensammlung. *Public domain*

The Persians, by contrast, used tattoos as a punishment. During his conquest of the Persian Empire, Alexander encountered an entire settlement of Greeks who had been mutilated and tattooed on the orders of the king of kings. A century and a half before, during the Persian invasion of Greece, Xerxes had a contingent of his Theban allies tattooed. If Herodotus can be believed, he also ordered the sea itself to be tattooed and whipped after a storm destroyed his bridge over the Hellespont.[2]

Before they encountered the Persians, the Greeks do not seem to have practiced tattooing. But by the beginning of the Classical period, they had begun to tattoo fugitive slaves, most often on the face or neck, with phrases like "Stop me—I'm a runaway."* Such

---

* Those who violated temples in the ideal city of Plato's *Laws* were to have the transgression tattooed on their faces and hands.

tattoos became familiar enough to be referenced both in a ribald Hellenistic poem—in which a woman summons a tattooist to punish her slave lover—and in the book of Revelation, which describes the tattooed forehead of the whore of Babylon. The Greeks also tattooed prisoners of war, typically with the emblems of their captors. Athenian soldiers seized in the wake of the disastrous Sicilian expedition, for example, were tattooed with the horse of Syracuse. Such tattoos were a mark of subordination: after defeating the Rhodians, Queen Artemisia of Halicarnassus reportedly set up a statue of herself tattooing a personified city of Rhodes.[3]

Like the Greeks, the Romans tattooed slaves; one of Caligula's many crimes was the tattooing of freeborn men. As in the Greek world, facial tattoos were most common. When the main characters of the *Satyricon*—a Roman novel—decide to disguise themselves as slaves, they shave their eyebrows and draw fake tattoos on their foreheads with ink. Constantine decreed that, since the human visage was made in the divine image, it should not be defaced with tattoos. A full half-millennium after Constantine, however, the Byzantine emperor Theophilus ordered twelve lines of (very bad) poetry to be tattooed on the faces of two monks who had defied his prohibition on icons.[4]

By the reign of Constantine, the Romans were also tattooing soldiers. A late antique military manual mentions marking recruits with the insignia of their units, and an imperial decree of the same era stipulates that all workers in arms factories be tattooed to prevent desertion. The practice continued for some time: a medical treatise from the following century defines tattoos as marks like those placed on the hands of soldiers.[5]

Former soldiers and freed slaves seem to have done everything they could to erase their tattoos.* Medical texts outlined various methods, which usually involved pricking the skin and rubbing the affected area with caustic substances. Alternatively, tattoos could be concealed with strategic bandages or long hair.[6]

---

* An inscription from the healing sanctuary at Epidaurus celebrates the miraculous disappearance of a hated tattoo.

There were a few Greeks and Romans, however, who were not ashamed of their ink. The semimythical sage Epimenides reportedly had himself tattooed with lines from his own poems. Ptolemy IV, king of Egypt, was tattooed with ivy leaves as a mark of devotion to Dionysus. And many early Christians, perhaps inspired by the penal tattoos of the martyrs, had their arms marked with a sign of the cross or the name of Jesus.* A more expansive devotional tattoo, which praised Mani as a disciple of Christ, revealed a certain African monk to be a heretic. A tattoo might even betoken a miracle: when a tumor in Saint Macrina's breast was suddenly healed, a tattoo-like mark appeared on the spot.[7]

Near the end of the sixth century, the emperor Maurice received a group of Turkish prisoners at Constantinople, and was surprised to see that many had crosses tattooed on their foreheads. When asked how they had acquired these marks, the Turks replied that a Christian had once told their tribe that the sign of the cross protected against plagues.† In this episode, with the cultural heirs of Classical Greece admiring the tattoos of a tribe that had replaced the Scythians, the ancient history of tattoos came full circle.[8]

---

* The Carpocratians, a heretical Christian sect, branded converts on the right earlobe with a red-hot razor.

† In this respect, the cross replaced images of Alexander the Great, which was worn for centuries as a talisman against the plague.

· 6 ·

Did They Have Newspapers?

$\mathscr{R}$ome was in danger. A rogue senator named Catiline was plotting to overthrow the government, and only one man had the courage, poise, and relentless eloquence to prevent revolution: Marcus Tullius Cicero, consul. At a meeting of the Senate, Cicero accused Catiline of fomenting rebellion, knowing that a network of informers, gossips, and couriers would carry his words to every corner of the city. His strategy worked all too well: Catiline fled Rome, but the news of his conspiracy generated so many rumors that Cicero had to reassure the people in a public address the following day.

In Cicero's Rome, upcoming elections and games might be publicized with streetside graffiti.* But in a world whose literacy rate likely hovered around 10 percent, most people learned by listening. Orators and heralds addressed the people during festivals, games, and assemblies, informing them of victories in the provinces, distributions of free grain, and other matters of public concern. The popular response, enthusiastic or otherwise, was part of the process: in late antiquity, members of the crowd sometimes bantered with the herald, or even with the emperor himself. Between games and assemblies, the hub of the hubbub was the Forum, where the stentorian voices of lawyers and politicians rang through forests of columns, and semi-professional rumormongers lingered around the rostra, voices all but

---

* The graffiti of Pompeii range far beyond such earnest announcements, from philosophical musings and love poems to praises of local gladiators and directions to the nearest prostitute.

lost in the buzz and hum of conversation. From the Forum, news spread as swiftly as tongues could wag—corroborated, contradicted, or condemned by the classical world's only newspaper.[1]

From the late Republic to late antiquity, the Roman government published the *acta diurna*, or daily gazette. Each issue began with the statistics for the day's births and deaths, along with such items of practical interest as the arrival of grain boats at Ostia. These particulars were accompanied by summaries of important court cases (especially, it seems, messy divorces) and significant decisions of the Senate. News relating to the imperial family was given a full treatment, even when the emperor was away from Rome, as was the progress of major building projects. In times of war, the gazette might describe Roman victories, along with any skirmishes or marches that the government saw fit to publicize.[2]

But it was the human-interest section of the gazette that, one suspects, the Romans followed most avidly. In addition to such prodigies as abnormal births and sacrificial animals with unorthodox organs, mention was made of any strange or surprising event. Examples mentioned by our sources include a rain of dirt from the sky, a dog that remained loyal to its master's corpse, a bloody brawl at a funeral, and an architect who straightened a leaning portico with a system of pulleys.[3]

The flavor of the gazette is captured by a parody in a Roman novel, in which the clerk of an obscenely wealthy freedman reads the daily report for his master's estates. After rattling off the statistics for births and harvests, he mentions—among much else—the crucifixion of a slave, a destructive fire, and the messy divorce of a woman who had been caught having an affair with a bath attendant.[4]

The gazette was produced by a small staff of minor officials, assisted by reporters who jotted shorthand notes at court cases and prowled the Forum in search of tips. Although their summaries were spare and concise, the gazette's writers were not above a bit of journalistic flair. Someone involved in a divorce, for example, might be described as "wounded at heart." We don't know how many copies were made of any given edition of the gazette, but the number was probably quite small. A few copies were sent to archives and libraries, where they could be consulted by historians and other researchers. The rest were posted on public notice boards to be read, recopied, and proclaimed.[5]

Since, as mentioned earlier, most Romans were illiterate, the contents of the gazette were broadcasted by street criers. Their patter was part of the daily din on the streets of Rome; one author compared an especially stentorian orator to someone "bawling the gazette into your ear." Although we don't know how they read the news, the epitaph of one crier may provide some idea: "Here lie the bones of Olus Granius the crier. He was modest, trustworthy, and honorable. That is all."[6]

Scribes—often the slaves of wealthy families—copied the gazette as soon as it was posted and sent facsimiles to the homes of the Roman elite. Since there was strong demand for news from the capital among Romans living in the provinces, merchants and couriers carried copies to every corner of the empire, and even to the legions on the frontiers.* As Cicero once said when describing a document he had publicized, "There is no place on earth, where the name of the Roman people is known, that it did not reach." He might have said the same about the daily gazette.[7]

---

* News could move very quickly. Cicero mentions a messenger who drove a chariot sixty miles in a single night to report a murder. Nero's death at Rome was known in Egypt within twenty-seven days.

Did They Attend Concerts?

𝒯he soloist stood center stage, feeling the eyes of the crowd. They had cheered when he entered, but were quiet now, watching as he poised his hands over the cithara. His rings flashed in the afternoon sun—the ring he had received from the emperor, the ring he had taken from that senator's wife, and the ring that he bought for himself, long ago, when he first became famous. He watched them glow for a moment. Then, almost casually, he ran a hand over the perfectly tuned strings, and the first notes shimmered through the theater . . .

The Greeks and Romans used dozens of musical instruments, from bugle-like signal horns to the clinking metal rattles that accompanied the hymns of Isis. Public performances, however, were dominated by three instruments. Foremost of these was the cithara, an elaborate lyre with seven or eight strings and an amplifying sound box at its base. It was played with both hands, the right plucking and striking strings, the left dampening unwanted notes. As the most prestigious classical instrument, the cithara was taught to the sons and daughters of the elite, and admired for its soothing* and subtle sound.[1]

Only slightly less prestigious than the cithara was the tibia, which the Greeks called the aulos. The tibia consisted of two pipes

---

* One famous citharode wrote a piece that imitated a storm at sea (and was mocked by a pipe player, who said that he'd heard worse storms in his cooking pots). Cithara, incidentally, is the source of the Italian *chitarra*, and thus of "guitar."

Fresco of a woman playing the cithara, from the Villa of P. Fannius Synistor at Boscoreale, now in the Metropolitan Museum of Art. *Public domain*

that were played simultaneously. The effect may have resembled modern bagpipes, with one pipe emitting a continuous drone and the other playing a melody. Virtuoso performers used both pipes in a fluttering counterpoint that ancient audiences found wildly exciting. Aristotle, in fact, thought the tibia too stimulating to use in schools.[2]

The newest and loudest concert instrument was the hydraulis, or water organ. Invented in Hellenistic Alexandria by the brilliant engineer Ctesibius, the hydraulis used a reservoir filled with water to regulate the air that was released through the pipes at the touch of the organist's keys.* Though never as prestigious as the pipe or cithara, organs became a staple of concerts and public shows, largely because they could be heard over the noise of a crowd.[3]

---

* Shortly before his fall from power, Nero spent a day displaying the latest organ models to his courtiers. He was also an avid cithara player, as were Titus and Hadrian.

Music was everywhere in the classical world. Hymns rose heavenward at festivals, pipes trilled at sacrifices,* and sacred processions filled the streets with the clamor of horns and drums. At the Roman games, trumpets bayed and organs roared as men and beasts battled on bloodstained sands. Beneath the bowers of villa gardens, slave orchestras serenaded the rich.† Musicians busked for coins at street corners, competing with troupes of mimes who sang and danced to the accompaniment of pipes, horns, and drums. Greek tragedies had choruses, and Roman comedy featured musical interludes.[4]

Famous musicians toured the great cities, demanding gargantuan fees and filling theaters wherever they went. Their arrogance was legendary; one singer refused to perform for Augustus, simply because he didn't feel like it. They engaged in fierce rivalries, which sometimes escalated to the point of sabotaging each other's performances. They had to work to please their audiences—crowds in the theater of Pompey, for example, were notorious for hissing performers off the stage—and some resorted to packing the seats with professional applauders. But the best musicians inspired something akin to Beatlemania, driving aristocratic ladies to fight for cast-off plectrums and lyre strings.[5]

A few singers became famous by performing choruses from the Greek tragedies or hymns for the gods.‡ Most of the great soloists, however, were instrumentalists. In the late second century, for example, an Egyptian playing a tall harp took Rome by storm; for months afterward, people could be heard humming his songs in the streets. Eminent pipe players frequently specialized in what we might call "classical music," presenting the compositions of masters like Timotheus, the court composer of Alexander the Great. Even if the melodies were not themselves classics, they tended to follow such

---

* In Rome, the men who played pipes on these occasions had their own guild, formally and quite specifically known as "the collegium of lyre- and pipe-players present at public sacrifices." At least once, they went on strike.

† One wealthy Roman owned so many musicians that music never stopped in his house. Another had a children's choir trained to sing for his guests after dinner. Yet another was lulled to sleep each night by slaves playing music in the distance.

‡ Singers were notorious for the intensity of their exercises, which ranged from speaking through a handkerchief to laying slabs of lead on their chests.

traditional forms as the Pythian melody, a stylized representation of the combat between Apollo and the monster Python.* Yet within the bounds of such conventions, songs were often the compositions of the pipe player himself, and might even be jazz flute-style improvisations.[6]

Cithara players were the most renowned, most lionized, and most insufferable of all soloists. They liked to appear in stage costume, complete with a jeweled crown, gold-fringed robe, and cloak of profoundest purple. Their instruments gleamed with ivory. They used traditional stage names[†] and had a repertoire of classics. But the best were poets in their own right, capable of composing lines and setting them to improvised music. One of the leading citharodes of the Roman imperial era was Mesomedes, a former slave who became Hadrian's court composer. Thanks to a quirk of the manuscript tradition and lucky finds from papyri, we possess several of his hymns, complete with musical notation. Even this meager sample offers a tantalizing taste of the elaborate poetry and intricate settings of a master musician.[7]

Famous pipe players and citharodes drew large crowds. But for centuries, the most popular musical performances were the ballets known as pantomimes. A pantomime stood onstage, robed in silk, wearing a mask with closed lips. To the accompaniment of a choir and orchestra, he performed elaborate dances that interpreted episodes from Greek myth. Although some pantomimes specialized in comic or romantic themes, like the love of Ares and Aphrodite, the repertoire was usually drawn from tragedy. "The madness of Ajax" and "Thyestes devouring his children" were crowd favorites. Pantomime was introduced to Rome during the reign of Augustus, and rapidly became popular, both in the great theaters and in the salons of the elite. From the beginning, however, it was controversial—partly because leading dancers indulged in a series of scandalous

---

* This was a piece with five parts, which represented Apollo choosing the place of combat, challenging the monster, battling to the death, emerging victorious, and dancing triumphantly.

† One famously vain pipe player in Rome had the stage name Princeps—"The Emperor."

affairs, but mostly on account of the fact that riots tended to break out during performances. At least once, all pantomimes were expelled from Italy. But they trickled back, and pantomime gradually claimed its place as a respectable art.[8]

Like so many other aspects of ancient music, the sounds of pantomime are lost to us. We know enough, however, to glimpse their emotional power. Imagine the beginning of a performance. A pipe sounds first, low and plaintive, filling the theater and stilling the whispers of the crowd. After a moment of silence, the rhythmic taps of the percussionists start to echo from the marble arcades. The pantomime stands alone, golden mask gleaming. The pipe resumes, and he bows with infinite grace, purple cloak brushing the stage. And then, as the chorus begins its melody, he whirls into a dance.

· 8 ·

Did They Attend Public Schools?

$\mathcal{A}$round the end of the first century, a marble tombstone was set up just outside Rome. The relief at its center, flanked by neat lines of Greek verse, showed a boy crowned with laurel, a scroll in his left hand. The epitaph commemorated Quintus Sulpicius Maximus, who lived eleven years, five months, and twelve days. Quintus had been a budding poet, performing with distinction at a famous competition for Greek verse. He had perished, the inscription claimed, from studying too hard.[1]

Quintus was far from alone in his dedication to his studies. Augustus wrote a tragedy, Claudius composed histories, and Hadrian fancied himself a poet. A Greek philosopher whose house had been destroyed proclaimed that he had lost nothing, for he retained his learning. Even the spirits of the blessed in the Elysian Fields were said to while away eternity discussing poetry and philosophy.[2]

Educational opportunity in the classical world mapped neatly onto social status. The rich were more likely to be educated than the poor, boys were more likely to be educated than girls, and free children were more likely to be educated than slaves.* In most periods and places, literacy—the most fundamental skill provided by a

---

* House slaves belonging to elite Roman families, however, were often highly educated, and might become readers, scribes, or tutors. The emperors had a dedicated school for slave children in the palace, which trained imperial accountants and administrators.

The tombstone of Quintus Sulpicius Maximus, now in Rome's Centrale Monte-martini Museum. *Public domain*

classical education—appears to have been restricted to about 10 percent of the population. The limited reach of education was reflected in an almost total lack of publicly funded schools. Wealthy private benefactors sometimes established free academies, and many late Roman cities appear to have maintained at least a few teachers from municipal funds. But in general, and almost everywhere above the primary level, education was organized privately. Dedicated school buildings were correspondingly rare. Most teachers taught under porticoes or in some other convenient public place, presiding from a tall armchair over a circle of students on wooden stools. Blackboards only began to appear in the Roman imperial era, along with busts of famous authors and wall maps.[3]

Especially at the primary level, teachers were poorly paid, sometimes to the point of having to take second jobs to make ends meet.* They were equally starved for prestige: a Greek proverb for someone who had fallen on hard times was "he's either dead or teaching."† In keeping with the job's low status, there was no qualifying process. Although employers might request a demonstration of their skills, most teachers were simply hired on the assumption that they possessed the requisite knowledge. This was not always the case: one Roman author mentions a grammar school teacher who refused to believe that sheep could have more than two teeth.[4]

Classes began soon after first light. Part of the morning might be given to exercise. Otherwise, lessons continued—with a break for lunch—until midafternoon. Discipline was harsh; and especially in Greek schools, where students were liberated only during religious festivals, holidays were few and far between. Roman students, by contrast, had every eighth day off, and enjoyed a summer vacation.[5]

---

* One inscription mentions a Roman teacher who drafted wills on the side. From the reign of Vespasian onward, teachers of grammar and rhetoric were at least exempted from taxation by their native cities. After cities complained that they were being deprived of tax revenue, however, the privilege was limited to only a few teachers in any given city.

† Supposedly, the deposed tyrant Dionysius of Syracuse became a schoolmaster. A few disgraced Roman senators were reduced to the same extremity. On the other hand, Eugenius, a teacher of rhetoric, managed to (briefly) seize the imperial throne at the end of the fourth century.

Although aristocratic families had hired tutors to introduce their sons to the poets and the sports of the gymnasium as early as the Greek Archaic period, the standardized curriculum that would dominate the Mediterranean world through the end of antiquity only emerged during the Hellenistic era. The primary stage of that curriculum, begun when children were six or seven, taught the basic skills of reading and writing. Learning to read started, of course, with the alphabet, which was learned literally backward and forward.* Then came syllables: every conceivable two-, three-, and four-letter pairing of consonant and vowel. Next, words, starting with monosyllables and working up to pentasyllabic tongue twisters. Then, and only then, were children introduced to texts, usually short passages that they were expected to memorize and recite. Students learned to write using a wax tablet and stylus or reed pen. As with reading, the process was maddeningly deliberate: a child first traced letters, then syllables, then words, and finally sentences. Egyptian papyri preserve some of the passages students copied out, which ranged from sober admonitions to dirty jokes.[6]

In some Roman schools, the agony of learning to read and write was doubled by repeating the process in both Latin and Greek.† Although the children of wealthy families, raised by Greek nannies, might learn Greek before their native Latin, children from less privileged backgrounds had to start their Greek in elementary school, where they were taught from bilingual manuals. Saint Augustine remembered the method as both painful and ineffective. Arithmetic at the primary level seems to have consisted of little more than

---

* As taught to young children, the alphabet had twenty-four letters in both Greek and Latin, since Y and Z, the last letters in the Latin alphabet, appeared only in transliterated Greek words. Wooden or ivory models were sometimes used to familiarize students with the shapes of the letters. One wealthy Roman bought twenty-four young slaves, named them after the letters, and introduced them to his son as playmates.

† Educated Romans were expected to know both Latin and Greek—what Horace called "our two languages." Cicero composed translations of the Greek classics, delivered orations in Greek, and sprinkled Greek liberally through his letters. Augustus composed a Greek tragedy, Nero preferred Greek to Latin, and Marcus Aurelius wrote his *Meditations* in Greek.

teaching students to read and write the names of the numbers,* though some Roman schools also covered the rudiments of adding and dividing fractions. A more substantial introduction to arithmetic operations and Euclidian geometry would come, if at all, at the school of the grammarian.[7]

Only a small fraction—perhaps 5 percent—of the students who learned to read and write moved on to the school of the grammarian, the secondary stage of a classical education. The grammarian's task was to teach the works of the poets. In the Greek world, the curriculum was dominated by the Homeric epics,† complemented by tragedies of Aeschylus, Sophocles, and Euripides; comedies by Aristophanes and Menander; and selections from the lyric poets. Roman students read Virgil, the comedies of Terence, selections from Horace and Ovid, and—in some cases—such prose authors as Sallust and Cicero.[8]

After students had read a given text, the grammarian began the exhaustive and exhausting process of explicating it. Proceeding line by line, he pontificated on each obscure word, every eccentricity of morphology, and any other pedantic picayune that occurred to him. These disquisitions alternated with lectures on the moral content of the poems. Homer, in particular, was regarded as the font of all wisdom and virtue, and misinterpreted accordingly. The poets were also used to introduce the formal study of grammar, which began with letters and syllables and proceeded relentlessly through all the categories, classifications, and conjugations of the parts of speech. The composition of short literary summaries—sometimes repeated, so that every noun could be declined into a different case—brought

---

* Greek thinkers—following Pythagoras, Plato, and other distinguished philosophers— were deeply impressed by the properties of numbers, and tended to assign an almost mystical value to one, three, four, and seven. One scholar composed an entire treatise on the theology of numbers.

† It would be difficult to overstate the influence of Homer, "the educator of Greece." Students memorized huge swaths of the epics, and were pitted against one another in city-wide recitation contests. Outside the dialogues of Plato—who was virtually alone among the major Greek authors in daring to criticize Homer—bardolatry reigned, not least in Egypt, where papyri of Homer still outnumber those of all other authors. A young Alcibiades reportedly beat a teacher who did not possess a copy of the *Iliad*.

the benumbed pupils to the end of their grammatical careers, and carried a select few to the threshold of the rhetorical school, the sum and summit of ancient education.[9]

The rhetor—the doctor of eloquence—was a more exalted being than a mere grammarian. The most distinguished practitioners were wealthy men, able to buy second homes in Athens, order papyrus directly from Egypt, and build artificial islands at their seaside estates. Their egos matched their affluence. One of the most famous, Polemon of Smyrna,* traveled in a silver-trimmed carriage accompanied by a baggage train and packs of hunting dogs, and was said to regard only emperors and gods as his equals.[10]

As might be expected from an educational system that never failed to start with first principles, students began their rhetorical training by memorizing definitions. Each type of oration was associated with an elaborate sequence of divisions, subdivisions, sections, and tropes, all of which had to be mastered before a budding orator could begin to study the exemplars of Greek and Roman rhetoric. Isocrates, the founding father of rhetorical education, had proclaimed the power of the spoken word to generations of Athenian youths. His works, the works of his students, and the orations of the great Demosthenes became the foundation of the rhetorical curriculum for the rest of antiquity, complemented—in Roman schools—by the towering figure of Cicero.

Once they had internalized these models, students moved on to the most important stage of their training: the rhetorical exercises known as declamations. There were two types, which the Romans called *suasoriae* and *controversiae*. *Suasoriae* were faux-political speeches, intended to persuade a fictional or historical audience to adopt a given course of action. A student might entreat Agamemnon to sacrifice his daughter Iphigenia, urge Alexander to march onward

---

* Polemon once dared to throw the future emperor Antoninus Pius out of his house for inconveniencing him, and only consented to see a king who wanted to become his pupil after the man paid an extortionate fee. Later in life, when he was afflicted with arthritis, Polemon was carried to speaking engagements in an elaborate litter. He ordered his family to bury him while he was still alive, so that the sun would never see him reduced to silence; as the tomb was being sealed, he is supposed to have cried out, "Give me a new body, and I shall declaim again!"

to the world's end, or ponder—in the persona of Cicero—whether he should beg Mark Antony to spare his life. Although *controversiae* were based formally on courtroom speeches, the imaginary scenarios with which they dealt tended to lack even a tenuous grounding in reality. In a characteristic example, a priestess accused of violating her vows is sentenced to be flung from a cliff. As she topples over the precipice, she calls upon the goddess Vesta. Miraculously, she survives the fall. Should she be flung from the cliff a second time? The orator had to argue for or against.[11]

Rhetorical training seems to have usually lasted four or five years. The schools of the most eminent teachers, concentrated in a few cultural centers, became the ancient equivalent of universities. Despite their small size and informal organization, they had something of the modern collegiate atmosphere, complete with lecture halls and tenured professors.* We read about students getting rowdy at the races, pulling pranks on their teachers, hazing freshmen, and throwing parties.[12]

After or instead of studying with a rhetor, a student who wanted to become a doctor might attend medical school. Although this entailed reading the treatises of Hippocrates and other authors, the training consisted primarily of following experienced physicians as they attended patients. The great Roman doctor Galen spent eleven years in his medical training, which took him from the healing sanctuary of his native Pergamum to the famous school at Alexandria.[13]

Traditionally, legal training had consisted of little more than an apprenticeship, during which a young man attached himself to an eminent lawyer and learned by listening to him as he met with clients and argued cases. During the Roman imperial era, however, instruction became more formal, with law schools emerging at Rome, Beirut, and (eventually) Constantinople. At the Beirut law school, students spent four or five years working through the curriculum,

---

* Although most rhetors supported themselves with the fees paid by their pupils, there were endowed professorships of Greek and Latin rhetoric at Rome and of rhetoric and philosophy at Athens, with generous salaries paid from the imperial treasury. At Constantinople, Theodosius II founded a state-run university with no fewer than thirty-one tenured faculty in Latin, Greek, philosophy, and law.

which began with the *Institutes* of Gaius and culminated in intensive study of the imperial edicts.[14]

Instruction in philosophy was never so systematic. Most schools consisted of a small group of thinkers, unified by fierce devotion to a master's teachings. Although students were expected to read a set of canonical texts, the essence of philosophical training was discussion. Teaching proceeded by conversation and debate, alternating with lectures on points of doctrine.

A classical education, philosophical or otherwise, struck some early Christian thinkers as superfluous or immoral. "What," thundered Tertullian, "does Athens have to do with Jerusalem?" This came, however, to be a minority view.* Saint Basil of Caesarea composed a famous treatise explaining that young Christians should read the Greek classics, since these texts prepared the mind to engage more deeply with scripture. So, as the Roman Empire became Christian, its educational system continued to be firmly rooted in the classical tradition. Although the collapse of the imperial order in the west would leave monasteries as almost the sole repositories of learning, the traditional curriculum persisted in the Eastern Roman Empire until the fall of Constantinople. And by then, thanks to the humanists of the Italian Renaissance, the great authors of Greece and Rome were being studied in western Europe, and beginning to serve again, as they had for so many centuries, as the basis of a classical education.[15]

---

* By the mid-fourth century, so many teachers of grammar and rhetoric were Christian that the pagan emperor Julian sought to exclude them from the profession. Two Christian teachers thus banished from the lecture hall used their newfound leisure to recast the Bible into the forms of classical literature: Genesis became a Homeric epic; the historical books of the Old Testament, Greek tragedies; the Gospels, Platonic dialogues. Although these experiments have not survived, we still have a late antique translation of the Gospel of John into exuberant Homeric hexameters.

· 9 ·

Did They Explore Distant Lands?

$\mathscr{I}$n the ninth year of the Yanxi era, the twentieth in the reign of Han Huan Di, twenty-seventh emperor of the Han dynasty, a small party of foreigners was received in the imperial palace at Luoyang. Although the gifts they brought—elephant tusks, rhinoceros horn, and turtle shell—were not especially impressive, they claimed to have come from a great realm in the far west, as vast and powerful as the Middle Kingdom itself, where an emperor named Marcus Aurelius reigned. We don't know who these Romans were, or why they traveled so far. But their presence at the court of the Chinese emperor illustrates the range and reach of classical merchants and adventurers.[1]

The Mediterranean—or, as the Romans called it, *Mare Nostrum* (our sea)—was always the heart of the classical world; Plato famously compared the Greeks, with their coastal cities, to frogs around a pond. By Plato's time, Greek scholars knew the whole span of the sea, from the Pillars of Hercules to the Nile delta, and had apportioned its coasts among the three continents of Europe, Asia, and Africa. The campaigns of Alexander the Great made the Middle East and central Asia familiar. The Romans, with their far-ranging conquests and massive trade networks, came to know even more: a map of the world produced by the second-century astronomer Ptolemy extended from the Canary Islands to western China, with more than eight thousand places plotted between.[2]

A fifteenth-century version of Ptolemy's world map. *Wikimedia Commons*

The Greeks and Romans knew that the world was round.* Thanks to Eratosthenes, who had calculated the circumference of the earth with remarkable accuracy, they also knew that the Mediterranean occupied a relatively small portion of the globe. And despite the agonies of ancient travel, a steady trickle of scouts, merchants, and missionaries ventured deep into the blank spaces of Ptolemy's map.[3]

Southward, as in every direction, geography and opportunity determined the distances that they traveled. Merchants based in Alexandria routinely visited Arabia Felix—modern Yemen—the land of frankincense and myrrh. Despite the fact that the spice-bearing regions were said to be tormented by flying snakes, Augustus sent an army to conquer the whole southwestern corner of the Arabian Peninsula. The failure of that campaign prevented the region from

---

* With the exception of a few stubborn flat-earthers—most notably, the Epicureans— the spherical shape of the earth was generally accepted by the fourth century BCE. By way of proof, Aristotle (who speculated about the possibility of sailing around the globe) pointed to the circular outline of the earth's shadow on the moon.

becoming part of the empire, but a legionary detachment was eventually stationed on the Farasan Islands, just off the Arabian coast.[4]

Roman merchants also followed the monsoon winds down the east coast of Africa. By the second century, they had crossed the equator, reaching the vicinity of Zanzibar. A few ventured even farther south, where the gargantuan Mountains of the Moon loomed on the horizon. These mythical peaks—possibly inspired by distant views of Kilimanjaro—were rumored to be source of the Nile. The Nile itself, of course, was the most convenient inland route into Africa. Although the province of Egypt reached only to the rapids of the Second Cataract, near the modern border between Egypt and Sudan, Roman influence extended much farther—especially during the reign of Augustus, when a Roman army marched through Nubia. Later, when Nero was considering an invasion of Ethiopia, a group of legionaries was sent as far as the Sudd, a vast swamp in what is now South Sudan that defied exploration until the nineteenth century.[5]

West of the Nile was the Sahara Desert, virtually impassable before the introduction of the camel around the beginning of the Roman imperial era. During the reign of Claudius, a Roman general ventured deep into the Sahara, where he reported finding plains blanketed in dust and mountains blackened by the heat. About a half century later, a Roman merchant set out from Libya with a caravan, spent four months in the desert, and emerged in a fertile land teeming with rhinoceroses*—probably the tropical savannah of what is now southern Chad.[6]

Southerly trade winds made it easy for ancient ships to sail down the Atlantic coast of Africa. The difficulty of returning north against those winds, however, limited the reach of exploration. After the Third Punic War, the historian Polybius led a Roman fleet as far as what is now southern Morocco. Centuries earlier, a Carthaginian navigator named Hanno had reportedly voyaged much

---

* Most of the African interior, however, remained unknown, giving rise to such bizarre legends as men with heads in their chests and a tribe that made a dog their king.

farther, passing a great volcano known as the Chariot of the Gods.* Although a few scholars think Hanno may have seen Mount Cameroon, it's unlikely that any ancient fleet could have sailed so far south and returned against the prevailing winds.[7]

An expedition sent by Juba—the African client king who married a daughter of Antony and Cleopatra—discovered the Canary Islands, named for the wild dogs (*canes*) that roved their shores. Spanish navigators had already encountered the Madeira archipelago, which came to be identified with the mythical Isles of the Blessed. The vast expanse of the Atlantic beyond, the void from which Plato had conjured Atlantis, was unknown. A few Greek thinkers speculated about a continent in the uttermost west, whose rivers choked the surrounding seas with silt. But to the best of our knowledge, no attempt was ever made to reach it.[8]

Although their existence had been known for centuries, the British Isles only became familiar to Mediterranean scholars after the Roman conquest of Britain. The process of reconnaissance continued for decades: long after the province had been established, Demetrius of Tarsus, a Greek scholar, was sent with a detachment of troops to reconnoiter the Isles of Scilly off the coast of Cornwall. It was only during the governorship of Agricola, a generation after the initial Roman invasion, that an imperial fleet circumnavigated Britain.[9]

Agricola's men were not the first Mediterranean sailors to reach the northern tip of Britain. Centuries before, Pytheas of Massalia—a Greek astronomer apparently motivated by scientific curiosity—had explored the British coast before continuing north to a mysterious island called Thule. Pytheas described Thule as a dismal place, shrouded in fog and soaked by freezing rains, where the summer sun scarcely set.† Although Thule has been variously identified with

---

* Hanno also claimed to have encountered a tribe with hairy bodies, whom the interpreters called "gorillas." The story is dubious, but it inspired the name later given to the largest living primates.

† Later authors wove colorful legends around Thule. According to Procopius, for example, Thule was ten times the size of Britain, and home to thirteen populous kingdoms, who celebrated the coming of the sun at winter's end with an annual festival. *Incredible Tales of the Lands beyond Thule*—a Greek adventure novel of the second century that has, unfortunately, been lost—described a fictional wanderer's journeys from Thule to the moon.

Shetland, the Faroe Islands, and Iceland, it's most likely that Pytheas reached the coast of modern Norway.[10]

After visiting Thule, Pytheas sailed east into the Baltic Sea, apparently as far as the vicinity of modern Hamburg. A Roman fleet replicated this feat in the reign of Augustus, and at least one Roman merchant ventured even farther east, traveling overland to what is now the north coast of Poland to gather amber for Nero. Despite these forays, Roman knowledge of northeastern Europe remained vague: Scandinavia was thought to be an island, and the regions east of the Baltic were said to be inhabited by men with the bodies of beasts.[11]

Much of central Asia was equally mysterious. Although the north coast of the Black Sea was seeded with Greek colonies, from which adventurous travelers ventured into the immensity of the steppe,* the lands to the east were cut off from the Mediterranean world by rugged terrain and the hostile power of Parthia. An inscription discovered near the shore of the Caspian Sea, however, documents the presence of Roman legionaries in modern Azerbaijan, and Roman troops may have briefly occupied what is now northern Iran during the reign of Nero.[12]

Roman geographers were familiar with the shape of the Caspian Sea and the courses of the great rivers around the lost Greek kingdom of Bactria.† But the northern reaches of central Asia were populated by monsters and legends. Even the relatively sober Pliny the Elder located Amazons and a tribe known as the Lice Eaters there. It was sometimes said that, beyond a range of mountains shrouded in perpetual night, the Hyperboreans dwelt in a land never troubled by cold. But by the Roman imperial era, it was known that an icy sea crowned the globe.[13]

---

* Herodotus devoted an entire book of his *Histories* to the Scythians, who dominated the Pontic-Caspian steppe during the Classical period. He may have drawn some of his material from informants closer to home, since the city of Athens used a band of Scythian slaves to control crowds at large gatherings. Even before the time of Herodotus, stories circulated about Anacharsis, a half-Scythian (and at least half-legendary) philosopher said to have traveled around the Greek world.

† Romans even (unwillingly) settled in the region: after the defeat of Crassus at Carrhae, some of his soldiers were sent to Merv in what is now Turkmenistan.

Siberia had little appeal for the Greeks and Romans. The spices and silks of the Far East, by contrast, held out the irresistible allure of enormous profits. Trade with India was especially lucrative. In the wake of Alexander's conquests—and, later, those of the Indo-Greek kingdoms, which briefly occupied territory as far east as the Ganges valley—the geography of northern India came to be fairly well known. But it was only during the first century BCE* that Mediterranean merchants began to cross the Indian Ocean routinely. Setting out from ports along the Egyptian coast of the Red Sea, they used the monsoon winds—which blow northeast in the winter, and southwest in summer—to navigate to and from India, where they traded for pepper, cinnamon, and Chinese silk. The immense value of this trade attracted captains and investors; by the reign of Augustus, 120 Roman ships were sailing for India every year. Although most trade was confined to ports along the west coast of the subcontinent, a few Roman merchants may have operated as far east as what is now southern Vietnam.[14]

Silk brought Romans even farther from the Mediterranean. After its initial appearance in Roman markets during the first century BCE, Chinese silk became an indispensable luxury, used in everything from legionary standards to the robes of the emperors. Supply, however, lagged far behind demand, since the flow of silk was controlled (and heavily taxed) by the Parthian Empire. In an effort to lower prices, Roman merchants developed trade routes that circumvented the Parthians. The most important of these, which reached China via central Asia, hinged on the ports of western India.

Very few Roman merchants traveled to China, since it was much safer and swifter to deal with central Asian or Indian middlemen.† A few, however, made the long journey. Sometime in the early imperial era, an enterprising businessman from Roman Syria crossed

---

* The route was pioneered by Eudoxus of Cyzicus, a navigator who later perished trying to circumnavigate Africa.

† Roman geographers tended to assume that China was much smaller than it actually was. They also confused the Chinese with the Tocharian merchants who brought silk to India, which helps to explain why they thought the Chinese people were tall and fair haired.

the Parthian Empire and made his way over the steppe to the Chinese frontier. The party of Romans that reached the court of the Chinese emperor during the reign of Marcus Aurelius was almost certainly composed of merchants. Another merchant reached China in the mid-third century, after the collapse of the Han dynasty. He was sent home with a Chinese officer as his escort.[15]

A troupe of acrobats from Roman Syria, sent by the king of Parthia, flipped and tumbled in the Chinese court. Syria also produced the Nestorian Christian missionaries who founded a cathedral in the Chinese capital. But the most poignant evidence of contact between China and Rome was discovered at the oasis settlement of Miran. There, on the rim of the bitter Taklamakan Desert, a Buddhist shrine, walls aglow with classicizing frescoes, was found buried in sand. The name of the artist, painted inconspicuously in a corner, was Titus.[16]

· *10* ·

Did They Practice Buddhism?

$\mathcal{S}$outheast of Mumbai, in a range of rugged hills, a winding path ascends to the mouths of the Karla Caves. On weekends and holidays, when pilgrims crowd the neighboring temple, the caves echo with footsteps and chatter. But when the monsoon shadows the valley, and waterfalls rush from the surrounding cliffs, it's easy to imagine the solitude that drew Buddhist monks to this place nineteen centuries ago. Although there are other cave complexes nearby, nothing else in India compares with the Grand Chaitya, or prayer hall, at Karla. It plunges deep into the cliff, its soaring ceiling ribbed with age-blackened teak, the richly ornamented pillars along its walls processing toward the stupa at the distant end, where monks once walked endless circles around a relic of the Buddha. High on the pillars, neat lines of Brahmi script commemorate the donors who contributed to the hall's construction. The inscriptions are terse, mentioning little more than name and native place. But in six cases, they note an additional detail: that the donor was a *Yavana*—a Greek.*

The Greeks first entered India in force four centuries before the Karla Caves were carved, when Alexander descended into the Punjab at the head of his invincible army. The conqueror spent a year and a half in the subcontinent, defeating local kings, subjugating cities, and leaving a string of garrisons in his wake. Then, he was gone. It

---

* The Sanskrit *Yavana*—like its Prakrit analogue *Yona*—derives from "Ionia," the native region of the first Greeks to visit India.

The Grand Chaitya at Karla. *Wikimedia Commons*

seemed, at first, that the Greek presence in India would be fleeting. Within a few years of Alexander's death, his Indian satrapies were absorbed into the growing empire of Chandragupta Maurya, whose successors would rule much of India for more than a century. But when the Mauryan dynasty began to crumble, Greeks were waiting on the frontiers.

Just northwest of India, in what are now Afghanistan and the central Asian republics, lay the Greek kingdom of Bactria, famous for its thousand cities.* The Bactrian kings were almost constantly at war, sparring with their Seleucid overlords, raiding the upstart Parthians, and pushing back incursions from the steppes. So when a political vacuum developed in northern India, they were quick to exploit it. The exact sequence of events is unclear, but it seems that the Bactrian king Demetrius I invaded India in the early second century BCE, conquering a large territory. Not long after, probably as a consequence of civil war, the Indian province became an independent Greek state. The rulers of the new Indo-Greek kingdom soon controlled more of India than Alexander ever had. Although their fortunes fluctuated, parts of northern India would remain under Greek rule until the first century CE.

Too few to remain a class apart, the Greeks in India adopted local customs.† Toward the end of the second century BCE, Heliodorus, ambassador of the Indo-Greek king Antialcidas, set up an

---

* One Greco-Bactrian city—Ai Khanoum, now in northern Afghanistan—has been excavated. The city stood at the confluence of two rivers, at the base of a hill that served as its citadel. The streets behind its tall mudbrick walls bounded blocks of low houses, many equipped with Greek-style bathing rooms. The main avenue, nearly a mile long, connected the gates with the main public buildings: a gymnasium, a theater with seats for five thousand spectators, and a palace with a majestic reception hall. Despite its remoteness from the rest of the Hellenistic world, Ai Khanoum was an emphatically Greek city. The excavators uncovered a public fountain with dolphin-head spouts, a mausoleum in the shape of a colonnaded temple, a monumental shrine inscribed with maxims of the Delphic Oracle, and even the imprint—pressed by chance onto mudbrick—of a philosophical treatise by a follower of Aristotle.

† Cultural syncretism had been the rule even in the stridently Greek city of Ai Khanoum, where ethnic Greeks were probably always a small minority. Almost all the buildings, even the theater, were built of mudbrick, in keeping with local custom. The grand reception hall of the palace was inspired by Near Eastern models. And despite a cult image modeled on the famous statue of Zeus at Olympia, the Temple of Zeus looked like a Persian shrine.

imposing stone pillar beside a temple honoring the Hindu deity Vasudeva. Most of the Greeks in India, however, were attracted to a different Indian religious tradition. Buddhism was already widespread in northwestern India by the time Alexander arrived, and continued to gain converts through the Mauryan era. Ashoka, greatest of the Mauryan emperors, was an energetic patron, founding monasteries, building stupas, and sending missionaries to every neighboring people—including the Greeks. Ashoka commissioned dozens of monumental inscriptions outlining the ethical precepts of Buddhism. Two of these—discovered near Kandahar, Afghanistan— were written in elegant and sophisticated Greek, a sign that at least a few native Greek speakers were involved in the king's proselytizing project. The inscriptions claim that missionaries were sent to all the Greek kingdoms of the east. According to later Buddhist tradition, some of these missionaries were Greeks themselves.

By the time the Bactrian kings annexed northwestern India, in short, many eastern Greeks were familiar with Buddhism. Within a century of the conquest, some of the most important men in the Indo-Greek kingdom identified themselves as Buddhists: a provincial governor named Theodorus is known to have dedicated a Buddhist reliquary, and another Greek governor established a stupa. Many wealthy Greeks, like the benefactors at Karla, were commemorated as donors in Buddhist cave monasteries. Menander, the ruler who brought the Greek kingdom in India to its apogee, was almost certainly a Buddhist. He patronized Buddhist shrines, put the eight-spoked Dharma wheel on some of his coins, and even appeared—long after his reign—as the protagonist of a Buddhist text, in which he shrewdly debates a learned monk. Upon his death, Menander's ashes were enshrined in stupas, where they were revered like the relics of the Buddha himself.* Menander's successors seem to have imitated his pro-Buddhist policies. Most of the later Indo-Greek kings describe themselves as "followers of the Dharma" on

---

* Menander's portrait is familiar from his coins, which circulated throughout northern India for centuries. It has also been suggested that the Bharhut Yavana—a relief of a Greek warrior with Buddhist emblems on the sheath of his sword—represents the king.

their coins. At Taxila, their capital, a Buddhist shrine and stupas stood beside temples to Hindu and Greek gods.[1]

During the first century CE, just as the Indo-Greek kingdom was collapsing,* contact between India and the Mediterranean world was renewed. Merchants based in Alexandria had discovered that the monsoon winds could carry ships swiftly and relatively safely from the mouth of the Red Sea to the western coast of India. Spurred by Roman demand for spices, hundreds of ships were soon crossing the Arabian Sea. Pliny the Elder complained that 100 million sestertii of gold and silver were being traded to Indian merchants each year. The substance, if not the scale, of his claim is confirmed by the hoards of Roman coins that are still periodically discovered across India.[2]

The Arabian Sea trade brought more than silk and spices to the Mediterranean world.† Indians also made the trip west, establishing a small community in Alexandria. One Indian visitor—possibly a Buddhist monk—made his way to Athens, where he caused a sensation by burning himself alive in the presence of Augustus. Despite this contact with India and Indians, the Greeks of the Mediterranean world remained virtually ignorant of Buddhism. Greco-Roman descriptions of Indian religions confuse the Hindu, Buddhist, and Jain traditions, and tend to be heavily influenced by accounts of Alexander's first encounters with the Indian ascetics whom the Greeks called "gymnosophists."[3]

The first explicit mention of the Buddha in a classical text was made by a Christian apologist, who noted that a sect of Indian philosophers revered a certain "Boutta" as a god on account of his holiness. Another stray reference appeared in a work of Saint Jerome,

---

* Greek cultural influence endured long after the dissolution of the Bactrian and Indo-Greek kingdoms. Many coins of the Kushan Empire, which ruled much of northern India and central Asia from the first to the third century CE, were basically Hellenistic: the legends were in good grammatical Greek, and Greek gods frequently appeared on the reverses. Greek, in fact, seems to have long been the administrative language of much of the Kushan Empire, and stray inscriptions suggest the existence of substantial Greek-speaking populations as late as the third century.

† An ivory statuette of a Hindu goddess, probably imported from India via Egypt, was discovered in the ruins of Pompeii. A Greek comedy set in India—and written partly in an Indian language (either Kannada or Tulu)—was performed in Egypt during the Roman imperial era.

who erroneously described the Buddha as the founder of a sect of gymnosophists.* Despite its obscurity, Buddhism may have influenced an important movement in Greek thought. The philosopher Pyrrho of Elis accompanied Alexander to India, where he conversed with monks and ascetics. When he returned to Greece, Pyrrho taught that the goal of existence should be freedom from worry, and that the only way to achieve such freedom was to suspend all judgment about the nature of reality. The parallel with Buddhism—in particular, the idea of virtue as an escape from suffering—is intriguing, though the degree to which Pyrrho was actually inspired by Buddhist doctrine remains unclear.[4]

In any case, even if the Indian roots of Pyrrho's skepticism can be proven, Buddhism was never a significant presence in the Greco-Roman Mediterranean. But in India, where so many Greeks became Buddhist converts and patrons, the encounter between east and west had lasting artistic consequences. For centuries, it had been customary to represent the Buddha with symbols—often footprints, an empty seat, or a Bodhi tree. But during the later years of the Greek kingdom, anthropomorphic representations of the Buddha began to appear. These first images of the Buddha, particularly associated with the Gandhara region, show clear signs of Greek influence.[†] They stand like Greek statues, have the expressions of Greek statues, wear the delicately draped tunics of Greek statues.

The fact that all the extant masterpieces of Gandhara-style art appeared after the fall of the Indo-Greek kingdoms has raised questions about the nature of Greek influence on Buddhist iconography.

---

* The life of the Buddha circulated in medieval Europe through the story of Barlaam and Josaphat, a romance about an Indian prince who became aware of the world's miseries and was converted to Christianity. For nearly a millennium, in his guise as Josaphat—the name is based on an Arabic transliteration of "Bodhisattva"—the Buddha was venerated as a Christian saint.

† The Gandhara style was prefigured in the art of the Kushan Empire. The courtyard of the Kushan palace at Khalchayan, in modern Uzbekistan, featured a splendid array of Greek-style sculptures, and the walls were adorned with paintings of Hercules, Athena, and Nike—among other Greek and Iranian gods—watching over Kushan rulers. The Buddhist stupas and monasteries that sprouted across the Kushan Empire often featured figural sculpture inspired by Greek models. On the Bimaran Casket, a golden reliquary discovered in Afghanistan, the Buddha appears in a pose and setting taken directly from classical sculpture.

It remains uncertain whether the earliest depictions of the Buddha emerged directly from a native Indo-Greek tradition, or whether ideas and craftsmen arriving via Roman trade routes played a significant role. Whatever its origins, the Hellenistic strain in Buddhist art would have a long history, moving with the faith into central Asia, China, and Japan. The image of the Enlightened One changed as it traveled. But even today, in shrines and sanctuaries across Asia and beyond, it bears traces, faint but unmistakable, of the Greek encounter with Buddhism two millennia ago.

· 11 ·

Did They Practice Astrology?

𝒯he new star was faint at first, little more than a glimmer in the summer sky. But as the Romans gathered to celebrate Caesar's funeral games, it blazed brilliantly—a sign, it was said, that the great man's soul had joined the gods. For seven days it burned over the tile roofs and umbrella pines, a rival to the setting sun. Then it faded, with the majesty befitting a god, into the shimmering calendar of the heavens.[1]

Although a few scholars flirted with heliocentrism, virtually all Greeks and Romans accepted that the earth occupied the center of the universe, and that it was orbited by the seven planets:* the moon, Mercury, Venus, the sun,† Mars, Jupiter, and Saturn. All the planets were thought to be embedded in "spheres" that carried them around the earth in a geometric dance of orbits and epicycles. The outermost sphere carried the stars,‡ which the definitive ancient catalog grouped into forty-eight constellations. Of special significance were the twelve constellations of the Zodiac, aligned with the tracks of the planets.[2]

---

* The Greeks seem to have adopted the practice of naming the planets after gods from the Babylonians. The Romans, as usual, followed the Greek precedent. The nature of the relationship between god and planet was always unclear, especially in the case of the sun.

† Aristotle described the sun as a globe of luminous ether. He was uncertain, however, how sunlight could warm the earth. A century before, Anaxagoras had claimed that the sun was a mass of red-hot metal.

‡ Ptolemy calculated the radius of the universe as about twenty thousand earth radii (less than the actual distance from the earth to the sun). Archimedes estimated that the number of sand grains needed to fill this sphere was 10^{63}.

Caesar's comet, as represented on a denarius of Augustus. *Public domain*

The Zodiac had first been defined in Mesopotamia, where scholars kept careful records of eclipses, planetary motions, and other heavenly phenomena for millennia. In the wake of Alexander's conquests, these records were absorbed by Greek astronomers, along with the Babylonian tradition of using the motions of the planets to foretell the future. From this marriage, astrology was born. Like its descendants, ancient astrology attempted to determine outcomes from the positions and interrelations of the planets and signs of the Zodiac. With knowledge of an individual's birth date, astrologers claimed that they could chart the whole future course of his or her life, and pick the most propitious time for anything from a voyage to a bath.[3]

Although some doubted that the stars influenced human affairs—pointing, for example, to the fact that twins born under the same sky often led very different lives—most Greeks and Romans regarded astrology as a natural and legitimate extension of astronomy. Astrologers were especially popular in early imperial Rome, where they became confidants of the emperors.* Augustus put Capricorn, his chosen Zodiac sign, on the Roman coinage. Scorpio, the birth sign of Tiberius, became the emblem of the Praetorian Guard. Hadrian confidently foretold the hour and day of his own death. Septimius Severus married a woman whose horoscope predicted she would become a queen.[4]

The astrological manual of Firmicus Maternus, who wrote in the fourth century, illuminates the degree to which the stars were thought to govern mortal lives. According to Maternus, for example, any man born in the first degree of Libra will be handsome and lovable. (If the ascendant is in the feminine stars, he is destined to be a male prostitute, albeit one loved by all for his sophistication and charm.) Those born in the seventh degree of Libra will be captured by pirates at some point, or possibly devoured by wild beasts. Those born in the twentieth degree will be great doctors—unless Mars is in that degree, in which case they are doomed to fall from a great height.[†] And so on.[5]

By the time Maternus wrote his manual, astrology had pervaded every aspect of Roman life. Parents took great care to note when their children were born, sometimes stationing a man with a gong to inform a waiting astrologer of the exact moment. Doctors studied astrological manuals to determine the moon's effects on the human body; Stoic philosophers hailed astrological predictions as manifestations of omnipotent fate. The seven laps in a standard chariot

---

* After a series of failed predictions, Tiberius threatened to have his court astrologer Thrasyllus flung from a cliff. Thrasyllus saved his life by declaring—correctly, as it turned out—that a ship which had just appeared on the horizon was bringing good news. Thrasyllus's son Balbillus became court astrologer to Nero. When a comet appeared in the sky over Rome, presaging the death of a great man, Balbillus helpfully advised the emperor to ward off disaster by executing a few eminent subjects.

† Some of Maternus's predictions are quite specific. Those born in the tenth degree of Capricorn, for example, will be rich and devastatingly effective adulterers, who will seduce all their friends' wives but never be detected.

race and the seven degrees of Mithraism were pattered on the seven planets, as was the seven-day week we still use, each of its days named for the planet that governed its first hour.[6]

During the early imperial era, astrologers were repeatedly expelled from Rome and Italy, largely from fears that their predictions would encourage plots against the emperors. Later, when the Roman world became Christian, they fell under suspicion again, since the idea that the stars influenced human affairs seemed to contravene divine omnipotence. Astrology, however, outlasted the emperors and their anxieties. Despite Copernicus, it remains with us still, an uncanny offspring of ancient science.[7]

· *12* ·

Did They Know When
the Pyramids Were Built?

$\mathscr{I}$n 357, Emperor Constantius II ordered an obelisk from Egypt's greatest temple to be set up in the Circus Maximus at Rome. After crossing the Mediterranean on a specially built barge, the obelisk was floated up the Tiber, rolled through the city on a wooden cradle, and raised onto a new base by thousands of men straining at capstans. Spectators marveled at the obelisk's size—it was 105 feet tall and weighed more than nine hundred thousand pounds—and puzzled over the hieroglyphs on its sides, which nobody in Rome could read. According to a treatise written in Egypt centuries before, the inscriptions on the obelisk recounted the deeds of a certain King Ramestes.* But who this king was, or when he had reigned, none could say.[1]

Like the Greeks before them, the Romans had an inexact sense of history's depth. They knew—or thought they knew—that Rome had been founded about eleven centuries before Constantius set up his obelisk, and that the Trojan War had taken place more than four hundred years before the foundation of Rome. But of the vast gulf

---

* The obelisk was actually set up by Thutmose IV. It had been removed from its original location on the orders of Constantine—who wanted it to adorn his new capital at Constantinople—but had been stranded in Alexandria by Constantine's death. After Constantine's son Constantius sent it to Rome, the obelisk stood in the Circus Maximus through late antiquity. Toppled by an earthquake or flood sometime during the Middle Ages, it was uncovered in the reign of Pope Sixtus V and reerected (sans part of its shaft) beside the Basilica of St. John Lateran.

The Lateran Obelisk, set up by Constantius II in the Circus Maximus. *Author's photo*

of time preceding the fall of Troy, they knew only what the Greek myths could tell them.*

Greek civilization had grown up among the empty tombs and tumbled palaces of the Mycenaeans. Some of these ruins came to be associated with the kings and heroes of the *Iliad*. Others, with their gargantuan stone walls, were said to have been built by the mythical cyclopes. A few were connected with the Pelasgians, the mysterious people thought to have inhabited Greece before the coming of the Greeks.[2]

Myth also provided a guide for chance discoveries of ancient tombs. The Athenians hailed the bones of a tall man buried with bronze weapons, for example, as the remains of the hero Theseus. A stone coffin uncovered by a flood on the outskirts of Rome was interpreted as the resting place of the legendary sage-king Numa

---

* The Hellenistic polymath Eratosthenes had set the date of Troy's fall as our 1183 BCE. Events before the Trojan War he assigned to "mythic time," an era in which exact chronology was impossible.

Pompilius.* Some antiquities, however, defied such ready identification. When the Spartan king Agesilaus opened a tomb traditionally associated with Alcmene, the mother of Hercules, he found a bronze tablet inscribed with mysterious symbols. No Greek scholar could make sense of it, so Agesilaus sent the tablet to be deciphered in the most ancient country he knew: Egypt.[3]

The classical experience of Egypt began in the seventh century BCE, when Greek merchants and mercenaries first traveled up the Nile. Alexander's conquest of Egypt set the stage for three centuries of Greek rule, and the establishment of Greek as Egypt's second language. After Augustus annexed the Ptolemaic kingdom, Egypt became a Roman province, and remained so for nearly seven hundred years. For a millennium, in other words, Egypt was an integral part of the classical world. Some classical authors mocked Egypt's animal-headed gods, or stereotyped the Egyptian people as mystics and thieves. But most Greeks and Romans seem to have regarded Egypt as a fascinating place—a land, to paraphrase Herodotus, filled with wonders. Under the emperors, this interest found expression in the obelisks set up around Rome, in the Nile scenes painted on the walls of villas, and in the pyramid tombs erected by members of the Roman elite.[4]

Although Pliny the Elder had criticized them as idle displays of wealth, the Pyramids—and especially the Pyramids of Giza—were universally ranked among Egypt's greatest marvels, and indeed as wonders of the world. Roman tourists paid local villagers to scramble up the smooth sides of the Great Pyramid, and carved graffiti into the casing blocks.† Like the Greeks before them, they knew that the

---

* Two stone chests were found together. One—supposed to be Numa's coffin—was empty. The other reportedly contained ancient manuscripts, which were burned. The so-called Chronicle of the Trojan War by Dictys of Crete claimed to be the translation of an ancient manuscript recovered from a tomb during the reign of Nero. Although the Chronicle is a work of the Roman imperial era, it is conceivable that actual finds of Minoan Linear A tablets inspired the story of its discovery. During the reign of Vespasian, finally, a tomb came to light that contained several vases, each painted—or so it was reported—with a figure who looked uncannily like the (elderly, bald, and rotund) emperor.

† Before they were stripped for building material in the fourteenth century, the limestone casing blocks of the Great Pyramid were covered in Greek and Latin inscriptions, which included a proclamation of a certain Roman governor's achievements and a poem eulogizing the brother of a Roman official.

Pyramids were the tombs of pharaohs. Their age, however, was a matter of controversy.[5]

Herodotus, the first Greek historian, thought that the first pharaohs had reigned around 15,000 BCE. Diodorus, writing four centuries after Herodotus, pushed the beginnings of the Egyptian monarchy back to around 23,000 BCE.* Since the Egyptian kingdom actually coalesced shortly before 3000 BCE, these were dramatic overestimates. But when describing the Pyramids at Giza—which we now know were built during the twenty-sixth century BCE—classical authors tended to miscalculate in the opposite direction. Herodotus believed that the pharaoh who built the Great Pyramid had reigned two generations after the Trojan War—by his reckoning, around 1200 BCE. Diodorus dated the same king to the ninth generation after the Trojan War, or sometime in the tenth century BCE. Other authors gave even more recent dates, especially for the Pyramid of Menkaure, which a long-standing tradition attributed to Rhodopis, a Greek slave girl who became a famous courtesan—or, by some accounts, wife of the pharaoh—during the sixth century BCE.[6]

In part, Greek and Roman ignorance about the age of the Pyramids reflected a broader breakdown of cultural transmission. Although many native Egyptians knew Greek, knowledge of how to read hieroglyphs was restricted to a small group of priests, whose numbers steadily dwindled.[†] Long before the last hieroglyphic inscription was carved at the end of the fourth century, the records inscribed on Egypt's ancient monuments were as inscrutable to most of their guardians as they were to everyone else. When the Roman prince Germanicus asked a priest to interpret an inscription in the ruins of Thebes, for example, he was fed an entirely fantastic tale

---

* These are far from the most extravagant estimates in classical sources for the antiquity of other civilizations. Pliny the Elder, for example, records that the Babylonian astronomical records went back 730,000 years.

† Greek and Roman scholars tended to assume that hieroglyphic signs were purely symbolic—instead of both phonetic and symbolic, as they actually are—and interpreted them accordingly. The only extant classical text that discusses the interpretation of hieroglyphs at length, a late antique treatise attributed to the Egyptian priest Horapollo, combines an accurate understanding of some signs with a great deal of misguided allegory.

about an ancient pharaoh who had conquered Bactria, Scythia, Syria, and Armenia.[7]

Not all Egyptian history, of course, was hidden behind hieroglyphs. Sometime in the third century BCE, a learned Egyptian named Manetho composed a history in Greek, which correctly dated the Pyramids to an early period of Egyptian history. But instead of consulting Manetho's treatise—which remained obscure until late antiquity—the Greeks and Romans preferred to read and reread Herodotus, whose chronologically chaotic account of Egyptian history was respected as a classic. The Greeks and Romans didn't know how old the Pyramids were, in short, because they preferred to perceive Egypt through the lenses of their own culture. What those lenses could not show, they had no wish to see.

· 13 ·

Did They Speculate about the Future?

$\mathscr{H}$ow will the world end? Reflecting on that somber topic during the reign of Nero, the Roman philosopher Seneca decided that the most likely cause would be a universal flood, in which rain and surging tides would merge with subterranean reservoirs to drown every land. After imagining the last survivors starving on mountaintops as lightning played over a swelling sea, Seneca looked further into the future. The earth, he believed, would be restored after the deluge, and humanity re-created. But the new men would be as corrupt as the old, and the world would be drowned again. Seneca also believed, however, that before the coming deluge, observation and research would reveal more and more of nature's secrets, solving puzzles that perplexed his own generation.[1]

Seneca's musings reflect the complexity of ancient ideas about the future, which differed profoundly from our own. Though prefigured during the Enlightenment, the modern assumption that the future will be more technologically advanced, if not materially better, than the present is a product of the nineteenth century, when the Industrial Revolution made a belief in continual progress both plausible and fashionable. Far from assuming progress, the foundational texts of classical literature proclaim the decline of human society from a primeval golden age. The most famous example, quoted and imitated throughout antiquity, is Hesiod's description of the ages of man, which presents humanity as the last and least in a series of mortal races. Decline was ongoing: soon, Hesiod claimed, mankind would lose its last semblance of morality, and be destroyed by Zeus.[2]

Greek thinkers often incorporated nostalgia for the lost golden age into a cyclical conception of history, which applied the human progression of youth, maturity, and old age to whole societies. The historian Polybius, for example, described a cycle of governments, from monarchy to mob rule, through which all states inevitably pass. Pre-Socratic philosophers applied the same paradigm to the universe itself. Heraclitus believed that matter was continually resolving from and dissolving into primordial fire, and Empedocles outlined a cosmic cycle of love and strife that caused all matter to unite and disintegrate in turn. Later, the Stoics held that the universe was consumed by a conflagration at the end of every eon, after which history repeated exactly: there would be another Athens, another Alexander, another Rome.[3]

Without necessarily arguing against a cyclical theory of history, a number of authors celebrated technological advances. Although there was some disagreement about the relative significance of ingenuity and serendipity in driving progress, it was generally acknowledged that human discoveries had altered life for the better. The long list of inventions in Pliny the Elder's encyclopedia, which ranges from the alphabet to catapults, attests to widespread awareness of technological change over time. Assertions that the future might be better than the present, however, emphasized moral or political, rather than technological, change. The most famous utopia in classical literature, the ideal city of Plato's *Republic*,* is if anything less technologically advanced than Classical Athens.[4]

The Romans inherited Greek ideas about the future, and infused them with a sense of political destiny. After the unrest of the late Republic, Roman poets hailed the peace brought by the reign of Augustus as a return of the primeval golden age, when war was unknown. Though intended to please the emperor, these evocations seem to have reflected genuine enthusiasm. Whether there was any

---

* Plato's more "realistic" ideal city—Magnesia, described in the *Laws*—is sited far from the sea, to discourage commerce and exposure to foreign ideas. Innovative technologies, like any other catalyst for change, would be unwelcome in such a closed community.

widespread expectation of actual improvement in the future, however, is difficult to say. The Romans imagined the original golden age to have been devoid of technology, since the earth had freely provided all things. Although the new imperial golden age was not associated with a rejection of existing comforts, neither was it linked with any expectation of technological progress.* What sufficed in the present would provide for the future.[5]

Long before the actual decay of Roman power, proclamations of a golden millennium coexisted with anxieties about future decline. The Romans liked to claim that their ancestors had been simple and virtuous, and seldom missed an opportunity to attack the corruption of their society—and especially its leaders—by modern luxuries. Such self-indulgence, they lamented, would doom the Roman people if not corrected. The series of disasters that overtook the empire in late antiquity seemed to vindicate this view—save in the eyes of the growing Christian community.

In contrast to the cycles of destruction and rebirth proposed by Greek philosophers, the early Christians had a resolutely linear conception of time, which traced a divine plan of salvation culminating in the Second Coming of Jesus. Christian scholars posited that human history would last six thousand years—one millennium for each of the six days of creation. Some believed that the sixth millennium was nearly ended, and that the Second Coming was at hand. Others, notably Saint Augustine, rejected any precise projections. Following a prophecy in the book of Daniel that foresaw the rise and fall of four great kingdoms, early Christians tended to identify the Roman Empire as the last power that would dominate the earth. When it fell, they predicted, the end times would begin.† This interpretation would have a long history in the Eastern Roman Empire, where the fall of Constantinople came to be closely associated with the apocalypse.[6]

---

* In the second century, the Greek satirist Lucian composed *A True Story*, a deliberately ludicrous tale involving travel to the moon, a war with the king of the sun, and a voyage (back on Earth) to visit the heroes on the Isles of the Blessed. Though often described as an early example of science fiction, *A True Story* is not—like modern representatives of the genre—informed by any assumption of technological progress.

† Several Roman emperors (most notably Justinian, rumored to be a demon in human flesh) were considered candidates for the Antichrist.

Although early Christians believed that the Gospels were destined to be preached in every land, and hoped for a universal community of believers, they did not expect the world to improve materially in the future. In this, at least, they agreed with the Romans. Despite poetic effusions about a new golden age, the Romans foresaw only decline. With reform and discipline, dissolution might be delayed. But inertia would prevail in the end. The empire would fall, the ordered symmetries of civilization would dissolve, and all would lie in chaos until the world was renewed, and history repeated again.

Did They Come Close
to an Industrial Revolution?

$\mathcal{A}$nthemius of Tralles was a patient man. He spent long hours composing mathematical treatises, watching light play over convex mirrors, and living out the quietly busy existence of a Roman gentleman scholar. When it came to his upstairs neighbor Zeno, however, Anthemius had no patience left. Their feud had begun with those little annoyances that apartment dwellers inflict on one another. It escalated when Zeno insisted on building a wall that blocked the light into Anthemius's rooms. Anthemius protested, to no avail. He brought the matter to court, and lost.* Finally, with no other options left, he activated his earthquake machine. One day, when Zeno was scheduled to have a dinner party, Anthemius brought a number of cauldrons into his rooms and filled them with water. Covering each cauldron, he connected it to a leather-encased pipe that ran up to the apartment's ceiling. Once Zeno's guests had arrived, Anthemius lit fires beneath the cauldrons. Steam rose through the pipes, swelling the leather covering their ends. As the steam pressure rose, the pipes began to pulse and vibrate, shaking the entire house. Zeno and his terrified guests ran down to the street, shouting about an earthquake—and Anthemius had his revenge.[1]

Anthemius's earthquake machine stood in a long line of classical steam-powered gadgets. Five centuries earlier, Hero of Alexandria had

---

* Anthemius probably didn't help his case by using mirrors to blast Zeno's windows with concentrated beams of light that temporarily blinded anyone who saw them.

written a treatise explaining how to open temple gates, play organs, and spin a turbine with steam. At the time Hero's treatise was written, the Romans were in the midst of what was—by ancient standards—an impressive economic expansion, marked by the mass production of certain goods, an enormous expansion in mining, and growing use of waterpower. In the light of these developments, steam-powered devices such as the earthquake machine might seem like tentative steps toward an ancient industrial revolution. As we'll see, this was always unlikely, though not for the reasons you might assume.

It is often claimed that the Greeks and Romans were uninterested in technological innovation. Members of the elite certainly tended to regard mechanical tinkering as a commoner's pursuit. They were, however, acutely interested in inventions and ideas that could make them money. The Roman Senate, for example, made a point of preserving and translating a Carthaginian handbook that outlined innovative methods of farming. The idea that ancient technology was stagnant is another myth. While there were few dramatic advances, the Roman imperial era alone witnessed the appearance of blown glass, the screw press for olives and grapes, the hydraulic concrete that built structures like the Pantheon, and many other inventions that impacted the lives and livelihoods of millions.* A third misconception is that the institution of slavery discouraged labor-saving devices. In most places and periods, slave labor was not cheap. Since slaves represented a serious investment, their owners were motivated to ensure that their labor generated the maximum possible profit. The slave-worked brick and tile yards established on many estates around Rome to feed the emperors' building projects illustrate the sensitivity of large landowners to economic opportunity.[2]

During the Roman imperial era—which, as the apogee of the classical world, will be the focus of this answer—certain aspects of the economy seemed to be primed for industrialization. Although

---

* Among the most striking of these inventions was the vallus, a reaping machine used widely in Roman Gaul. This first mechanized harvester consisted of a two-wheeled wooden frame whose front was fitted with a bin and rows of knives. As the frame was driven forward by a mule, the knives cut through rows of wheat, tipping the heads into the bin.

most economic activity was always local, there was intense long-distance trade in grain, wine, olive oil, and other goods, driven largely by the need to supply both the city of Rome and the legions on the frontiers.* And although small workshops were the backbone of the ancient economy, several Roman industries featured examples of what might reasonably be called mass production.† The sprawling fish-processing factories that dotted the shorelines of what are now Spain, Portugal, and Morocco featured purpose-built areas for gutting and preparation, concrete salting vats, and rows of vessels in which garum—a sauce made from fermented fish guts—ripened. The salted fish and garum these facilities produced was often shipped as far as Rome. Mass production also characterized the manufacture of terra sigillata pottery, a glossy red tableware made in northern Italy and Gaul during the early imperial era. The pots were produced in enormous quantities by workshops using standardized molds, and fired in kilns capable of handling as many as forty thousand vessels simultaneously.

The Romans mined gold and silver on a proto-industrial scale, driving shafts thousands of feet into hard rock and pumping out groundwater with slave-worked treadwheels.‡ Carts carried ore to the surface, sometimes trundling along primitive railroads in the form of tracks cut into the tunnel floor. The colossal mine at Las Medulas in northwestern Spain, more than a mile across and up to 650 feet deep, was ringed by no fewer than seven large aqueducts. These fed reservoirs perched along the rim of the pit, which were periodically emptied, sending water downhill with a force that stripped away debris and exposed the gold-bearing deposits below.[3]

---

* The scale of this trade is visible at Monte Testaccio, an artificial hill on the outskirts of Rome made up of more than fifty million broken oil amphorae.

† In late antiquity, when the emperors established a network of arms factories, mints, and weaving centers, standardized goods were manufactured on a grand scale under the auspices of the government.

‡ The mines at Rio Tinto were drained by eight pairs of treadwheel pumps, which collectively raised water about one hundred feet. It has been estimated that they could remove about 2,400 gallons per hour. Pliny the Elder describes a Spanish silver mine with a gallery more than a mile long, drained by slaves working in shifts measured by lamplight.

Equally striking, if less dramatic, was the widespread Roman use of power sources beyond human and animal muscle.* Water mills for grinding grain could be found in every part of the empire. A famous example—at Barbegal, near Arles—was served by a purpose-built aqueduct more than five miles long, and consisted of two parallel rows of millhouses, each equipped with an overshot waterwheel. Together, its sixteen mills were capable of producing enough flour each day to feed more than ten thousand people.[4]

Finally, as mentioned earlier, Roman scientists experimented with steam power. An especially intriguing product of their tinkering was the device known as Hero's aeolipile, a hollow sphere mounted on a pivot over a covered cauldron. When the water in the cauldron was heated, steam was forced through pipes into the sphere. As the steam escaped through a pair of angled outlet vents, it caused the sphere to spin—making this device the first known steam turbine.[5]

To summarize: far from being opposed to technological innovation, the Romans welcomed it, especially when it promised a clear financial reward. The Roman economy was characterized by the mass production of certain key goods, by large-scale mining, and by extensive use of waterpower. And there was, at least in some academic circles, an understanding of the basic principles of steam power. In view of all this, it might seem as though the Romans were on the cusp of a British-style industrial revolution. But that was never the case.

Hero's aeolipile, to begin with, was too inefficient to ever be developed into a practical power source—which is hardly surprising, since there is no reason to think that Hero intended it to be anything of the sort. Had he wanted to create a steam engine, Hero likely could have done so. It simply never occurred to him that such a device would be worth making. Hero was a product of a society in which technological innovation—though sometimes welcome, at least when it offered the elite ways to make more money—had a limited place. The Ptolemies had supported a few mechanically inclined scholars at the Library of Alexandria, and one of them—the

---

* Wood and charcoal were the primary means of generating heat everywhere except Roman Britain, where surface coal deposits were mined.

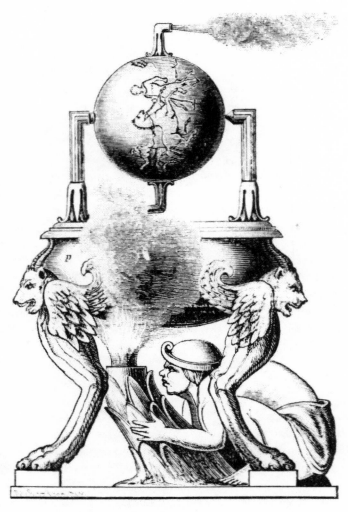

A reconstruction of Hero's aeolipile. *Wikimedia Commons*

brilliant Ctesibius—had rewarded their patronage by inventing the force pump, the hydraulic organ, and the first accurate water clock. This sort of state-financed research and development, however, was virtually nonexistent in the Roman world.[6]

Most members of the Roman elite saw no reason to encourage mechanical experimentation. They tended, like the Greeks before them, to regard such things as unworthy of a gentleman's attention— what Plato and Aristotle had called "banausic." Seneca dismissed the invention of plate glass, for example, as a contrivance of slaves, unworthy of educated minds. Such snobbery reflected a generally cautious attitude toward innovation. According to an anecdote repeated by several ancient authors, Tiberius destroyed the workshop of a craftsman who developed a flexible form of glass, fearing that it would reduce the value of gold and silver. Vespasian was said to have once rejected a new device for lifting columns, since he wanted to keep the Roman commoners employed. Although it's unlikely that either story has basis in fact, both are characteristic of a culture that did not necessarily regard technological progress as positive.[7]

There were other impediments to an ancient industrial revolution. Thanks to poor communications, a machine or method developed in one part of the empire had no guarantee of reaching the rest of the Roman world. The famous Antikythera Mechanism, an elaborate astronomical clock sometimes described as the first analog computer, is the only device of its kind ever discovered, since knowledge of how to create machines like it was probably limited to a small circle of craftsmen on the island of Rhodes. On the theoretical side, the nature of Greco-Roman higher education, which emphasized the practice of rhetoric and close reading of classical texts, encouraged those few students who contrived to be interested in mechanics and the physical sciences to refine the work of their great predecessors instead of pioneering new lines of research. More fundamentally, there was no economic incentive in the classical world to pursue anything like the industrial ventures that transformed Britain during the eighteenth century. For all its sophistication, the Roman economy was, in modern terms, underdeveloped. Most of the population lived near the subsistence level, and the vast majority of all wealth was held by a small landed aristocracy. Commerce was mostly localized; industry, mostly small scale.

The British Industrial Revolution was initially stimulated by the cotton textile industry, which awarded spectacular profits to entrepreneurs who pursued the most efficient methods of mass-producing cloth. Those profits were made possible by a thriving international market and by financial institutions that facilitated large-scale investment in new technologies. Nothing in the Roman economy enabled or repaid such investment. As we've seen, there were a few examples of what could be called mass production. But these were exceptional, for the simple reason that the Roman market for mass-produced consumer goods was vastly smaller than the global market that made British cotton cloth so profitable in the late eighteenth century.* The majority of Romans, after all, were poor farmers with little disposable income. And in any case, the difficulties and expense of transport made marketing manufactured goods cost-ineffective almost anywhere outside a major city.

Even if there had been a more promising market for mass-produced manufactures, the Roman world lacked a class of entrepreneurs ready to exploit it. Although the Roman elite sometimes invested in industrial enterprises, these invariably produced basic and inexpensive goods that did not drive technological innovation. Nor did they create a separate entrepreneurial class, since the slaves and contractors who managed them had to surrender most of their profits to aristocratic owners. The Roman elite's participation in manufacturing, in any case, was always limited and opportunistic. Wealthy men preferred to invest in land—the ancient world's most reliable asset—or in some combination of money-lending and luxury commerce, which were far more lucrative than any manufacturing enterprise known to the Romans. And instead of reinvesting their profits in business ventures, Roman aristocrats tended to pour them into lavish villas, extravagant banquets, and other forms of conspicuous consumption.

---

* There was a substantial textile industry in the Roman world, which witnessed the appearance of the labor-saving horizontal loom. But almost all the workshops involved seemed to have been quite small, and no aspect of the industry was ever mechanized.

Although there were prosperous merchants and freedmen outside the traditional aristocracy, these outsiders never formed a distinct group, and the wealthiest among them imitated the attitudes and investing habits of the elite. Unlike eighteenth-century Britain, in short, the classical world had neither a class of entrepreneurs ready to invest in innovative technologies nor any industry that rewarded such investment. British society had been primed for industrialization by a host of factors—ranging from a history of coal mining to a growing population of landless agricultural workers—but the critical catalyst was the emergence of the cotton textile industry, which offered profits on a scale that drove generations of investors into a frenzy of competition and innovation. Nothing remotely comparable existed in antiquity.

Although we have been conditioned to expect it, technological advance is not inevitable. New technologies do not appear spontaneously when a society reaches a certain level of prosperity and knowledge. Invention needs to be stimulated by a clear need or opportunity. Lacking that, and lacking entrepreneurs motivated to invest in new technologies, stagnation is as natural as progress. Nor is progress, as we see it, the goal of every society. The technologies of the Greeks and Romans were perfectly adequate for the needs they perceived. Their failure to industrialize was not a missed opportunity. In their eyes, there was no opportunity to miss.

II

HOW DID IT WORK?

· 15 ·

How Did They Prove Their Identity?

$\mathcal{B}$y the time he died, Nero had been the most famous person on the planet for nearly fourteen years. His name prefaced inscriptions from Spain to Syria, his statues stood in every province, and tens of millions of coins bearing his likeness were circulating throughout the empire and beyond.* News of his death rippled across the Roman world as swiftly as speeding ships and galloping riders could carry it. Yet despite Nero's notoriety, or because of it, no fewer than three pretenders emerged. The first false Nero appeared in Greece, where the emperor had recently spent more than a year touring cities and competing at festivals. He looked like Nero, could sing and play the lyre like Nero, and managed to persuade several units of Roman soldiers that he was the genuine article before being captured and executed. The second false Nero, from the province of Asia, resembled the former emperor closely enough to gain a small army of adherents and the support of a Parthian usurper. A generation later, the third false Nero also enjoyed Parthian aid.[1]

Nero's case is of course exceptional, and political factors clearly influenced the acceptance of the various pretenders. But the fact that the most recognizable man on earth could be imitated so successfully indicates the difficulties of proving identity in the tenuously interconnected classical world. Some of the most dramatic examples

---

* Despite his posthumous infamy, Nero's coins continued to circulate for centuries, especially in Egypt, where they outnumbered all others for decades after the emperor's death.

involve slaves, who were—for obvious reasons—exceptionally moti-vated to assume false identities. Pliny the Younger, a provincial governor, wrote a letter informing Trajan that two slaves masquerad-ing as Roman citizens had been discovered in a group of legionary recruits. On another occasion, Pliny notified Trajan that an escaped slave found working in a local bakery claimed to have been stolen from a distinguished Roman years before by barbarian raiders. Cicero complained about the disappearance of one of his household slaves, who had disguised himself as a free man and vanished into the Dinaric Alps. The reverse also occurred: freeborn travelers on lonely roads ran the risk of being captured and enslaved by bandits. In one notorious instance, the household steward of a Roman consul washed up on a lonely shore after a shipwreck, and was chained in a window-less workhouse by local slavers.[2]

Even when identity theft was less distressingly literal, the stakes of demonstrating status were high. Pretending to be a Roman citizen, for example, was a capital offense. Being able to prove one's freedom, citizenship, legal status, and—in some periods—religious convic-tions* might mean the difference between life and death. At least in theory, Roman citizens could verify their identity and status with official documents. From the reign of Augustus onward, legitimate children were registered as citizens soon after birth. Parents could request documentation in the form of a declaration issued by a local magistrate and validated by seven witnesses—the equivalent of a birth certificate. Those who gained citizenship later in life were also enrolled on the official lists, which were kept both in their home-towns and at the state archives† in Rome.[3]

Throughout the republican period, the citizen lists were revised on a semiregular basis by the census, a national register that

---

* During the persecution of the Christians ordered by Decius, for example, every inhab-itant of the empire was expected to obtain a written form, signed by a magistrate, attesting that they had sacrificed to the traditional gods.

† Census records were sometimes kept for hundreds of years. Justin Martyr, writing in the second century, claimed that tax records from the time of Christ's birth could still be consulted. In late antiquity, the legal records of the Eastern Roman Empire were kept in vaults beneath the Hippodrome of Constantinople. By the reign of Justinian, thousands of cases of documents—some more than two hundred years old—were stored there.

determined—among other things—tax obligations. In Italy, the census fell into abeyance during the early imperial era, not least because Italians were exempt from direct taxation. Censuses continued to be held, however, in the provinces, whose inhabitants were still liable to the land and poll taxes. Although census returns were not typically used as means of establishing identity, they were available for reference in provincial capitals.

The best-documented ordinary Romans were those serving in the imperial army. On enlistment, a recruit's name and physical characteristics were entered in his unit's records. An Egyptian papyrus, for example, reports that one new soldier had a scar on his left eyebrow, while another had a mark on his left hand. Once he had sworn the military oath, each soldier was given the ancient equivalent of a dog tag: a lead tablet, inscribed with his personal details, that was kept in a leather pouch around his neck. Upon discharge, auxiliaries—men, in other words, who had enlisted as noncitizens—received Roman citizenship. Veterans seem to have often commemorated the occasion by commissioning "diplomas"—small bronze tablets recording their citizen status, certified by the names and seals of seven witnesses.[4]

Roman citizens, in short, were at least theoretically able to prove their identity with government records. Such documentation, however, was often inaccessible, outdated, or lost. This seldom mattered in a person's native place, where friends and relatives could be called upon as character witnesses. Away from home, the most effective way to demonstrate identity was to exhibit the appropriate social cues. When Saint Paul, for example, told a centurion who was about to scourge him that he was a Roman citizen, he seems to have been believed because he acted the part.* Someone who claimed to be a Roman citizen but couldn't speak Latin,† on the other hand, was likely to encounter skepticism.[5]

At last resort, identity could be proved in court. A collection of wax tablets from Herculaneum documents a legal case centered on

---

* Paul's father may have gained Roman citizenship by making tents for the army of Pompey.

† Claudius once revoked the Roman citizenship of a Greek provincial for his inability to speak Latin.

Petronia Iusta, who sought to prove that she had been born after her mother—a former slave—had been freed. The defense countered that her mother had still been a slave when Petronia was born, and that she was thus a freedwoman, rather than freeborn. Since there was no written documentation of Petronia's birth, both sides were forced to rely on the testimony of witnesses.[6]

The relative insignificance of written documentation in such cases is also apparent in Cicero's defense of Archias, a poet accused of not being a Roman citizen. After bringing forward witnesses from the poet's town of residence to attest that he was a citizen there, and thus a citizen of Rome, Cicero dismissed as irrelevant the fact that Archias had never been registered by the censors, since he had been away from the capital during each recent census. And in any case, Cicero declared, even if Archias were not already a Roman citizen, he deserved to be one, since he was a skilled and patriotic writer. Not incidentally, several prominent Romans were willing to vouch for him. In the Roman military, likewise, personal connections were more important than documents. When Titus Flavius Longus, an Egyptian legionary, was accused of not being a Roman citizen, he defended himself by having several of his fellow soldiers—including a discharged veteran—swear to his citizen status by Jupiter and the emperor.[7]

"It can be difficult," one Roman jurist noted, "to distinguish a free man from a slave." Yet the Romans never ceased to conceptualize status as an attribute that could be performed and recognized. Nor did they ever cease to believe that, even in the most distant places, safety and assistance would come rushing in response to that simple phrase: "I am a Roman citizen."[8]

How Did They Invest Their Money?

*W*hen a certain wealthy freedman died during the reign of Augustus, it was discovered that he had owned 4,116 slaves, 3,600 pairs of oxen, 257,000 other cattle, and 60 million sestertii* in cash, along with vast estates and many other assets. His will stipulated that 1.1 million sestertii were to be spent on his funeral. At a time when many Roman men earned less than 1,000 sestertii in an entire year, riches on this scale were staggering. And there were other Romans who were even wealthier. Crassus, for example, owned estates worth 200 million sestertii, along with many thousands of slaves, hundreds of buildings in the city of Rome, and dozens of silver mines in the provinces. The wealthiest Romans, in short, possessed fortunes on a scale excelled only by kings, emperors, and modern billionaires.[1]

In the Roman world—the focus of this answer—elite men were expected to devote their lives to public affairs. For many, such service, whether on a city council, within the imperial chancery, or in the Senate itself, was the only real job they ever had. Especially during the late republican era, when governors were more or less expected to plunder their provinces, a public career could be very lucrative. But under the emperors, despite the large salaries paid to high officials, only a handful of court favorites grew rich this way.

---

* The Romans reckoned costs in sestertii, big brass coins worth a quarter of a denarius. During the early imperial era, a sestertius could buy two loaves of bread, four cups of cheap wine, or a single cup of good wine. A tunic cost about 15 sestertii, and the annual rent for a decent apartment in a provincial city was probably 300–500 sestertii.

Most elite Romans made their money in the private sphere. Although the great majority had inherited wealth, few were complacent about their fortunes. It was normal for a wealthy Roman to act—in some ways—much like a modern investor, diversifying assets and seeking high returns. Although there were bankers in every substantial Roman city, the elite tended to use them only for a few specialized transactions, such as making payments at a distance. They preferred to keep their ready cash at home, often in iron safes containing a few gold bars and stacks of coins. One first-century senator never left home without a wagon carrying gold worth a million sestertii. Usually, however, wealthy Romans stored only a small fraction of their wealth in cash.* When they purchased a house or estate, they performed the transaction on paper, either issuing a promissory note or exchanging debts and property titles.[2]

Like most premodern elites, rich Romans kept the majority of their wealth in property. The safest investments were country estates, normally worked by some combination of free tenants and slaves. The wealthiest owned whole networks of estates, scattered across the empire.† Though not especially profitable—the typical annual return was probably 5 or 6 percent—revenue from these properties added up. One magnate is known to have earned 3 million sestertii every year in rents from his estates. Especially in the city of Rome itself, elite Romans also invested in urban real estate: baths, warehouses, and—above all—apartment buildings. Crassus famously owned teams of slaves trained as firemen and builders. Whenever a tenement caught fire, he would rush to the scene, purchase the burning structure at a steep discount, and then send his slaves in to extinguish the blaze and reconstruct the building. Even Cicero, who was only modestly wealthy for a senator, owned about a million sestertii of

---

* At one point, Julius Caesar forbade any Roman to keep more than 60,000 sestertii in silver or gold coins at a time—an illustration of the relatively minor role of cash in elite portfolios.

† When Melania the Younger, an immensely wealthy late Roman heiress, decided to become an ascetic, she sold extensive estates in various parts of Spain and Gaul, but kept her properties in Sicily, Africa, and southern Italy to finance the monasteries she had founded. At the same time, she freed eight thousand of her slaves. Her mansion in Rome was so palatial that no buyer could be found; it burned, unsold, during Alaric's sack of Rome.

rental properties in the city of Rome.* One Roman entrepreneur made a lucrative career of buying houses, adding heated baths, and selling them for large profits. On a less exalted economic scale, middle-class investors might buy and manage a single building: we know, for example, of a freedman who left his daughter an insula with six apartments, eleven shops, and a latrine.[3]

Besides the omnipresent threat of fire, fluctuating prices represented the greatest risk of investing in real estate. Political circumstances occasionally brought about the ancient equivalent of a housing crash. This first occurred in 82–81 BCE, when the dictator Sulla had hundreds of political opponents executed. The sale of their property to Sulla's cronies at steeply reduced prices—Cicero mentions a villa worth 5 million denarii that was auctioned for 2,000—caused real estate values to plummet. An even greater housing crash took place a generation later, during the civil war between Pompey and Caesar. After Pompey abandoned Rome, fears that Caesar would cancel all debts or confiscate properties drove panicked sales of estates and mansions. The effects were felt all over Italy, as villa owners tried to anticipate the seizure of their assets by selling them to anyone who would buy.[4]

Alongside real estate, elite Romans invested in slaves. Although their numbers were greatest during the late Republic, there were millions of slaves in all periods, performing every conceivable job from field laborer to imperial accountant. Crassus regarded slaves as the most valuable part of his property. Besides the thousands who worked his estates, he had hundreds of his slaves trained to serve as readers, table servers, stewards, scribes, and silversmiths—among other professions—and hired them out by the day. Other wealthy Romans trained slaves to serve as quasi-independent artisans, setting them up in shops with a small stock of borrowed capital. These slaves were allowed to keep part of their earnings, and could eventually use their savings to buy their freedom. Even after they were free, however, they retained economic ties to their former masters, who might loan them money to invest in commercial ventures.

---

* Cicero seems to have been something of a slumlord, noting in one letter that two of his properties had collapsed and another was cracking.

Whether in the form of slaves or land, property was the foundation of most wealthy Romans' fortunes—or that, at least, was what they liked their peers to think. Trade was not regarded as a respectable occupation, and Roman senators were actually prohibited by law from direct involvement in commerce. But since there were immense profits to be made this way, members of the elite found ways to participate. Cato the Elder—a senator—set up an investing association, whose members financed ventures in overseas trade. The scale of such enterprises could be impressive. An Egyptian papyrus preserves part of a contract between a Roman investor and a merchant sailing from Egypt to India. The merchant's profits from that single voyage were at least 7 million sestertii—equivalent to the value of a large estate in central Italy.[5]

Some wealthy Romans also earned income from the interest on loans. During the late Republic, senators loaned money to provincial cities and foreign kings. Typically, however, loans were made to private individuals, often at the standard interest rate of 12 percent.* Debt claims—written records of outstanding loans—made up an important part of many investment portfolios, and circulated almost as freely as cash, being transferred and sold. The philosopher Seneca reportedly held 40 million sestertii of debt claims in a single province. A few Roman magnates became, in effect, one-man banks, with agents working in the Forum, and even in the provinces, to loan portions of their wealth to promising clients.[6]

To discourage excessive lending, Julius Caesar passed a law ordering creditors to invest most of their capital in Italian estates. When this statute, ignored for decades, abruptly began to be enforced during the reign of Tiberius, it sparked a crisis. Wealthy investors scrambled to assemble the funds they needed to buy land, calling in their outstanding loans. Many of their debtors found themselves unable to pay and had their properties confiscated. The flood of confiscated properties caused land prices to plummet and encouraged investors to wait until the last possible moment to buy

---

* Brutus, the future assassin of Caesar, lent more than 2 million sestertii to the city of Salamis at an ambitious 48 percent interest rate.

estates, in the hope that prices would fall further. While they waited and husbanded their resources, interest rates shot up, as the few remaining creditors took advantage of a credit-starved economy. The crisis only eased after Tiberius created a system of public banks,* deposited 100 million sestertii in them, and authorized the banks to make three-year, interest-free loans.[7]

The investments of a wealthy Roman, in short, could be impressively diversified. Income streamed in from the revenues of his estates, the rents of his urban properties, the earnings of his slaves, the profits of his commercial enterprises, and the interest of his loans. In combination, perhaps, with a government salary and legacies from well-placed friends, all this was normally more than enough to finance conspicuous consumption in the finest aristocratic style.

---

* Although the Roman emperors did not have financial policies in the modern sense, they did what they could to ensure the basic stability of the economy. Domitian, for example, was so worried by a glut on the wine market that he banned the planting of new vineyards in Italy and ordered the destruction of half the vines in the provinces.

· *17* ·

How Did They Deal with Inflation?

$\mathcal{I}$ have a collection of Roman coins. Although nothing in it is valuable—rarities are far beyond this starving author's budget—I've managed to assemble a scattering of common types, arranged chronologically from the late Republic to the reign of Justinian. When I'm writing about a given theme, I like to flip through my album to see whether any of my coins illustrates the topic. As I began to outline this chapter, I opened to the page reserved for coins of the mid-third century. At the top is a row of gleaming silver antoniniani, the two-denarius pieces that dominated the era's economy. The coins in the middle rows are duller, their silver heavily alloyed. The bottom of the page holds ragged bits of bronze, some only a third the size of the antoniniani issued a few decades before. Here, in miniature, is antiquity's greatest inflationary crisis.

Unlike modern governments, which issue currency to serve as a medium of exchange and value storage throughout the economy, the Roman Empire minted coins primarily to pay its own expenses. Although the emperors recognized that it was a good thing to have money circulating through the provinces, not least because it made taxes easier to collect, the nature and the number of coins they issued were always determined by their financial obligations.

The emperors had many sources of income. The most important was taxation, levied both directly (in the form of land and poll taxes) and indirectly (through customs duties and taxes on inheritances, auctions, and the manumission of slaves). Tax revenue was

Three coins from the author's collection. From left to right: an antoninianus of Gordian III (r. 238–244), a debased antoninianus of Gallienus (r. 253–268), and a "barbarous radiate"—a provincial imitation of an antoninianus struck during the rampant inflation of the 270s. *Author's photo*

supplemented by income from the vast network of properties owned directly by the imperial house, which included everything from massive estates and marble quarries* to tenements in Rome. The revenues produced by taxation, the imperial estates, and the occasional war were balanced, and sometimes dwarfed, by expenditures. The emperors had to pay a small but elite bureaucracy. They had to finance massive building projects. They had to sponsor gladiatorial combats and beast hunts. They had to subsidize the grain that fed the city of Rome. And above all, they had to pay the troops.

By ancient standards, the Roman army was enormous. The nearly half million men permanently under arms by the early third century represented a colossal investment, and a gargantuan burden. Soldiers were paid well, earning about as much each year as a skilled craftsman, and officers were paid vastly better, to the point that their salaries alone accounted for almost a quarter of the total payroll. In addition to wages, the emperors had to meet the costs of provisions and retirement bonuses. As a result, even in peacetime, at least two-thirds of the imperial budget was always dedicated to military costs.

---

* The emperors imported hundreds of thousands of tons of marble from every corner of the Mediterranean to supply their building projects at Rome. The imperial marble yards, which sprawled along the Tiber near the base of the Aventine Hill, still contained thousands of blocks when they were discovered in the nineteenth century.

To pay the troops and meet their other obligations, the emperors minted coins. The gold coin, the aureus, was used for high-value payments and to store wealth. The brass sestertius and its fractions facilitated everyday transactions. But it was the silver coin, the denarius, that was the real foundation of the monetary system, and the currency in which soldiers and officials were usually compensated.* For nearly two and a half centuries, the Roman monetary system, anchored by the denarius, was remarkably stable.† Even at the best of times, however, imperial expenditures tended to exceed revenues. To make up the difference, the emperors relied on fresh supplies of gold and silver from mines and successful wars. When these fell short, there were only two possible solutions: deferring payment (always dangerous, since unpaid soldiers were mutinous soldiers) or debasing the currency—producing coins, in other words, that contained less gold and silver.

There were a few episodes of debasement in the early imperial era. After the Great Fire of Rome, for example, Nero reduced the weight and fineness of the aureus. The silver content of the denarius fell slowly but steadily after the reign of Domitian. But these changes were minor, and caused no lasting economic problems. The crisis came in the mid-third century, when a seemingly endless series of disasters brought the Roman Empire to the brink of collapse. Invaders breached every frontier. Cities from London to Antioch were sacked, and whole provinces abandoned in the face of the barbarian onslaught. Behind the shattered border defenses, a parade of pretenders and usurpers battled for the throne.

The economy withered, cutting tax revenues at a time when the emperors desperately needed gold and silver to pay the troops. The supply of precious metal was further diminished by the need to buy off enemies with stipends, and by the depletion of the mines on which the mints had relied for centuries. As the supply of precious

---

* As established by Augustus, 1 aureus = 25 denarii = 100 sestertii = 200 dupondii = 400 asses.

† It was also remarkably exportable: Roman coins have been discovered as far afield as Thailand, China, and—in one instance—Japan. As late as the nineteenth century, worn Roman coins could be found circulating in the bazaars of northwestern India and Pakistan.

metals dwindled, military expenses soared. During the second century, legionary pay had been stable at 1,200 sestertii a year. It rose dramatically under Septimius Severus and Caracalla, to the point of increasing the imperial budget by something like 70 percent in a few decades. By the end of the third century, in the wake of additional increases, soldiers were being paid about eight times what they had received a hundred years before.

Faced with ballooning expenses and dwindling stocks of silver and gold, the emperors did the only thing they could: they debased the currency. The aureus, whose size and quality had been stable for 250 years, was reduced from a pure gold coin weighing slightly more than seven grams to an alloyed fragment weighing as little as a gram. The silver currency was debased to oblivion. During the reign of Marcus Aurelius, the denarius had been about 80 percent silver. To facilitate their massive increases in military pay, Septimius Severus and Caracalla had reduced the silver content to about 50 percent. Caracalla had also introduced the antoninianus, a coin worth 2 denarii. Originally, the antoninianus was about half silver. But over the course of the mid-third century, as the antoninianus replaced the denarius as the most important coin in the Roman economy, and continual warfare kept military expenditures high, it was rapidly adulterated. In 250, under Decius, the antoninianus was about 40 percent silver. Only a few years later, under Valerian, its silver content had fallen to 20 percent. By the reign of Claudius Gothicus (268–270), the antoninianus was only 2 percent silver—a sorry billon fragment of its former self.

The runaway debasement of the currency was accompanied, and partly driven, by inflation. Debasement and inflation, it should be noted, were not automatically correlated.* Although the Romans knew and cared how much precious metal their coins contained, it was only when trust in the government failed—as it did during the third century—that coins came to be valued purely by bullion

---

* In Roman Egypt, which had its own currency system, the equivalent of the denarius was the tetradrachm, an originally silver coin that was debased until it contained little precious metal. Thanks, however, to public trust in the government (and a lack of competition from higher-quality coins), tetradrachms circulated at face value for centuries.

content. Inflation had been present in the early imperial era, most notably after Augustus's annexation of Egypt and Trajan's conquest of Dacia, when the economy struggled to absorb huge influxes of gold and silver. Less dramatically, there are signs of a slow rise in prices. At Ephesus, for example, the price of bread seems to have risen from 2 to 5 obols over the course of the second century. The smallest Roman denominations, the quadrans and semis, were no longer struck after the mid-second century, which suggests that rising prices had made them obsolete.

Inflation accelerated in the third century, as both the quality of the coinage and faith in its value plummeted. As prices continued to rise, the sestertius fell out of production, followed by the denarius itself. With gold marginalized and bronze increasingly worthless, virtually the only coin left in circulation was the antoninianus. But as their silver content fell, antoniniani were increasingly unlikely to be accepted at face value. To compensate, the emperors minted more and more, sometimes producing over a million coins a day.* This, of course, drove prices even higher.

By 268, the Roman world stood at the brink of disintegration. The empire had broken into three parts. A German tribe was ravaging northern Italy, Gothic marauders were plundering the ancient cities of Greece, and a huge barbarian horde was massing along the Danube. Emperor Claudius Gothicus, a skilled general, beat back the invaders, but died after a short reign. It was left to his successor, a cavalry commander of peasant origins named Aurelian, to save the empire. Against all odds, he did. After conquering the breakaway provinces and crushing the latest round of invaders, Aurelian decided to end the economic chaos that had plagued the Roman

---

* Ancient coins were struck on flans—blank metal disks—which were positioned between two engraved dies and struck with a mallet. Since the dies were engraved separately, design differences visible on surviving coins allow us to estimate the number of dies used for a given issue. It is generally assumed that a single obverse die could produce twenty to thirty thousand coins before wearing out. On this basis, it has been estimated that an average of 1.1 million aurei and 16 million denarii were struck each year during the reign of Hadrian. The number of coins produced escalated dramatically amid the disasters of the third century, when it seems to have become fairly routine to issue as many as a million antoniniani in a single day. During a reign of less than two years, the Gallic usurper Victorinus may have produced nearly half a billion heavily debased coins.

world for decades. Among other reforms, he replaced the antoninianus with a heavier coin that had its silver content—5 percent—stamped on the reverse.

Over the following decades, Aurelian's reforms were extended by Diocletian and the tetrarchs, who would reissue nearly a billion coins in the course of a massive overhaul of the currency. Inflation, however, remained a problem—Diocletian himself felt compelled to issue an edict decreeing the death penalty for any merchant who charged too much. But the edict proved unenforceable. Prices continued to rise, and the economy limped on toward the Middle Ages.*

---

* The cycle of debasement and reform was only ended when the Eastern Roman emperor Anastasius I (r. 491–518) issued a stable bronze currency ultimately modeled on the coins of the early empire.

· *18* ·

How Did They Deal
with Chariot Traffic?

In the heart of Rome, not far from the Basilica of Santa Maria Maggiore, the Via in Selci winds through a neighborhood of ageless ochre buildings. Especially around sunset, when coppery light splashes weathered brick, and bells toll in the distance, it's a peaceful street. But it wasn't always so. Two thousand years ago, this was the Clivus Suburanus, the busy thoroughfare that connected the Forum with the teeming tenements of the Esquiline Hill.* All the life of ancient Rome coursed along this street—the swirling masses, the swaying litters, priests, pontiffs, and praetorians. All that, on a street so narrow that it can only carry a single lane of traffic today.

There were, according to an ancient estimate, about sixty miles of streets in Rome. There were the ends of the mighty consular highways, aimed like arrows at the restless empire. There were winding lanes, old as the city itself, along the crests of the seven hills. There were dusty alleys in the concrete creases of the warehouse district. There were boulevards lined with marble monuments. And there were the countless unassuming streets that bound and tied a million

---

* A close look at the Via in Selci reveals ancient paving stones beneath the modern asphalt and a Roman building on one side, preserved to the height of thirty feet. Originally either a civil basilica or the reception hall of a late antique mansion, this structure was converted into a church sometime in the Middle Ages, and incorporated into a convent during the Renaissance. It still houses nuns today.

92

lives into a single urban fabric.* Most of these streets were narrow and twisting. Roman authors blamed the Gauls, who had burned the city early in its history, leaving a mass of haphazardly overbuilt ruins. The real culprits, however, were the rapid growth of Rome's population and the absence of anything resembling urban planning. Despite the passage of laws—streets, for example, were supposed to be at least eight feet wide—and despite the best efforts of the officials responsible for enforcing those statutes, the sheer inertia of the teeming, crumbling, overcrowded city defied all management.[1]

Although most of Rome's streets were paved by the imperial era, their stones were caked and slicked with a proprietary blend of excrement and mud,† moistened by the oozing overflow of hundreds of fountains. Pedestrians were often spattered to their knees, and sometimes to their necks, with filth. The greatest danger on Rome's streets, however, was the sheer number of Romans. In a famous passage, the satirist Juvenal describes the experience of negotiating a crowded street: "One man jostles me with his elbow, another jabs me with a pole, a third wallops me with a board, and a fourth whacks my forehead with a wine jar. My legs are caked with reeking mud, huge feet trample me from every side, and a soldier grinds his hobnails into my toes." Members of the Roman elite sometimes found it useful to join the crowds on the streets, especially when they were campaigning for office. But if they wanted to avoid the omnipresent muck, they used litters, which glided over the chaos of the street as quickly as cudgel-wielding guards could beat a way.[2]

---

* Street names were often descriptive, like Via Nova ("New Street," built to serve the Baths of Caracalla), Alta Semita (the "High Street" along ridge of Quirinal), or the self-explanatory Vicus Longus ("Long Lane"). Streets might be named for the merchants who had shops along them, like the Vicus Frumentarius ("Grain Merchant Lane") near the Tiber docks, where wholesalers in grain were based. Alternatively, they might be called after a nearby landmark, as in the case of the Vicus Honoris et Virtutis ("Lane of Honor and Virtue"), named for a nearby sanctuary of—you guessed it—honor and virtue.

† Many streets must have resembled slot canyons between cliffs of tenements. When Nero created wide boulevards after the Great Fire of 64, there were complaints about the excessive amount of sunlight reaching the pavement. However wide the street, the filth was inescapable. Caligula once ordered an unfortunate urban aedile to be plastered with muck from the alleys and avenues of Rome as a punishment for neglecting his duties.

Thousands of vehicles shuttled goods and people around Rome, and many more arrived at the customs posts outside the city every day. From the pedestrian's standpoint, it didn't matter whether a wagon was one of the fine traveling coaches favored by the aristocracy, sparkling with silver filigree, or a rough construction cart with wheels of solid wood, heavy enough to rattle the subterranean sewers: the approach of any vehicle meant being shoved to the wall until it passed.

Recognizing the problems they caused, Julius Caesar passed a law restricting the use of wheeled vehicles on the streets of Rome. With the exceptions of carts involved in public construction projects, the carriages of priests and priestesses, and chariots employed in certain rituals, wheeled vehicles were banned within the city limits between sunrise and late afternoon.* Eventually, riding a horse or mule was also banned, and the heaviest carts were prohibited from entering at any time. Although members of the imperial family and leading senators came to regard themselves as exempt, Caesar's law remained in effect through late antiquity.[3]

There must have also been regulations, or at least conventions, about traffic flow on individual streets. In Pompeii—whose paving stones provide our best evidence for how Roman traffic actually worked—ruts reveal that most streets were one-way. Large parts of the city, including the Forum itself, were closed to wheeled vehicles, and curbs and barricades guided them elsewhere. On the relatively few two-way streets, traffic kept to the right, as seems to have been the rule in most parts of the Roman world.† Although Pompeii had no parking lots, ramps connected the streets with stables and yards where drivers could leave their teams. There were loading zones, in the form of curbside tethering holes for horses and donkeys.

---

* Litters could be hired and wagons rented at stands just outside the city gates.

† Then as now, Britain may have been an exception. On the road leading into a Roman quarry near Swindon, centuries of cart traffic wore two sets of ruts. One set—on the left, looking out from the quarry—was much deeper than the other. This, archaeologists realized, reflected the traffic pattern on the quarry road: carts loaded with stone had exited by the left-hand ruts and returned empty on the other side.

There were crosswalks on stepping stones between the ruts. There were even traffic tickets, issued for blocking public thoroughfares and other infractions. As far as we can tell, however, there were no addresses* or street signs.[4]

Although Rome's streets probably resembled Pompeii's, nothing in the empire could compare with Roman traffic. The sheer congestion caused by a million pedestrians was bad enough. But Rome also suffered from numerous chokepoints—the worst were the gates of the old republican walls—and from the building programs of the emperors, which tended to either block existing streets (like the imperial forums) or attract enormous crowds (like the imperial baths). Accidents were predictably frequent. Pedestrians slipped and fell in the muck. Wagons careened out of control, maiming and killing those in the way. During festivals, when the streets were even more crowded than usual, visitors were often trampled to death.[5]

But despite every disaster, the traffic never ceased. As soon as the sky brightened, as soon as the shop windows opened, as soon as the first clients reached their patrons' doors, the streets began to fill. As the sun rose, traffic slowed to a crawl. Every alley and lane became a gauntlet of barbers and bearers, stray pigs and street performers, and crowds, unbelievable crowds, knotted and tangled by festivals, funerals, and miscellaneous pomp. In late afternoon, just as the pedestrian riot subsided, carts and carriages thundered onto the scene, their dull roar persisting insistently, incessantly until the final wagons rumbled away through the predawn light of another day.[6]

---

* A bronze nameplate was discovered beside the door of the House of Lucius Satrius Rufus at Pompeii. But in general, as far as we can tell, people simply navigated by landmarks. In one Roman comedy, for example, a character receives a long list of directions, which include such instructions as "turn at the big fig tree." A graffito in Pompeii urges passersby to seek a certain prostitute "on Venus Lane by the Rome Gate."

· 19 ·

How Did Their Aqueducts Work?

The Trevi Fountain is one of Rome's most spectacular sights. Across a pale green pool, between two tritons wrestling with winged horses, from beneath the feet of the mighty sea god Oceanus, a silver cascade sweeps over steps of stone. Impressive though all this is, the most remarkable part lies behind the riot of statues, where the water that feeds the fountain flows, as it has for more than two thousand years, through the concrete channel of a Roman aqueduct.*

Greek engineers began building aqueducts as early as the sixth century BCE. A stone-lined channel carried spring water to Archaic Athens, and Samos was served by an aqueduct that plunged through a tunnel two-thirds of a mile long. Even more impressive systems appeared during the Hellenistic era, when the acropolis of Pergamon was supplied with water flowing under pressure through huge lead pipes. Roman aqueducts differed from their Greek predecessors in their use of arches and hydraulic concrete, but it was sheer number and scale that truly set them apart. Hundreds were constructed, some well over fifty miles long and capable of delivering millions of gallons each day. Although they provided drinking water to public fountains, most of these spectacular aqueducts were luxuries, designed primarily to supply bath complexes, nymphaea, and the mansions of the elite.

---

* The Trevi Fountain is fed by the Aqua Virgo, completed in 19 BCE. Although the Aqua Virgo is the only one of Rome's aqueducts to have remained in service more or less continuously since antiquity, several other ancient aqueducts were restored to service by Renaissance popes. These still serve the fountains of the city center, though they are no longer sources of drinking water.

The time-consuming and expensive* process of building an aqueduct began with locating a usable water source. Lakes were almost never chosen—stagnant water was regarded as unhealthy—and rivers were tapped only in exceptional cases, since they carried sediment and fluctuated seasonally.† The preferred source was a hillside spring. A Roman aqueduct was an artificial river, flowing downhill with a gradient that had to be both gentle and consistent. If the channel was too steep, the mortar lining would erode; if too gentle, the water within would stagnate. Most Roman aqueducts descend five or ten feet every mile, and some have slopes as gradual as 1 in 20,000—that is, a few inches per mile. To maintain such minuscule gradients, Roman engineers relied on the dioptra and the chorobates. The dioptra—an ancestor of the modern theodolite—was a sighting platform used to measure the relative position and height of distant points. The chorobates, a long table with a central channel, was a water level. With competent use of these instruments and adequate stocks of manpower and money, an aqueduct could be built almost anywhere.[1]

For most of their length, Roman aqueducts ran underground, following the contours of the landscape as they descended from their sources. Although the water flowing through them was rarely more than knee deep, their channels were usually made tall enough for

---

* A modest mausoleum along the Via Appia cost 10,000–20,000 sestertii to build. A wealthy senator might spend 300,000 adding a private bath to his house. A large public bath could cost 2 million. But Pliny the Younger mentions a modest provincial aqueduct that, while still far from finished, had already cost more than 3 million sestertii—as much, in other words, as a mansion in the heart of Rome. The Aqua Marcia, which cost 180 million sestertii, was the most expensive building project ever undertaken by the Roman Republic. Even this was dwarfed by the Aqua Anio Novus and Aqua Claudia, which cost the imperial treasury a staggering 350 million sestertii.

† There were a few exceptions. At Subiaco, in the hills east of Rome, Nero constructed a series of spectacular dams—one of them 140 feet high—to create pleasure lakes for one of his villas. Later, water from these reservoirs was channeled into the Aqua Anio Novus. Although the great dam at Subiaco washed out in 1305, a few Roman reservoirs are still extant, including two that fed the aqueducts of Emerita Augusta (Mérida) in Spain. An interesting demonstration of the Roman preference for spring water could be seen at the head of the aqueduct at Side (in modern Turkey), which was located across a river from a copious spring. Since an aqueduct bridge would have been prohibitively expensive, the engineers positioned the channel in the exact place where the water of the spring, flowing with such force that it formed a separate layer on top of the river current, could be captured and diverted.

maintenance workers to walk without stooping. To minimize leakage, the masonry walls were coated with waterproof cement. When an aqueduct had to cross a valley, its gradient was maintained by elevating the channel on arches made of local stone or brick-faced concrete. The most spectacular example is the Pont du Gard, just outside Nimes. No less than 160 feet high, it consists of huge blocks of limestone laid without mortar, which support a channel so carefully graded that its level descends less than an inch from one end of the bridge to the other.

Where an aqueduct crossed a valley too deep for a bridge, Roman engineers built an inverted siphon—a pipe running at ground level from a header tank on one side of the depression to a receiving tank on the other.* As long as the receiving tank was at least slightly lower than the header, the water in the pipe would rise to its own level, flowing up the slope and out of the valley. The counterparts of the siphons and bridges that carried aqueducts over gorges were the tunnels that funneled them through hills. Unless the cutting was exceptionally deep, the usual construction method involved excavating a series of shafts and boring in both directions from the bottom. This didn't always go as planned: an inscription from North Africa records how two work gangs, tunneling from either side of a mountain, became disoriented and began digging in opposite directions.[2]

When—having hewn through hills, vaulted valleys, and marched majestically over the plains—an aqueduct finally reached the city it was to supply, its terminus was often marked by a spectacular fountain.† Most of its water, however, was channeled into the distribution tanks that the Romans called *castella*. These fed batteries of pipes, which in turn led to smaller distribution tanks. Pompeii

---

* The Romans generally preferred arcades to siphons, since siphon pipes required huge quantities of lead, which was heavy, difficult to transport, and time consuming to cast and join. If a siphon clogged, moreover, it was very difficult to fix.

† The ruins of one such fountain—the so-called Trophies of Marius—can still be seen in Rome. The terminal tank of the Aqua Claudia, destroyed during the eighteenth century, was a huge rectangular structure with five chambers, each feeding distribution pipes. Some of these pipes were gargantuan: an example from the reign of Hadrian, discovered in the nineteenth century, was more than a mile long and contained over two hundred tons of lead.

The Pont du Gard. *Wikimedia Commons*

had 12 of these; Rome, 247. In the northwestern provinces, water pipes were often made of tree trunks joined with iron bands. In the eastern Mediterranean, they might consist of long lines of hollowed stone blocks. Most Roman pipes, however, were made of terra-cotta or lead. Although they knew that lead caused health problems, the Romans persisted in making pipes from it, simply because lead was cheap, was easy to work, and didn't rust. They were only saved from mass lead poisoning by the swiftness with which water flowed through the pipes, and by the calcium deposits that tended to coat their insides.[3]

Although the majority of cities with aqueducts also had wells or cisterns, aqueduct water was regarded as healthier and better tasting. By one count, Rome had 1,352 aqueduct-fed fountains. In Pompeii, it has been estimated, there was a fountain for every 160 inhabitants.* Aqueduct-fed baths were almost equally abundant. In Rome alone, aside from the colossal imperial thermae, there were more than 850

---

* An inscription from Cirta (now Constantine, Algeria) describes an elaborate public fountain with six golden drinking goblets—chained to the wall for security—six marble statues, six bronze statues, six bronze water spouts, and a single bronze cupid.

neighborhood baths by late antiquity. The largest complexes used so much water that they required dedicated aqueducts. The Baths of Caracalla, for example, were fed by a spur of the Aqua Marcia, and featured a reservoir with thirty-two chambers and a capacity of more than two million gallons. The outflow of wastewater was copious enough to power watermills.[4]

Private connections to aqueduct water were relatively rare. At Rome, the process for installing a tap involved appealing to the emperor, bringing the emperor's authorization to the water commissioner, and finally receiving a calix, a bronze nozzle stamped with the owner's name.* The grant was not permanent: as soon as the recipient died or sold his home, his calix was removed. Although some private connections were granted to the owners of industrial facilities, most belonged to members of the elite, who used the water to supply the gardens, fountains, and private baths of their mansions. The situation seems to have been broadly similar in Pompeii, where only 10 percent of households had access to piped water, but that 10 percent used it so extravagantly that one house had no fewer than thirty-three faucets.[5]

Maintaining the aqueducts was a constant struggle. In the city of Rome, a permanent staff of seven hundred installed new pipes, braced buckling arches, and kept the channels clear. Mud and stones had to be removed from the settling tanks—depressions in the channel designed to catch suspended sediment and debris—and mineral deposits were periodically scraped from the walls.† Although Rome's aqueducts seem to have been fairly well maintained until late

---

* Lacking precise timekeeping instruments, and so unable to measure head or velocity of flow, the Romans could only estimate the water being supplied to a house by the diameter of its calix. A calix was always made of bronze, probably because bronze (unlike lead) was difficult for unscrupulous homeowners to stretch. Some Romans found a way around the regulations by angling their calix into the aqueduct channel to capture more water.

† During the nineteenth century, the owner of an estate beside the ruins of the Aqua Anio Novus discovered huge piles of sand and gravel on his property, left there from ancient cleanings of the aqueduct's settling tanks. Pebbles from these piles paved a mile of the estate owner's drives. Heaps of sinter—deposited calcium carbonate—have also been discovered around the manholes of Roman aqueducts; at the Eifel aqueduct, which served Cologne, a centimeter of sinter (a sintermeter, if you will) accumulated every thirteen to fourteen years. Since aqueduct sinter was a smooth, attractive stone that could be easily carved, it was used as a building material during the Middle Ages.

antiquity, not all cities were so scrupulous, and some allowed their aqueducts to become completely clogged with debris.[6]

When they were functioning as intended, however, the aqueducts were awesome manifestations of the Roman knack for practical engineering on a monumental scale. The aqueduct that served Carthage ran fifty-five miles from a sacred spring to the cavernous cisterns of the city's great baths. The aqueduct that Augustus built along the Bay of Naples was even longer, and featured at least a dozen branches supplying the naval station at Misenum, the elaborate seaside villas at Baiae, and the doomed cities of Pompeii and Herculaneum. The aqueduct of Constantinople, whose channels had a combined length of over three hundred miles, filled a series of covered reservoirs and artificial lakes.

Most impressive of all were the eleven aqueducts of Rome, which may have collectively carried as much as a million cubic meters of water each day. Tapping springs and streams in the surrounding hills, and carried over suburban villas and market gardens on seemingly endless arcades, Rome's aqueducts entered the city proper in a spectacular array of pipes, conduits, and distribution tanks. Since only a few of the aqueducts were high enough to supply all fourteen of the city's regions, most had a fairly localized distribution network. The whole system, however, was interconnected, so that if one aqueduct were shut down for repairs, another could be diverted to replace it. This feature was not always appreciated, since Rome's aqueducts ranged in quality from the Aqua Marcia—fed by the emerald pools of a delicious mountain spring*—to the Aqua Alsietina, whose water was so muddy that it was considered undrinkable. But thanks to hundreds of millions of sestertii in funding, endless maintenance work, and the basic quality of their construction, the aqueducts continued to flow long after the emperors were gone.[7]

---

* Nero once bathed in that delicious spring. A subsequent outbreak of disease was blamed on the incident.

How Did Their Public
Toilets Work?

*O*stia, the ancient port of Rome, had every amenity of a respectable classical city: a forum with a lofty temple, a theater ringed by bustling porticoes, sprawling warehouses, sumptuous baths, well-appointed apartments—and a healthy consistency of public latrines. A nearly intact example near the Forum Baths has become a favorite of modern visitors, who pose for pictures by the marble seats. An ancient customer would have been less impressed by this facility, which—with a mere twenty seats and no decoration to speak of—was only a modestly commodious commode.

The most common means of managing human waste in antiquity was the simple but dependable chamber pot—a large vessel, usually made of clay, but sometimes of bronze or even silver, that was stowed in a corner, used as needed, and emptied when convenient. Though attested in the Bronze Age palaces of Minoan Crete, toilets of any kind seem to have been uncommon in the Greek world before the Hellenistic period, and it was only during the Roman imperial era that the classical world came to be flush with latrines. Toilets were tucked into many Roman houses, often in or near the kitchen, so that food scraps could be tipped down the hatch.* Few of these

---

* Even on the second or third floors of buildings, some Roman apartments were provided with toilets, connected by terra-cotta pipes with a sewer or cesspit.

The latrine near the Forum Baths at Ostia. *Wikimedia Commons*

toilets were connected to sewers, since—lacking traps—they were distressingly accessible to noxious gases and clawing rats.*

Public toilets began to appear during the late republican period.† Although some were quite small, like the tiny latrines perched atop the Aurelian Walls or the neighborly two-seaters on the ground floors of many apartment buildings, most had at least a dozen seats. A handful were considerably larger, like the fifty-seater (complete with a heated floor) in the Forum of Julius Caesar and the sixty-eight-seater in the Roman Agora of Athens. The most capacious facilities may have had as many as eighty places.

Though not all Roman latrines were architecturally ambitious, a remarkable number were equipped with marble paneling, mosaic floors, and even statues. One at Timgad featured fancy toilet armrests in the shape of leaping dolphins. A few latrines in Hadrian's Villa,

---

* Most private toilets emptied into stone-lined cesspits. An example in Herculaneum was found still half-filled with trash and human waste, which contained traces of sea urchins, eggs, olives, walnuts, and figs.

† By one late antique count, there were 144 public latrines in the city of Rome. Presumably, this number excludes the many latrines in bath complexes.

designed for the emperor's exclusive use, were favored with marble seats, frescoed walls, and windows framing ornamental pools.* The goddess Fortuna was often painted on the walls of latrines, apparently in the hope that she would guard the health of those using the facility. A less reverential attitude was on display in the latrine of a bath in Ostia, where frescoes of the seven wise men of Greece were captioned with sage advice about such matters as farting stealthily. We even have a few examples of bathroom graffiti, including one from Herculaneum that reports, "Apollinaris, doctor of Emperor Titus, shat well here."[1]

Public latrines were normally located in high-traffic areas, often near fountains or baths, whose wastewater could be channeled under the seats and into the nearest sewer.† Most facilities had a swinging door or curtain at the entrance, watched—if it was a pay toilet—by an attendant. The interior was almost always quite dim, which provided a measure of privacy. So did the nature of Roman clothing, which covered patrons more or less completely as they did their business. This helps to explain the fact that—as far as we can tell—men and women used the same latrines. Around the Mediterranean, toilet seats were usually stone. Wood was more common in northern Europe, not least because it was unpleasant to sit on stone during a northern winter. There was usually a slot beneath the seat to allow discreet use of the latrine sponge.

---

* A red marble seat is displayed in a quiet corner of the Vatican Museums. Originally, it was one of two; the other was stolen by Napoleon. Both seats originally served as toilets in an imperial villa. After they were rediscovered during the Middle Ages, they were moved to the chapel of St. Sylvester in the Lateran Palace and incorporated into the papal investiture ceremonies (presumably on the theory that they were the more literal sort of imperial thrones). A new pope sat first in the seat on the chapel's right side, and was given the staff of Saint Peter and the Lateran keys. He then shifted to the seat on the left, where he was girded with a gem-studded sash, and received the homage of palace officials. Finally, still enthroned, he cast silver coins into the crowd. Leo X, elected in 1513, was the last pope to perform this ritual. But by then, it had begun to be rumored that when a pope first sat on one of the seats, a dutiful junior cleric would reach through the hole and confirm that the new guy had the right set of genitals for the job. Once this had been ascertained, it would be proclaimed: "He has the pontificals" or—less ambiguously—"He has two testicles, and they hang well."

† The sewers of Rome—including the famous Cloaca Maxima, which drained the Forum—were designed to carry away excess water, not waste. But in a city like Rome, whose population produced an estimated 110,000 pounds of excrement each day, every little bit helped.

The sponge on a stick* that served as the equivalent of toilet paper is one of the more notorious aspects of daily life in ancient Rome. The sponge pressed into service was normally, it seems, a pleasingly absorbent Mediterranean Sea sponge, which was moistened before use and rinsed after. Though doubtless filthy and wriggling with parasites,† sponges were at least soft—which could not be said of the pottery shards and seashells that some Romans used instead to scrape themselves clean. A less abrasive alternative involved splashing one's undercarriage with small jugs of water. There may have even been toilet paper, in the form of a dampened cloth. If old papyrus was ever used for the purpose, it must have chafed terribly.[2]

The Romans attempted to keep their latrines clean. Most were equipped with a basin for cleaning hands and/or latrine sponges. The floors were designed to be easily washable, often with drains beneath each toilet seat. Though usually small and high, windows ensured basic ventilation. Scented candles may have sometimes been burned to control odors. By our standards, however, latrines must have almost always been unpleasant places—dim, crowded, and reeking.‡ There were hazards, too, that would have given even the boldest Romans pause. On at least one occasion, a hapless latrine user was bitten in a sensitive spot by a snake hiding in the toilet channel. And thanks to buildups of hydrogen sulfide and methane in the sewers, latrines were occasionally rattled by explosions that sent gouts of flame roaring through the seats. No wonder so many latrines had frescoes of Fortuna—if there was ever a place where divine protection was needed, it was a Roman toilet.[3]

---

* The assumption that the Romans typically used a sponge on a stick to clean themselves in the lavatory is based on a handful of literary references, most notably an anecdote in Seneca about a German prisoner who committed suicide by swallowing "the vile sponge." Corroborating evidence seems to be inherent in the design of Roman toilets, which conventionally have a stick-sized slot beneath the seat.

† Traces of intestinal parasites such as roundworm and whipworm have been found in Roman-era fecal matter at multiple sites.

‡ One early Christian priest reportedly encountered a demon in a public toilet.

How Did the Romans Build Such Durable Roads?

$\mathcal{I}$ come from Chicago, where there are two seasons: winter and road construction. Every spring, seemingly the day after the last snow melts, orange cones appear along the highways, lanes close, and big yellow machines set to work. They grind up asphalt, batter down curbs, and lay endless loads of gravel and concrete. When their work is done, the road is a thing of beauty—for a few months. Then a new crop of cracks and bumps and potholes sprouts, and the cycle of rebuilding begins anew. Often, when admiring the fitted paving stones and timeless bridges of a Roman road, I've found myself wondering whether the highway engineers of Illinois could learn a thing or two from their ancient predecessors.*

By the second century, there were well over fifty thousand miles of Roman roads, radiating out from the golden milestone in the Forum to every corner of the empire. Conduits of trade, instruments of rule, monuments to the imperial order, they ran in uncompromising lines through every terrain. Roman roads skirted the burning edge of the Sahara, where sand drifted among the milestones. They

---

* Modern expressways, of course, are fundamentally different from Roman roads. First and foremost, they're designed to carry motor vehicles, which are far heavier, faster, and more numerous than the horse-drawn carts of antiquity. A busy section of American highway takes more punishment in a day than any Roman road did in a century. Modern roads are engineered to handle those enormous stresses without being prohibitively expensive to build. In practice, that means a lot of reinforced concrete and asphalt. Though highly effective, and cost effective, these materials begin to break down fairly quickly under heavy traffic. Even expressway bridges are designed to last only a half century or so. In this sense, the highways of Chicago really are less durable than the Roman roads.

penetrated the marshes of northern Europe, suspended over seas of mud on wooden pilings. They climbed the passes of the Alps, grooved and banked to prevent wagons from hurling over icy cliffs. Perhaps the best sense of the network's scale comes from the Peutinger Map, a medieval copy of a late Roman atlas. Though distorted to fit a narrow scroll, the map is remarkably detailed, featuring the names of regions, peoples, and some 2,700 places, all connected by the red lines of the Roman roads. The distances between towns are carefully marked, as are the waystations along the highways.[1]

Roman roads were equally impressive on the ground. Designed by legionary surveyors and engineers and often built by detachments of troops, they were marvels of practical engineering. The most familiar method of constructing them, used for the great highways of central Italy, began with digging the roadbed down to a firm layer of subsoil. This trench was then filled with compacted layers of rubble and capped by a pavement of local stone, wedged between curb blocks and crowned to shed water. Outside Italy, roads were often surfaced with gravel or packed dirt instead of paving stones. In deserts, they might be little more than a track cleared of rocks. In swamps, on the other hand, they had to be supported with an intricate underpinning of pilings and beams. On the approaches to large cities and in the most hazardous mountain passes, ruts were sometimes carved into the pavement to control traffic and prevent accidents. The main highways were paved to a standard width of fourteen Roman feet and flanked by gravel paths for riders and pedestrians.* Tall milestones stood along the shoulder, inscribed with the distance to the nearest town or landmark. Groves of trees marked roadside inns and shrines. And when tombs started to appear among the milestones, a city was seldom far away.[2]

The Roman road network was designed for military use. Soldiers built the roads, guarded their strategic points, and used them constantly. The undeviating lines and long, straight slopes of the main highways were shaped by the single aim of allowing infantry to

---

* A few especially busy roads were given discrete lanes, separated by a depression in the pavement. Other roads featured pullouts on viaducts and steep passes, to allow animals to rest and vehicles to pass each other.

The Via Appia just outside Rome. *Author's photo*

march as quickly as possible from point to point.* They were used, however, by all kinds of traffic. On any given road, we might imagine a farmer and his mule bringing a load of vegetables to market, a woman walking to visit her mother in the next village, a wealthy man being carried in his litter to a fashionable healing sanctuary, a shepherd herding his flock along the roadside, and occasionally—galloping along the bridle paths—a rider of the imperial post, the Roman Empire's swiftest and most secure way of sending messages.

Many aspects of the Roman highways seem modern. They had waysides, highway police, and tolls. And they were characterized by feats of civil engineering that would not be excelled until the nineteenth century. The Roman road to the St. Bernard Passes of the Alps, for example, sprang over mountain chasms, drove up boulder-strewn

---

* Roman roads went straight up hills because it was quicker for marching soldiers and their mules to march to the top, rest briefly, and move on than to wind their way up a series of switchbacks.

slopes, and culminated in a spectacular rock cut more than seven hundred feet long. Hundreds of Roman bridges are still extant. The bridge at Mérida, which carried traffic until 1991, is more than half a mile long. The Bridge of Augustus at Narni, up to 110 feet high, featured a central arch 105 feet wide. The Romans also carved road tunnels through dangerous mountain terrain. A famous example is in the Furlo Pass, where a tunnel 130 feet long and wide enough for two lanes of wagon traffic carried the Via Flaminia through a high ridge. The tunnel was used by cars until the 1980s.* Perhaps the most awe-inspiring section of the entire Roman road network was located on what is now the border of Serbia and Romania, where the Danube rushes through the rugged gorge called the Iron Gates. Just below the Gates, Trajan erected the greatest of all Roman bridges, a leviathan nearly four thousand feet long supported by twenty immense piers. Upstream, Trajan's engineers hacked a highway through the riverside cliffs, suspending part of the roadbed on beams cantilevered over the water.[3]

Roman roads were designed to carry the traffic of their day—riders, wagons, and marching soldiers—in any weather. They were meant to be both convenience and symbol, and served both purposes well. The sheer durability of the system is remarkable. But the Roman roads, like any roads, were far from immortal. Milestones record numerous reconstructions, which repaired damage caused by heavy rain, flash floods, and simple wear. The famous Via Appia, which ran from Rome to Brindisi, was renewed many times over the centuries, and repeatedly improved with new bridges and viaducts.[†] One inscription notes the resurfacing of a worn-out section of limestone paving with harder-wearing basalt.[4]

---

* The longest Roman road tunnel is the so-called Grotta di Cocceio, which connected Cumae with Augustus's harbor at Lake Avernus. About two-thirds of a mile long, and wide enough for loaded carts to drive through, it was ventilated and lit by a series of light wells up to one hundred feet deep, and paralleled by an aqueduct channel. Though neglected after the fall of Rome, the tunnel survived the Middle Ages virtually intact, and was reactivated as a road tunnel in the nineteenth century. During the Second World War it was used to store munitions, which were touched off by retreating Nazi soldiers in 1943. The Grotta di Cocceio suffered catastrophic damage, and has remained closed ever since.

† The cost of repairing a paved highway in the imperial era has been estimated at roughly 20 sestertii per foot of road. A new highway was considerably more expensive, perhaps as much as 500,000 sestertii per mile.

Despite the awesome longevity of their bridges, most Roman roads vanished during the Middle Ages, their paving stones buried or pulled up for reuse, their grassy beds running straight to nowhere.* Yet when European engineers began to build new highways in the early modern period, they consciously imitated the Romans. The pioneering methods of John McAdam, the father of modern road construction, were partly inspired by Roman techniques. So, ultimately, were the expressways of the Windy City.

---

* During the Middle Ages, Roman roads were usually attributed to a mythical king or to the devil. Even after the pavement had vanished, the roadside ditches were often still visible, especially when they shone with morning dew. These gleaming swales were said to mark the paths walked by ancient saints.

How Were the Roman Catacombs Constructed?

The bedrock beneath many ancient cities was honeycombed with caves and passageways. Under the Umbrian hill town of Orvieto, for example, is a labyrinth that remained in use through the Renaissance, when warring noble families cut private escape routes through the maze. The tombs and tunnels under Naples sheltered much of the city's population during the air raids of the Second World War. But far more expansive than these, more enticing than the half-submerged funerary chapels and hypogea below the streets of Alexandria, more impressive than even the cave cities of Cappadocia, were the sprawling subterranean cemeteries we know as the Catacombs of Rome.

The full extent of the Roman catacombs is a mystery. The Catacomb of St. Callixtus alone contains about twelve miles of passageways, and housed an estimated five hundred thousand burials. About sixty other catacombs have been at least partially explored, and more—perhaps many more—still await discovery.* Altogether, the tunnels of the Roman catacombs may be nearly as long as the Italian Peninsula. Antonio Bosio, an early explorer, was once lost underground for two full days, groping blindly among the bones and broken lamps of the city of the dead.

---

* At the end of the nineteenth century, seventeen catacombs were open to the public. Only five can now be routinely visited; a few more are accessible by advance booking or special application to the Pontifical Commission of Sacred Archaeology. Access to the other catacombs is strictly forbidden, often because the complex is in a state of collapse or still unexplored.

The catacombs came into being at a moment of transformation in Roman burial customs. For centuries, it had been customary to cremate the dead. There were exceptions to this rule—some noble families, for example, had traditions of inhumation,* and victims of lightning strikes were buried on the spot—but for most Romans, a funeral involved buying wood from the priests of Libitina, carrying the funerary couch to one of the public burning places, and kindling a pyre.† From the early second century onward, however, cremation was gradually displaced by burial. The reasons behind the transition are obscure. Christians, believing in the resurrection of the body, rejected cremation; but there were too few of them to drive trends at that early date. The strong cultural influence of the eastern provinces, where inhumation had long been standard, may have been partly responsible. Ultimately, it may just have been a matter of fashion.¹

Whatever its cause, the transition from cremation to burial placed unprecedented demands on the crowded cemeteries that ringed Rome.‡ Grave plots were already so expensive that cremated members of the middle classes were often interred in columbaria, "condominiums of the dead" with hundreds, and sometimes thousands, of niches for funerary urns. As burial replaced cremation, demand grew for an equally cost-effective means of entombing unburned bodies. From that need, the catacombs emerged. The first Roman catacombs were family tombs, excavated to extend the capacity of a small grave plot. Gradually, larger catacombs were constructed as inexpensive alternatives to surface tombs. These early catacombs seem to have had no particular religious affiliation. By the late first century, however, Rome's Jewish community had

---

* Nero had the body of his wife Poppaea embalmed, and the discovery of several embalmed bodies—including a perfectly preserved woman found just outside Rome in the fifteenth century—suggests that the custom was far from unknown among the Roman elite.

† Sometimes, in keeping with an ancient tradition of disputed significance, a finger was cut from the corpse for separate burial. Several hundred vessels discovered along the Via Appia, each containing a single finger bone, may bear witness to the custom.

‡ Law and custom forbade burial within the city limits, with the exceptions of vestal virgins, emperors, and men who had celebrated a triumph or performed some other signal service for the state.

begun to create its own catacombs. This precedent, and the hypogea constructed by certain polytheist sects, likely inspired the Christian catacombs, which were developed on a grand scale from the beginning of the third century.[2]

A nineteenth-century drawing of a Roman catacomb. *Wikimedia Commons*

The city of Rome stands on thick deposits of the soft volcanic stone known as tufa. Into the tufa, within a half day's walk of the city and twenty to seventy feet underground, the Christian catacombs were cut. Often starting from quarries or sandpits,* they were excavated piecemeal, gradually expanding outward and downward. Though seldom more than a few feet wide, the passageways could be twenty feet high, and were laid out on as many as five levels.

The walls of the passageways were lined with rows of burial niches, or loculi. A body was dusted with quicklime, wrapped in a sheet, and laid in its niche, often with a few bottles of perfume to mask the stench of decomposition. The niche was then sealed with tiles or stone slabs. Wealthier Christians and martyrs were laid to rest in arcosolia, alcoves framing a sarcophagus. Chambers set off the main passageways served as private mausoleums for families and guilds.

The catacombs contain some of the earliest examples of Christian art. Simple motifs—the fish, the dove, the anchor—were etched or painted onto tomb slabs to symbolize elements of the Christian faith. More interesting, from an art historical perspective, are frescoes illustrating episodes from the Bible, often using conventions and figures from the repertory of classical art. In this sense, though few of them can be called masterpieces, the frescoes of the catacombs anticipate the brilliant paintings of the Renaissance. Equally intriguing, at least for historians, are the tens of thousands of inscriptions that have been discovered in the catacombs.† Although the earliest, in keeping with the eastern origins of Rome's Christian community, are in Greek, the majority are Latin. Most consist only of the deceased's name and the words "in peace," but a few are more elaborate, like the lengthy poetic epitaphs that a fourth-century pope composed for the tombs of the martyrs.

---

* The early Christians called the catacombs *coemeteria*. The word "catacomb" originates from *kata kumbas* ("by the quarries" in Greek), the name of the district around the Catacombs of St. Sebastian. During the Middle Ages, when the Catacombs of St. Sebastian, known as the *coemeterium ad catacumbas*, were the only catacomb still accessible to visitors, "catacomb" began to be applied to similar burial places in Rome and elsewhere.

† In place of inscriptions, some loculi were identified by tokens—coins, glass bottles, or statuettes—pressed into the cement around their tiles.

Contrary to a persistent legend, the catacombs were never used as places of refuge during the persecutions of the third and early fourth centuries, not least because the Roman authorities were well aware of their locations.* The martyrs of the persecutions, however, were buried in the catacombs, and eventually drew pilgrims in such numbers that air shafts and wider staircases had to be built to cope with the crowds. The massive expansion of the Church after Constantine's legalization of Christianity was mirrored underground, as miles of new corridors and hundreds of thousands of tombs were cut into the straining tufa. The apogee, however, was short lived. Interments diminished through the fifth century and stopped in the sixth, thanks to a combination of changing burial customs and the erosion of Rome's population.

Parts of the catacombs were already closed in late antiquity, as the spoil from new graves was heaped in disused passageways. After the fall of the empire, as Rome's hinterland became depopulated and dangerous, the bones of the martyrs were moved to churches within the city and the catacombs were abandoned. Though never completely forgotten,† they all but vanished from the popular consciousness until 1578, when part of the Catacomb of St. Priscilla collapsed, revealing a bone-strewn passageway aglow with ancient frescoes.

---

* The catacombs, however, witnessed several martyrdoms. During the Great Persecution of Diocletian, Pope Sixtus II and his deacons were captured and executed in a catacomb. Saint Candida reportedly met her end when persecutors flung her down a catacomb air shaft.

† As mentioned earlier, the Catacombs of St. Sebastian remained open throughout the Middle Ages. During the Renaissance, intrepid souls ventured deep into some of the "lost" catacombs. The humanist Julius Pomponius Laetus, for example, held clandestine meetings with fellow lovers of antiquity deep in the Catacombs of St. Callixtus. It was only in the nineteenth century, however, that the upper levels of the largest catacombs were cleared of bones and debris, and tour groups began to visit.

III

WHAT HAPPENED?

· 23 ·

Did Atlantis Exist?

$\mathcal{B}$y the time he wrote the book that made him a household name, Ignatius Donnelly had suffered through several careers. He had abandoned his practice as a lawyer, gone bankrupt as a land speculator, and been voted out of the United States Congress. At first sight, his book seemed no likelier to succeed. It was nearly five hundred pages long, filled with references to obscure scientific literature, and written on a subject most people had barely heard of. But when it appeared in 1882, it was an immediate success. Despite a few dissenting voices—Charles Darwin was skeptical—the critical response was positive. And the public loved it: Donnelly's book would go through dozens of printings in the next decade alone. The title of his unlikely bestseller was *Atlantis: The Antediluvian World*; and its purpose was to prove that Atlantis—the island-empire described by Plato—had actually existed.*

Most modern enthusiasts believe that Atlantis was a seafaring civilization that flourished in the twilight before recorded history. On these articles of faith are founded countless theories. Atlantis, it is

---

* Atlantis, Donnelly claimed, had been a large island off the coast of Spain. The people of Atlantis had invented writing, bronze working, and monumental architecture before proceeding to colonize most of the world. After a terrible disaster destroyed the island of Atlantis, the survivors preserved memories, later remembered as myths, of their vanished civilization. The Pyramids of Egypt and Central America, the Phoenician alphabet and Mayan hieroglyphs, the Garden of Eden, Mount Olympus, and much, much more were all, Donnelly insisted, legacies of Atlantis. Even in 1882, it was clear that there was no real evidence—geological, archaeological, or otherwise—for a lost continent or prehistoric supercivilization. But the idea of an ancient empire lost beneath the waves was too fascinating to ignore, and many readers were convinced.

variously claimed, was annihilated by asteroid, burned by barbarians, or crushed in a chasm. Its ruins are awash in Antarctic ice, or slumbering beneath Spanish sands, or bleaching on the beaches of Bimini.

Determining whether any of these theories has basis in fact means going back to our only sources for the story of Atlantis: the dialogues of Plato. Born into one of Athens's leading families, Plato was a brilliant student, a gifted poet, and a champion wrestler.* He seemed destined for a successful political career—until he fell under the unlikely spell of Socrates. More than forty years Plato's senior, Socrates refused to engage in any profession other than philosophy, and spent most of his time lounging or strolling barefoot in public places, engaging anyone who stood still long enough in discussions about things like the definitions of courage and piety. To Plato and a small group of other philosophically inclined youths, he was a fascinating friend and teacher. To most other Athenians, however, he seemed a nuisance, and possibly a menace. In 399 BCE, a jury condemned Socrates to death on charges of impiety and corrupting the youth of Athens. Though able to escape, he chose to accept the penalty; and after about a month in prison, he calmly drank a fatal dose of hemlock.[1]

The execution of Socrates convinced Plato to devote his life to philosophy. Inspired by the Socratic habit of seeking truth through discussion, Plato presented his ideas in the form of conversations between two or more characters. The most important speaker in these dialogues is usually, but not always, Socrates. Plato himself never appears. The reader is presented with a long and detailed discussion of some philosophical concept, and left to ponder its implications. This format allowed Plato to explore complex issues without committing himself to a single interpretation. Equally importantly, it drew readers into the conversation, urging them to consider the issues at stake for themselves.

The two dialogues that describe Atlantis, *Timaeus* and *Critias*, are among the last Plato wrote. Both reflect his deep interest

---

* Plato was also a bit of a rebel, if we can believe the later claim that he wore an earring in his wayward youth.

in politics. Earlier in his career, in his famous *Republic*, Plato had described a utopian society. In his old age, however, he seems to have become increasingly interested in the practical problems of governing a city. The *Timaeus* and *Critias* are products of this new approach to the perfect state. The *Timaeus*, presented as a continuation of the *Republic*, features Socrates and three other characters. Socrates begins the dialogue by summarizing the ideal society outlined in the *Republic*. Their discussion, he suggests, is incomplete, since they have yet to consider how effective such a city would be in a crisis.

One of the other characters, Critias, replies that he knows a relevant example. An ancestor of his had once visited Egypt. There his ancestor had fallen into conversation with some priests, who told him that their records preserved many things the Greeks had long forgotten. Nine thousand years before, the priests claimed, Athens had been a great city. The ancient Athenians had performed many noble deeds; but their most famous exploit was the defeat of a mighty empire called Atlantis. The Atlanteans, from an island in the far west, had conquered most of the known world. When they sought to add Greece to their empire, however, the Athenians had thrown them back, and finally led a war that liberated Europe from Atlantean tyranny. Not long after this victory, both ancient Athens and Atlantis were destroyed by terrible earthquakes and floods. A few Athenians survived by fleeing into the mountains. But Atlantis and its people sank beneath the waves.[2]

Critias continues his story in the next dialogue, which is named after him. He begins by presenting ancient Athens as an example of the ideal society described in the *Republic*. Then he turns to Atlantis, which he now describes in detail. Atlantis, he says, was founded by Poseidon, who set ten of his mortal sons on the thrones of its kingdoms. To the eldest of his children, Poseidon gave a spectacular natural fortress surrounded by concentric rings of seawater. This became the heart of the Atlanteans' greatest city, and was duly crowned with a temple of Poseidon. Around the metropolis stretched a vast plain, traversed and irrigated by a network of canals. In times of war, Atlantis's chief kingdom could muster a navy of 1,200 ships and an army of well over a million men. The other kingdoms were equally populous and powerful. The ten kings of Atlantis, however, maintained a truce among themselves, meeting every few years to sacrifice bulls to Poseidon and confirm their alliance. The Atlanteans grew steadily in wealth and might. In time, however, they became corrupt, and the gods were stirred to anger. Zeus convened a heavenly council, and—the dialogue ends. Plato never finished the *Critias*, and never mentioned Atlantis again.[3]

References to Plato's Atlantis story appear sporadically in other ancient authors. Aristotle seems to have dismissed Atlantis as fictional. But in later centuries, there was a range of opinion. According to a late antique commentary on the *Timaeus*, some philosophers thought that the Atlantis story was literal truth, others regarded it as an outright fable, and still others interpreted it as a more or less convoluted allegory. Neither in this commentary nor in any other ancient text, however, is there a sign of widespread interest or belief in Atlantis.[4]

Virtually all modern classicists agree that Atlantis was a parable. Plato's dialogues were designed to engage readers, and so guide them to the benefits of philosophy. In keeping with this purpose, Plato sometimes had one of his characters tell a story that illustrated or complemented the discussion. Some of these stories were framed as myths or allegories. Others, though fictional, were described as true. As a writer of dialogues, Plato did not have to commit himself to the truth of any of these tales: he could simply put a story in a character's mouth, and treat it as a point for discussion. Wanting to explore how an ideal state would function in a time of war, Plato described ancient Athens as a virtuous and well-governed city. He seems to have invented the empire of Atlantis, mighty but corrupt, as a counterexample. Atlantis, in short, was an illustration of how not to govern. It may have also been a caricature of contemporary Athens, which Plato regarded as badly managed and morally bankrupt. But there is no reason to assume that it was a historical place.[5]

It has sometimes been suggested—most cogently by Irish classicist John Luce—that Plato modeled Atlantis on the Minoan civilization of Bronze Age Crete. Minoan society was centered on colossal palaces, which served as ritual and economic centers until they were destroyed by a series of disasters. Pointing to a few Minoan-looking

Santorini, looking toward the caldera of the Thera volcano. *Wikimedia Commons*

customs in the *Critias*,* Luce claimed that either Plato or one of his ancestors had traveled to Egypt, and there encountered a garbled description of Minoan Crete that became the basis of the Atlantis story. It was also in Egypt, Luce believed, that Plato learned about the eruption of the Thera volcano.[6]

The island of Thera, located about ninety miles north of Crete, is better known today as Santorini. Every summer, thousands of visitors shuffle up and down the whitewashed streets of Santorini's towns, squinting appreciatively at towering black cliffs and a turquoise bay. This picturesque landscape was created some thirty-six centuries ago, when a cataclysmic eruption tore the island apart, blackening the sea with ash and sending tsunamis toward the palaces of Minoan Crete.†

---

* Luce suggested, for example, that the Atlantean kings' strange habit of hunting sacrificial bulls with lassos reflected memories of a Minoan custom, since Minoan frescoes depict what appears to be a similar ritual.

† We have no accounts of the Thera eruption. Some sense of its intensity, however, is provided by descriptions of the apocalyptic eruption of Krakatoa in August 1883. Falling ash shrouded the sun. Beneath the sudden gloom, the sea, lit by eerie tendrils of static lightning, churned uneasily. Hour after hour, the air shuddered with percussive blasts. When four colossal explosions finally shattered the volcano, tsunamis up to 150 feet high engulfed the neighboring coasts. The final explosion was heard over three thousand miles away, and generated a pressure wave that traveled around the world three times before dissipating. Debris from the eruption lingered for months in the upper atmosphere, depressing the average global temperature by a degree Fahrenheit. The eruption of Thera was considerably more powerful than Krakatoa's.

Yet there is no reason to assume that either the Thera eruption or Minoan Crete inspired Plato's Atlantis story. First, Crete bears no resemblance to Plato's Atlantis. It is not located in the Atlantic Ocean, is not the size of a continent, and does not—as Plato claimed of Atlantis—have herds of elephants cavorting on its plains. Second, Minoan civilization survived the eruption of Thera. Although the eruption's date is disputed, it almost certainly occurred more than a century before the burning of the Minoan palaces. Finally, it is hard to see how any description of Minoan Crete or the eruption of Thera could have reached Plato. If there had been a tradition known to the Greeks about a great civilization on Crete and its sudden destruction, it seems likely that there would be traces of it in other ancient sources. But there are none.*

This does not mean, however, that Atlantis was invented out of thin air. Twice in Plato's lifetime, parts of Greece were devastated by disasters reminiscent of the one said to have drowned Atlantis. In 426 BCE, an earthquake and tsunami overwhelmed a small island named Atalante. And in 373, about two decades before Plato wrote the *Timaeus* and *Critias*, an earthquake caused the city of Helike to sink into the sea. The submerged ruins became a tourist attraction; and for centuries, local fishermen snagged their nets on a statue of Poseidon beneath the waves. Perhaps the fate of Helike inspired Plato to drown Atlantis. Or maybe the terrible flood and earthquake described in the *Timaeus* were just literary flourishes. Whatever his inspiration, Plato can never have imagined the afterlife of his parable.[7]

---

* John Luce tried to sidestep this problem by suggesting that either Plato or his ancestor Solon traveled to Egypt, and learned about the Minoans there. Solon probably did visit Egypt, and Plato may have. Neither man, however, is likely to have picked up the basis of the Atlantis legend from Egyptian priests. Although the Egyptians had traded with Minoan Crete, there is no sign in any extant inscription or papyrus that they regarded the Minoans as powerful or dangerous.

Was There a Trojan War?

$\mathcal{E}$arly on the morning of May 31, 1873, a glimmer caught Heinrich Schliemann's eye. About thirty feet below the surface, in the rubble beneath the great ramparts, a corroded copper vessel protruded from the trench wall. As he began to move it, he glimpsed gold beneath. Thinking quickly, he ordered the workmen to take their breakfast break. Then he pulled the vessel aside, exposing a jumbled mass of precious metal. Using a knife to dislodge the treasure, he gathered it up by the armload, and hid it in his hut. After a delay of several days, Schliemann had the treasure smuggled to his home in Athens, where he was finally able to examine it closely. When he did, he was astonished by its richness: bronze spearheads, daggers, and axes; vessels of silver, gold, and electrum; silver ingots and gold bracelets; basket earrings, a diadem, and splendid headdresses of gold. As the glittering piles grew, his doubts vanished. This was the proof he had sought for the past three years. He had found Homer's Troy.[1]

"Priam's Treasure,"* as Schliemann's find came to be known, made headlines around the world. For centuries, it had been assumed that the Trojan War was more or less fictional. But this spectacular discovery on the traditional site of Troy, found alongside impressive stone walls and what appeared to be the remains of a sacked and burned palace, seemed an eloquent argument to the contrary.

---

* The treasure was displayed in Berlin until the Second World War, after which it was seized by the Soviets and taken to Moscow. Some of the most spectacular pieces can now be seen at the Pushkin Museum.

Schliemann's wife Sophia wearing a golden diadem and earrings from "Priam's Treasure."
Wikimedia Commons

Much later, it would be realized that Priam's Treasure was at least a thousand years older than any conceivable date for the fall of Troy. By then, however, Heinrich Schliemann was widely thought to have proven that the *Iliad* was rooted in fact.

Although the Greeks and Romans assumed that the Trojan War was historical, they were aware that many centuries lay between them and the ruined fortresses and tombs they associated with the Homeric heroes. Only Homer bridged the gap—and Homer, they suspected, hadn't gotten all his facts right. One Greek historian claimed that Helen never made it to Troy. Another thought that Helen had never even existed, and that the Trojan War had been a straightforward political struggle. Virtually all ancient scholars agreed, however, that the little city of Ilion stood atop the ruins of Troy.[2]

Although Ilion was not an especially important or impressive place, its Homeric associations drew a series of eminent tourists. The Persian king Xerxes visited just before his invasion of Greece, and sacrificed a thousand oxen at the Temple of Athena. Alexander the Great—so obsessed with the *Iliad* that he kept a copy beneath his pillow—also came, and took part in a naked footrace to the Tomb of Achilles. Julius Caesar, who claimed descent from the Trojan hero Aeneas, was another visitor, as was the emperor Caracalla, who cremated one of his courtiers on a Homeric-style funeral pyre just outside the city. So many tourists came to Ilion, in fact, that the city began to mint coins showing Homeric heroes as souvenirs.* Tourists were still coming in the fourth century, when Ilion's bishop gave the emperor Julian a grand tour. Soon after, however, the city began to decline; and by the time Schliemann set eyes on its ruins, it had been abandoned for more than a millennium.[3]

Almost as soon as he began his excavations at Ilion in 1871, Schliemann realized that the site was covered by the superimposed ruins of many settlements. Convinced that Homer's city would be found at the bottom of this archaeological jumble, he hacked a broad trench, up to forty-five feet deep, through the center of the site. Using crowbars, pickaxes, and improvised rams, his workmen scraped and battered their way to bedrock. They soon discovered, however, that the first settlement on the site had been a simple fishing village. Homer's Troy, Schliemann decided, must have actually been the second settlement. This was much more promising: it had been destroyed by fire, its buildings were large, and it was surrounded by a massive wall. Once he discovered Priam's Treasure just outside that wall, Schliemann was convinced that he had found the setting of the *Iliad*.

He was, however, unable to investigate further for some time. Warned that the Ottoman government, furious over his illegal removal of Priam's Treasure, would arrest him if he returned to Turkey, Schliemann suspended the excavations at Troy and turned his

---

* One Roman visitor mounted a series of coins from Troy and other cities in what is now western Turkey on the outside of a ceremonial vessel as a sort of commemorative album of his travels.

attention to sites in Greece. In 1876, he began a large-scale dig at Mycenae, described by the *Iliad* as the capital of the Greek war leader Agamemnon. Almost at once, he discovered the fabulously wealthy tombs of Mycenae's Bronze Age kings. Each tomb yielded marvels: exquisitely worked swords and daggers, cups and vases of gold, gorgeous amulets and diadems. The most wonderful find of all, however, came to light in what Schliemann called the first shaft grave. Here, seventeen feet below the surface, he found the bodies of three men, two buried with heavy gold masks.* Schliemann was entranced, and sent the king of Greece a message later abbreviated into his most famous words: "Today, I have gazed upon the face of Agamemnon."[4]

Over the next few years, Schliemann excavated at two other sites associated with the Greek heroes of the Trojan War. In combination with the discoveries at Mycenae, his finds made it clear that Greece had been home to a sophisticated civilization centuries before the rise of the classical city-states. The rulers of this society had occupied lavish fortified palaces. They had engaged in lucrative trade with Egypt and the Near East. And, as the colossal walls around their palaces and the weapons in their tombs indicated, they were no strangers to warfare. These Mycenaeans, as they came to be known, looked rather like the Greek chieftains of the *Iliad*. Just after Schliemann's death, shards of Mycenaean pottery were discovered at the site of Troy. The Trojan War, it seemed, was real.

Soon, however, new scholarship on the *Iliad* began to raise doubts. It had long been recognized that the *Iliad* emerged from a tradition of oral poetry—poetry, that is, composed and transmitted without the aid of writing. But only in the 1930s did the implications of this fact for understanding the Homeric epics become clear. The impetus was the research of a young Harvard professor named Milman Parry, who conducted fieldwork on the illiterate bards of Bosnia.

---

* Two of the bodies had been reduced to fractured bone. When Schliemann lifted the mask off the third man, however, he discovered that some quirk of the soil had preserved the head beneath. An artist was hurried in from a nearby town to sketch the remains before they decayed. His drawing, included in Schliemann's publication of the excavations a few years later, shows a broad face incongruously perched on a bare spine. Although the nose and hair are gone, the skin and eyelids are intact, and the perfect teeth are bared in a rather unsettling grin.

These men, Parry found, sang about some very Homeric subjects, including long sieges. He even discovered a Bosnian Homer—an exceptionally talented bard who could compose poems nearly as long and elaborate as the *Iliad*. Although the Bosnian bards claimed to recite their songs from memory, their performances—Parry soon realized—were basically improvised. Every bard had internalized a vast stock of formulaic phrases, lines, and scenes. As he sang, he combined and recombined these elements, crafting around them a poem that was at once completely traditional and completely new. The works of Homer, Parry thought, must have been created in a similar way.[5]

These conclusions called into question the idea that the *Iliad* could have preserved historical information. Homer, it was clear, stood at the end of a long tradition of oral poetry. Even if aspects of that tradition extended back to the Mycenaean period, centuries of illiterate bards, each freely adapting his songs, stood between the *Iliad* and its original sources. Parry's studies suggested that oral poetry seamlessly blended the very old with the very new—and this is exactly what scholars began to find in the *Iliad*.* Homer, scholars realized, was not remembering a distant past; he was inventing it. The argument against a historical Trojan War was strengthened by the discovery at several Mycenaean sites of clay tablets covered with strange symbols. These proved to be inventories, written in an early form of Greek, of trade goods entering and leaving the palaces. They revealed that the Mycenaean kings—unlike the petty warrior-chieftains of the *Iliad*—presided over centralized states with substantial bureaucracies. And unlike Homer's heroes, those kings— or at least their scribes—could read.[6]

In the wake of these discoveries, a historical Trojan War was hard to imagine. Over the past few decades, however, additional sources of information have come to light. Archaeologists have identified nine more or less discrete cities on the site of Troy, each built on the ruins of its predecessor. New excavations have revealed that one

---

* For example, Homer's heroes, like the Mycenaeans, have chariots. Instead of using those chariots in Mycenaean-style combat, however, they ride them to the battlefield, dismount, and—like the Greeks of Homer's own time—fight on foot.

of these cities, Troy VI,* was much larger than previously believed, with a residential area adjoining the citadel that may have housed up to ten thousand inhabitants. Recently deciphered Hittite documents suggest that Troy VI was the center of a small kingdom, which flourished at a time when at least one Mycenaean kingdom was attempting to expand into the area. A letter in the Hittite archives, written around the beginning of the thirteenth century BCE, notes that Troy was occupied by a rebel prince with close ties to the Mycenaeans. Another letter, composed a few decades later, mentions a dispute between the Hittites and Mycenaeans over the city.[7]

We have, in short, archaeological evidence that late Bronze Age Troy was a large and wealthy city, which was attacked and captured at least once by invaders. Hittite records confirm the presence of Mycenaean Greeks near Troy, and indicate Troy as a target of Mycenaean aggression. The *Iliad*, finally, contains apparent echoes of a conflict or series of conflicts between the Mycenaeans and Trojans.[†] Although none of this proves that anything like the war described in Homer's poem took place, it is not beyond the realm of possibility that one or more of the conflicts around Troy achieved epic scale, with thousands of Mycenaeans and local allies arrayed against the Trojans and their neighbors. At least once, Troy was captured. And however the city fell, it survived as ruins—and in song.[8]

---

* Troy VI, a large and massively fortified city, was destroyed shortly after 1300 BCE. The culprit was almost certainly an earthquake, though invaders or a popular uprising may have contributed. The survivors of this disaster immediately rebuilt their city, creating the settlement known as Troy VII. Though about the same size as its predecessor, Troy VII was considerably less grandiose. Many of its houses had storage vessels built into their floors, which suggests that the inhabitants lived in fear of a siege. They had good reason to worry: Troy VII was destroyed around 1180 BCE by a violent sack. Some scholars believe that this destruction inspired the Trojan War tradition. But since it took place after the collapse of Mycenaean civilization, Troy VI seems to have better Homeric credentials.

† The oral tradition seems to have preserved at least faint memories of the Bronze Age, including accurate descriptions of Mycenaean weapons and artifacts. The Mycenaeans spoke Greek and had a tradition of oral poetry. Perhaps some of their songs were inspired by a conflict or conflicts around Troy. Perhaps these songs did not die with the palaces, but were passed on, ever changing, to Homer's time.

What Was Sparta Really Like?

$\mathcal{A}$round the beginning of the second century, the scholar and biographer Plutarch collected hundreds of sayings associated with notable Spartans. They make for colorful reading, as a few examples will illustrate:

> Agis once said: Spartans do not ask how numerous their opponents are. They ask, "Where are they?"

> When Cleomenes was asked why he hadn't eliminated the people of Argos, who had often attacked Sparta, he replied, "Oh, we would never kill them all. We need them to train our boys."

> Asked how far the borders of Sparta extended, Agesilaus held up a spear and exclaimed, "As far as this can reach!"

The two most famous sayings in Plutarch's collection are attributed to Leonidas, the Spartan king immortalized by his last stand against the Persians at Thermopylae:

> When someone told Leonidas that the Persian arrows blotted out the sun, he said, "Then won't it be nice to fight in the shade?"

> After Xerxes demanded that the Spartans surrender their weapons, Leonidas answered, "Come and take them."

Plutarch's collection epitomizes the popular image of Sparta: a society of hardened soldiers and their selfless wives, trained and eternally ready to fight and die for their country. Though idealized, and partially misleading, this image has some basis in fact.[1]

For two centuries, Sparta was the most powerful, most famous, and most feared city-state in the Greek world. Spartans led the coalition that broke the gargantuan armies of the Persian king of kings. Spartans destroyed the Athenian Empire and its proud fleets of triremes. Twice, Spartan armies dared to invade Persia itself. Even after Spartan power dwindled, the Spartan legend continued to grow. Ancient observers marveled that a few thousand citizen-warriors, living in a cluster of villages in a single mountain-rimmed valley, had shaped the whole course of Greek history. They were even more impressed by Sparta's political stability, which they regarded as an expression of Spartan self-discipline.[2]

That discipline was taught. At age seven, the sons of Spartan citizens were enrolled in a state-sponsored education system. Although they learned to read and write—possibly from private tutors—their training was primarily and relentlessly physical. Boys lived in communal barracks, where they slept on heaps of dry rushes. Even in winter, they were forbidden to wear shoes or any clothing besides a single thin tunic. They were fed little, and expected to forage and steal for sustenance. Around the age of twenty, young Spartans joined one of the communal dining halls. In these close-knit organizations, each consisting of about fifteen men, members contributed a set amount of food and wine to the common table, and dined together almost every evening of their adult lives. They also went to war together. Spartans were eligible for military service from the ages of twenty to sixty. When not on campaign, they were expected to maintain their fitness and readiness for battle.* A Spartan's service to the state ended only with his death, when he was lowered into a simple pit and covered with his red military cloak. Only men who died in battle were allowed a headstone, and only one inscription was permitted: the name of the deceased, followed by the words "in war."[3]

---

* Just before the last stand at Thermopylae, Persian scouts were shocked to see Spartan warriors exercising nude on the battlefield.

Since it was assumed that only strong mothers could give birth to strong sons, Spartan girls also took part in a state-sponsored physical education regimen. They ran, threw, wrestled, and danced,* wearing the loose clothes that earned them the nickname (in Athens) of "thigh flashers." Both these garments and public athletics, however, were set aside at marriage. Raising children was seen as a service to the state: women who died in childbirth, like men who fell in battle, were honored with a tombstone. The duty of producing strong sons outweighed all other obligations, to the point that it was acceptable for a Spartan to ask a man whose strength or courage he admired to sleep with his wife, and conceive a better child than he could himself.[4]

Early in their history, when they were conquering their territory, the Spartans had made the inhabitants of some nearby towns *perioikoi*—free, but deprived of citizen rights—and had reduced the mass of the rural population to the status of helots, serfs compelled to surrender their crops to Spartan masters. Each Spartan citizen went to war with a helot servant, and bands of helots were sometimes employed as light infantry. In times of peace, however, helots were periodically forced to humiliate themselves by getting drunk and singing crude songs in the dining halls. Those judged insubordinate or dangerously talented were murdered.[†] Every year, in fact, Spartan officials formally declared war on the helots, so that they could be killed with impunity.[5]

Despite these brutalities, Sparta has often been admired. To many Greeks and Romans, and to those among their intellectual descendants who admired order and hierarchy above all else,[‡] the Spartan citizen-soldiers seemed to epitomize obedience, courage, and patriotism. In several key respects, however, the Sparta applauded

---

* The Athenians were especially amused by an energetic dance Spartan girls performed at festivals, during which they leapt and kicked their own buttocks.

† Some of these murders were carried out by the Krypteia, a band of elite soldiers who prowled the countryside, armed only with a dagger. At least once, thousands of helots were executed in cold blood.

‡ Infamously, Sparta was upheld as a model by Nazi Germany, to the point that Hermann Göring could liken the German troops at Stalingrad to Leonidas's Spartans in a major radio address.

since antiquity bears little relation to historical reality. Since the Spartans themselves produced no historians or philosophers, all the ancient sources on which our understanding of their society is based were written by outsiders. Sources contemporary with the Spartan apogee in the fifth and fourth centuries BCE do not present a coherent picture, and works produced after Sparta's decline—such as Plutarch's enduringly popular *Lives*—tend to idealize. The biases and limitations of these texts have simplified, obscured, and misled.

Our ancient sources, for example, emphasize the austerity of the Spartan citizen-soldiers. They wore rough cloaks. They gnawed on barley bread and guzzled pig blood soup.* Their dishes were clay, their money was iron, and their houses were hewn from rough wooden beams. Citizens were forbidden to own gold jewelry, engage in commerce, or practice a trade. Their days were spent preparing for war. The fact remains, however, that Spartan citizens were a leisure class. Each citizen possessed an estate—always substantial, and sometimes very large—that produced a profitable surplus. Their cloaks might be rough, but their hair was carefully combed and dressed.† Their meals might begin with barley and broth, but they usually ended with delicacies. Their houses might look rough-hewn, but their interiors were often filled with rich furniture and stocks of foreign coins. Their preparations for war were not constant military drills, but leisurely hunting expeditions and exercises in the gymnasia. Some Spartans even found the time and money to dabble in chariot racing, the most expensive of all Greek sports.[6]

From a cursory reading of the ancient sources, it might be assumed that the Spartans were invincible in battle. Though not professionals like Roman legionaries, Spartan hoplites certainly tended to be far better trained and more disciplined than their opponents,

---

* The soup's ingredients appear to have been pig blood, salt, and vinegar. The resultant black broth was regarded as a delicacy by the Spartans and precisely nobody else. A king once imported a Spartan cook expressly for the purpose of making it, and regretted his investment at the first sip.

† Spartan citizen-soldiers wore their hair long, a habit they maintained centuries after short hair became fashionable in the rest of Greece. Even under duress, they took great pains to tame their luxuriant locks. Before Thermopylae, for example, a Persian messenger witnessed the Spartans combing their hair. A Spartan general in captivity was said to have exchanged his precious signet ring for a comb.

Leonidas, a statue of a hoplite set up at Sparta during the era of the Persian Wars, now in the Archaeological Museum of Sparta. *Author's photo*

who were usually inexperienced volunteers. To other Greeks, there were few sights were more terrifying than a Spartan army marching onto a battlefield in perfect order. In combination with their reputation for victory at all costs—fed, above all, by the legend of Thermopylae—the Spartans' discipline made them formidable opponents, and allowed them to go undefeated in any major land battle for nearly two centuries at the height of their prestige. Yet the Spartans did lose, sometimes spectacularly. They were bested several times in early clashes with neighboring city-states, and were capable of surrendering a significant part of their army even in their period of greatest dominance. From the mid-fourth century BCE onward, they suffered a series of defeats catastrophic enough to undermine the very bases of their power.* Afterward, they never again won a major battle.[7]

Nor, contrary to what readers of Thucydides might assume, was Sparta the antithesis of Athens. The laws and institutions of both cities were shaped to maintain the privileges and cohesion of a relatively small class of male citizens. For all its infamous ferocity, the Spartan system of physical education seems to have been complemented by a rather Athenian-looking course of literary studies. And regimented though aspects of their lives undoubtedly were, adult Spartan citizens lived much like wealthy Athenians, hunting, exercising at the gymnasium, and dining with their fellow citizens.[8]

The Spartans attributed their laws and institutions to Lycurgus, a reformer said to have lived in the distant past. Although modern historians agree that he almost certainly never existed, the date and purpose of the reforms associated with his name remain controversial. It seems likely that the state-sponsored education system, communal dining halls, and other iconic features of Classical Sparta emerged quite late, possibly not until the eve of the Persian Wars. It also seems likely that the underlying goal of these reforms was not military

---

* At the Battle of Leuctra (371 BCE), the most notorious of these defeats, nearly half of Sparta's citizen-soldiers died, along with the myth of Spartan invincibility. The battle's impact was magnified by the fact that the Spartans—thanks to the concentration of wealth (and thus, citizen status) in the hands of progressively fewer families—could not replace their losses.

effectiveness, but political harmony. Sparta's culture of austerity, in other words, may have been a cousin of Athenian democracy.

The Sparta Plutarch knew looked little different from any other modestly prosperous regional center in Roman Greece. It had a theater, baths, and porticoes. Its leading citizens revered the emperors and lived in villas with fine mosaic floors. The Spartan past, however, had not been forgotten. A regular festival honored Leonidas, and featured orations on the heroes of Thermopylae. At least twice, when the Romans campaigned against the Parthian Empire, a contingent of Spartan soldiers was sent to do battle with these latter-day Persians. And every year, Spartan boys displayed their contempt for pain by being whipped bloody at the ancient Sanctuary of Artemis Orthia.* Artificial though all this was, it was nothing really new. The Spartans had always lived in the shadow of their own myths.[9]

---

* This infamous "endurance contest" evolved after the Classical period, apparently from an older ritual that involved stealing cheeses. In the bloody variation known to Plutarch and his contemporaries, boys competed to see who could endure whipping the longest without crying out. The contest became such a tourist attraction that tiers of theater-like seating were built around the altar where the boys were lashed.

Was Caligula Insane?

$\mathcal{D}$uring the summer of 39 CE, one of the strangest construction projects in Roman history took shape along the northern shore of the Bay of Naples. From the resort town of Baiae to the bustling port of Puteoli, a distance of about three miles, hundreds of boats were anchored in a double line. The spaces between them were bridged with planks, their decks were packed with earth, and a roadbed was laid on top, complete with fountains and wayside inns. When the floating highway was ready, a young man appeared onshore. He wore a spectacular gilded breastplate, stolen—it was said—from the tomb of Alexander the Great. A cloak of cloth of gold spilled from his shoulders and over his caparisoned horse. An oak leaf crown perched on his balding brow. He paused a moment at the bridgehead; and then, cloak streaming, an army of praetorians at his back, Caligula galloped onto the sea.[1]

Ancient authors struggled to explain why Caligula built his colossal bridge. One speculated that he wished to demonstrate his power over the elements. Another suggested that he was trying to intimidate the barbarians beyond the empire's frontiers. But the most popular explanation, then as now, was simple: he was insane.

The brief reign of Caligula, the third Roman emperor, is one of the most notorious eras in ancient history. The son of a famous and popular general, Caligula was hailed as Rome's savior when he came to the throne at the age of twenty-four. But by the time he was assassinated less than four years later, he had carved out a reputation for tyranny and cruelty that would outlast the Roman Empire itself.

Caligula ruled with dictatorial disdain for any power or prerogative besides his own. Soon after becoming emperor, he reportedly told someone who dared to give him advice, "Remember—I can do whatever I want." He showed particular contempt to the Roman aristocracy, making distinguished senators hold his napkin at banquets or hitch up their togas and jog beside his chariot. Eventually, he began to present himself as a living god, receiving the veneration of his subjects from a throne flanked by statues of the divine twins Castor and Pollux. His private life was equally unrestrained. Caligula bathed in perfumed oil, dissolved pearls in his wine, and gilded the foods served at his banquets. On Lake Nemi, just outside Rome, he ordered the construction of two magnificent luxury barges. When their remains were uncovered in the early twentieth century,* archaeologists found traces of heated marble floors, rotating statue platforms, and pumps for hot- and cold-water baths.[2]

Caligula's casual disregard for human life was legendary. Once, when beef and pork prices were high, he decided to save money by having prisoners fed to the lions and bears scheduled to appear in the arena. He executed scores of political opponents, sometimes forcing

---

* Caligula's barges were recovered piecemeal. In 1446, inspired by the Renaissance enthusiasm for all things Roman, a cardinal attempted to raise one of the ships by building a large floating platform on the surface of the lake and hiring divers to attach chains to the wreck. Almost as soon as the men on the platform began to winch the ship upward, however, the chains snapped, and only a few fragments were brought to the surface. Another attempt, equally unfruitful, was made in 1535 using a primitive diving bell. A more successful effort to recover artifacts from the wrecks was mounted in 1895, when an enterprising explorer managed to recover some of the ships' elaborate mooring rings, railings, and bronze fittings. In 1928, after Mussolini ordered the recovery of Caligula's barges by any means necessary, it was decided that the only practical method was to drain Lake Nemi down to the level of the shipwrecks. Since one of the ships was more than thirty feet underwater, and the other—half-buried in muck—was sixty-five feet below the surface, this was a major undertaking. A pumping station on the lakeshore began funneling water out through an ancient drainage tunnel. After six months of continuous pumping, the prow of the first ship appeared. Another six months revealed the rest of the ship, which was reinforced with modern timbers and moved ashore on a specially built railway. The other ship was more difficult to recover. The pumps soon exposed most of the hull; but before it could be freed from the mud, the drying lake bottom shifted, stopping the work and allowing water to cover the wreck again. It was only in late 1932, a year and a half after it first surfaced, that the second ship could be recovered. The two ships were moved into a specially constructed museum, which opened with great fanfare in 1936. Only eight years later, during Allied shelling of a nearby German artillery post, a fire destroyed both ships, leaving only a few bronze fittings.

parents to watch the deaths of their sons.* He burned a man alive for composing a poem that poked fun at his regime, beat slaves to death with chains, and had prisoners bled dry with countless tiny cuts.[3]

The emperor's eccentricities were even more notorious than his cruelty. On some occasions, he wore silks dripping with precious stones; on others, the costume of a tragic actor. He liked to dress as a god, and could be seen sauntering about with the trident of Neptune, the caduceus of Mercury, or the golden beard and thunderbolt of Jupiter. His belief in his own divinity was so strong that he was said to stand at windows after dark, calling the moon goddess down to his bed. Once, in the middle of the night, Caligula summoned three senators to the palace. As they stood in the audience hall, sure that they were about to be executed, the emperor emerged in a flowing tunic, performed a dance to the tune of flutes and cymbals, and flitted from the room without saying a word.[4]

After Caligula was safely dead, historians of his reign agreed that he had been mad. Some speculated that a fever had been the cause. Others blamed a love potion administered by his wife. Still others thought that his madness stemmed from innate character flaws. Representations of the emperor in pop culture—most famously, the movie *Caligula* and the BBC series *I, Claudius*—have followed the ancient sources, and presented the emperor as insane. As so often, however, the historical truth is less straightforward.[5]

Any assessment of Caligula's mental condition has to begin with his political position. For the first few centuries of its existence, the Roman Empire was a military autocracy masquerading, ever less convincingly, as a republic. Emperors were expected to at least gesture toward including the traditional ruling class, embodied by the Senate, in important decisions. That fiction, transparent though it was, continued to be important: it mattered whether the aristocracy felt respected, not least because aristocrats tended to write the histories. Caligula, who ignored the political compromises underpinning his power, was never destined to be remembered fondly by senatorial

---

* Supposedly, Claudius discovered a huge chest filled with poisons in Caligula's rooms. He ordered it flung into the sea, where its contents killed thousands of fish.

historians. Assassination guaranteed his lasting infamy. Claudius, the next emperor, had to distance himself from his murdered predecessor, and did so by labeling Caligula a tyrant. Historians followed the court's lead.* Their accounts should be read with corresponding caution.

Take, for example, the allegation—repeated by several of our sources—that Caligula was involved in an incestuous relationship with his sister Drusilla. Suetonius's biography lists the evidence, which boils down to a rumor that the emperor's grandmother had caught him in the act, to the favor Caligula showed Drusilla during his reign, and to his grief when she died. This is hardly compelling, especially when combined with the fact that a number of other ancient authors fail to make any mention of Caligula's relations with his relations. The most notorious instance of the emperor's supposed madness is equally suspect. That Caligula made his racehorse a consul is a staple of pop history. Suetonius, however, makes it clear that he never actually did this, but was only rumored to have considered it. He was certainly fond of racing in general and of his horse Incitatus in particular, going so far as to build a palatial stable with marble stalls and ivory mangers. But the rumor that Caligula intended to appoint Incitatus to high political office seems to have originated from nothing more than one of the emperor's sardonic puns.[6]

Explanations can be posited for the most outlandish of Caligula's exploits. Sometime in the spring of 40, for example, the emperor led a large army to the English Channel. If we can believe our sources, he drew the troops up in full battle array, then ordered them to gather shells from the beach, as spoils of their victory over the ocean. This puzzling episode has generated dozens of interpretations. Some—such as the theory that Caligula wanted his soldiers to use the shells as missiles in their military exercises—seem unlikely. But others are plausible: since the Latin word for "shell" can also

---

* All three of our most detailed sources on Caligula's reign are problematic. Seneca—who had been exiled by Caligula, and wrote many of his works during the reign of Claudius—had both personal and professional reasons to present Caligula in the worst possible light. Suetonius, writing long after Caligula's death, could never resist a scandalous anecdote. Cassius Dio, writing even later, was less scrupulous and equally susceptible to reproducing rumors.

mean "boat" or "hut," for example, some commentators see Caligula's command as an order to gather an invasion fleet or break camp.* Perhaps the most likely explanation is that Caligula really did order his soldiers to gather shells—not from some megalomaniacal delusion, but as part of a ceremony centered on the surrender of a British king.[7]

Even the colossal floating bridge at Baiae likely had a symbolic purpose. Caligula crossed it twice—first at the head of an army, then in a chariot followed by wagons of treasure. Both crossings were clearly pageants, borrowing motifs from history and ritual to imitate—respectively—a battlefield charge and a triumph. Although the precise significance is uncertain, the basic meaning of both processions and bridge is clear: they were statements, blatant but not irrational, of imperial power.[8]

For all their silences and distortions, our sources present a basically coherent portrait of Caligula. To the extent that this picture was drawn from life, we can glimpse the historical emperor: a strange and unsettling figure, witty, even charming, but untroubled by the slightest sense of moral responsibility. Caligula was erratic, eccentric, megalomaniacal, and murderous. But there is no reason to assume that he was insane.

---

* The same word was also a slang term for female genitalia, prompting a few bold interpreters to suggest that Caligula was ordering his men to visit the local brothels. One suspects that no encouragement was needed.

How Deadly Was the Eruption
That Destroyed Pompeii?

$\mathcal{D}$arkness came first, as the gigantic cloud over Vesuvius devoured the sky. A gentle snow of ash drifted through the twilight. Then pumice began to rattle on the rooftops. Most of Pompeii's citizens fled, warding off the falling stones with cushions or cloaks. But many, unwilling or unable to leave their homes, remained. As pumice piled on buildings and smothered streets, some Pompeiians were trapped behind buried doors or crushed by collapsing roofs. Others tried to escape through the sea of stones, groping and stumbling as lightning arced overhead. All night, pumice fell. All night, the mountain thundered. Shortly after dawn, a new sound filled Pompeii. A few may have seen the fiery cloud just before it killed them. For everyone else, it was only a sound—indistinct at first, then resolving, in the last few seconds, into a chorus of howling wind and disintegrating buildings and human screams. After that, nothing at all.

Beneath southern Italy, continents are colliding. Africa is plunging under Europe, throwing up mountain ranges, spawning earthquakes, and sending stray plumes of magma through the fractured crust. Where those plumes reach the surface, a volcano is born. The most active Italian volcano is Stromboli, which has been erupting continuously for thousands of years. The largest is Etna, which looms eleven thousand feet over the Sicilian coast. The most dangerous is Vesuvius.* Vesuvius has existed for tens of thousands of years, bursts

---

* For tens of thousands of years, there have been two volcanic hot spots on the Bay of Naples. Vesuvius marks one. The other is the collapsed caldera known as the Campi Flegrei, still frothing with hot springs and fumaroles. In 1538, a sudden eruption in the Campi Flegrei created Monte Nuovo, a 440-foot hill that rose in a single day, burying the village of Tripergole.

The Forum of Pompeii, with Vesuvius looming beyond. *Author's photo*

of furious activity alternating with long periods of dormancy. The mountain last came to life in March 1944, in the midst of the Allied invasion of Italy. Although lava flows damaged several villages and ash disabled dozens of military aircraft, this was a relatively minor episode.

Geologists rank the severity of eruptions by the Volcanic Explosivity Index (VEI). The scale increases logarithmically, so that an eruption with a VEI of 2 is ten times the size of an eruption with a VEI of 1.* The eruption of Vesuvius in 1944 had a VEI of 3—substantial, but not very remarkable, since several eruptions of that size occur somewhere on earth almost every year. Vesuvius alone has produced about two dozen eruptions on the same scale over the past four

---

* The most severe mega-eruptions in geological history, which only occur about once every fifty thousand years, are assigned a VEI of 8. The most recent event with a VEI of 7 took place in 1815, when Indonesia's Mount Tambora exploded with a roar heard more than one thousand miles away. So much sun-shrouding ash was ejected into the atmosphere that 1816 was nicknamed "the year without a summer."

hundred years. The volcano's last major eruption, which took place in December 1631, had a VEI of 5. The eruptive column blotted out the sun, sending ash as far as Constantinople. Torrents of lava and clouds of superheated gas rushed downslope, killing thousands. There were other major eruptions during the early Middle Ages, including one that sent mudflows surging through the heart of Naples. But none of these could compare with the eruption of 79 CE, which entombed Pompeii and Herculaneum. This was Vesuvius's most violent historical eruption, with a VEI approaching 6. It produced about thirty times the debris generated by the 1631 eruption, devastated a vast area, and sent ash as far as Syria and Egypt.

Before the eruption of 79, Vesuvius had been dormant for many centuries. Vineyards climbed its slopes, a forest flourished in its crater,* and the lands in its shadow were a patchwork of farms and villas, threaded together by the busy roads leading to Pompeii and Herculaneum. Neither town was especially large—Pompeii, with perhaps twelve thousand inhabitants, was about three times the size of Herculaneum—but both were prosperous centers of the fertile region around the volcano. In the decades before the eruption, several Roman authors noticed similarities between the rocks of Vesuvius and the volcanic debris spewed forth by Mount Etna. There seem, however, to have been no fears of an eruption, not least because the Romans, like the Greeks before them, were mystified by volcanic activity.† So when the mountain began to stir in the autumn of 79, the warning signs were neither understood nor heeded.[1]

One of those surprised by the eruption was Pliny the Younger, a youth staying with his uncle—Pliny the Elder—at Misenum, across the Bay of Naples from Pompeii. When a cloud appeared over Vesuvius, the elder Pliny, who was commander of the local Roman fleet,

---

* Spartacus and his army of escaped slaves camped in the volcano's crater, which was then wooded and overgrown with wild grapevine. A few decades later, perhaps due to stirrings of volcanic activity, the forest was gone, revealing an expanse of charred rock.

† The oldest explanations of volcanism were mythological: it was said, for example, that Typhoeus lay broken beneath Mount Etna, spouting flame from his sulfurous lips. The volcanoes of the Aeolian Islands were sometimes associated with the workshop of Vulcan. The most prevalent scientific theory posited that the earth was honeycombed with hollows and passages, where subterranean winds ignited flammable stones, sparking eruptions.

sailed to investigate on a fast warship. As he approached the volcano, he found the sea choked with floating pumice. Undeterred, he landed at Stabiae, a few miles past Pompeii, and slept in a friend's villa, ignoring the drifts of debris building up outside. At last, afraid that the house would be buried, Pliny and his companions tied cushions to their heads and ventured into the pelting stones. Unable to escape by sea, they were overtaken by a cloud of hot ash, and Pliny the Elder died by the shore.

Back in Misenum, Pliny the Younger—unaware of his uncle's fate—was becoming worried about his own safety. A series of earthquakes shook the house, tsunamis battered the shore below, and pumice clattered on the roof. On the morning of the eruption's second day, a menacing black cloud began to glide across the bay. Pliny and his mother fled, but the cloud overtook them on the road, wrapping them in darkness and buffeting them with grit. When the shadow passed, Pliny found himself in a landscape shrouded with ash.[2]

From Pliny's account, and with the geological evidence of the debris around Vesuvius, we can track the progress of the eruption fairly closely. It began with a column of pumice and hot gases that punched twenty miles into the atmosphere. Pushed by a steady northwest wind, the eruptive column drifted over Pompeii. Pumice began to fall from the cloud, accumulating at a rate of about six inches an hour. By the morning of the eruption's second day, Pompeii had been smothered beneath more than nine feet of debris. The worst, however, was yet to come. It struck Herculaneum first. Though closer to Vesuvius than Pompeii, Herculaneum had been upwind of the eruptive column and had only experienced a light rain of pumice. Most of the inhabitants had taken the opportunity to flee, but hundreds remained, sheltering in a row of boat houses along the harbor. Early on the second day, death came to these fugitives in the form of a pyroclastic surge.

A pyroclastic surge is a superheated cloud of ash and volcanic gas, often accompanied by a chaotic avalanche of debris. It moves with incredible speed, sometimes upward of four hundred miles per hour, and is lethally hot, with temperatures that can exceed 750 degrees Fahrenheit. Its passage is apocalyptic. During the 1902 eruption of Mount Pelée on the Caribbean island of Martinique, a pyroclastic surge swept over the city of Saint-Pierre, battering down masonry walls, scything through the ships in the harbor, and instantly killing all but two of the twenty-eight thousand inhabitants.

The surge that struck Herculaneum was equally destructive. In a matter of seconds, as the burning cloud cascaded over the buildings and found the refugees in the boathouses, every living thing in the city died. Pompeii's turn came a few hours later, when another pyroclastic surge roared over the city. As at Herculaneum, it killed everyone it caught, whether they were hiding in half-buried houses or trying to escape across the dunes of pumice. Their bodies dropped in beds of glowing ash, and the world collapsed around them, roofs and walls, columns and trees, tumbled and broken by the fury of the eruption.

Then, little more than a day after it began, the worst was over. Ghostly curtains of ash frayed in the gathering light. The waves of the bay beat their ancient rhythm against a newborn shore. And a red-rimmed sun settled, cinder cold, over the buried city of Pompeii.

The plaster cast of a body found at Pompeii. *Wikimedia Commons*

In the years after the eruption, when some of Pompeii's buildings were still visible, scavengers burrowed into the rubble to recover valuables.* But by the time the ash and pumice ripened into soil, and a new generation of settlements sprouted over the ruins, all knowledge of the city's location had been lost. An irrigation channel was dug through the site in 1592, turning up inscriptions that at least one scholar connected with Pompeii. Yet despite his insight, and despite other chance discoveries, Pompeii was only identified in the mid-eighteenth century, when the first excavations began.† After a slow start, a grand aristocratic villa came to light, followed by a monumental theater and a temple with vibrant frescoes. Gradually, inexorably, Pompeii became famous.

From the beginning, the bodies found among the ruins were part of the site's mystique.‡ Early descriptions were often fanciful. Four skeletons lying beside iron shackles, for example, were interpreted as the remains of prisoners left chained in their cell. A jewelry-draped woman found in the gladiator barracks was described as a wealthy matron caught in the act of visiting her gladiator lover. A skeleton discovered near one of the city gates was enthusiastically misidentified as a soldier who had remained at his post, spear in hand, through the horrors of the eruption.

The best known of all the victims discovered during the early days of the excavation at Pompeii came to light in the Villa of Diomedes, a lavish aristocratic residence just outside the city walls. Here, the bones of twenty people were found in a subterranean

---

* The Latin message "house tunneled" was found scratched beside the door of one Pompeian mansion. Archaeologists suspect that at least a few of the skeletons discovered in Pompeii's houses belong to scavengers who dug too enthusiastically.

† In 1709, workmen digging a well uncovered four beautiful marble statues in what proved to be the theater of Herculaneum. Excavations were initiated in earnest a quarter century later, when teams commissioned by the king of Naples began to bore tunnels through the deeply interred city, seeking ancient sculptures and fine marble for the royal palaces. The next few decades witnessed a spate of finds at Herculaneum, culminating in the Villa of the Papyri. Gradually, however, the difficulties of the work encouraged the king to focus his attention on Pompeii, whose remains lay much closer to the surface.

‡ It became customary to stage discoveries of bodies for prominent tourists. When Joseph II of Austria visited in 1768, for example, a skeleton was disinterred from the pumice as he watched. It was so obvious that the skeleton had been placed there, however, that the emperor saw through the ploy immediately. Another skeleton was "discovered" on three separate occasions for the benefit of royal guests.

wine cellar, lying where they fell when the pyroclastic surge came howling through the skylights. As they began to clear the skeletons, the excavators noticed that exact impressions of the victims' long-vanished clothes and flesh had been imprinted in the volcanic debris. One young woman had left an almost perfect image, down to the features of her face and folds of her tunic. Although the diggers shattered this mold as they tried to remove it, they managed to save a few pieces, including the impression of one breast. This became a highlight of the site museum, and eventually inspired an eccentric French novella.*

The sensational finds in the House of Diomedes were the first of many. As more of Pompeii was cleared, the excavators noticed that skeletons were often found in body-shaped hollows, made when the ash of the pyroclastic surge hardened around clothing and flesh. In 1863, the director of the excavations had the idea of filling these hollows with plaster, creating a haunting mirror image. This was the origin of the famous plaster casts, which convey, more powerfully than any description, the anguished final moments of the victims of Vesuvius.†

Herculaneum was thought to be almost devoid of human remains until 1980, when workers digging a drainage trench uncovered the jumble of skeletons in the boathouses along the city's ancient seafront. Like the vast majority of the dead found in Pompeii, these victims had been caught by the pyroclastic surge, their lungs seared by burning ash, their bodies blackened by fourth-degree burns. Forensic analysis of their skeletons revealed some interesting facts: the people of Herculaneum ate quite a bit of fish, were mostly free of lead poisoning, and were—on average—slightly taller than the modern inhabitants of Naples.

Beyond such details, the bodies found at Herculaneum and Pompeii humanize the eruption and the world it destroyed. Take, for example, the very first group of plaster casts made in Pompeii. It

---

* Théophile Gautier's *Arria Marcella.* The breast has vanished, probably thanks to inexpert nineteenth-century chemical treatments.

† No casts could be made at Herculaneum, where the high post-antique water table obliterated the impressions left by the victims' bodies.

was a family of four. The father was carrying the house keys, a few pieces of golden jewelry, and about 400 sestertii—probably the family savings. The mother held a bag with more valuables—a mirror, some silverware, a figurine made of amber. Their two young daughters had their hands free as they scrambled with their parents over the heaped debris. The pyroclastic surge caught them all in a street near the forum.

A rich man, carrying a fortune in gold and silver coins. A slave, iron shackles on his ankles. A doctor, his box of instruments beside him. A soldier, sword and dagger at his belt. A boy, sick in bed. All victims of the same disaster, all participants in the same tantalizingly familiar world. To date, about 1,150 bodies have been found in Pompeii, and 350 in Herculaneum. Hundreds, perhaps thousands, are still buried. Roughly a quarter of Pompeii and three-quarters of Herculaneum remain unexcavated, along with dozens of villas and small settlements. Many more victims must lie along the ancient roads.

On a humid July morning a few years ago, I walked up to the summit of Vesuvius. With the exception of a few silently steaming fumaroles, all was stillness in the crater. Below, the glittering arc of the bay swept toward the tower blocks of Naples. After a few minutes of squinting, I was able to pick out the site of Pompeii, all but submerged beneath a choppy sea of modern development. The same sprawl has crept to the very foot of the volcano, directly in the path of the next eruption. But for now, the mountain is as quiet as the painted hills in a Roman fresco, just as it was before that crisp October afternoon, nineteen centuries ago, when it destroyed Pompeii.

Were There Ancient
Conspiracy Theories?

$\mathcal{A}$ncient history is full of conspiracies, in the sense of coordinated plots against power. Famous examples include the Catilinarian Conspiracy, an attempt to overthrow the Roman Republic; the Pisonian Conspiracy, which sought to supplant Nero; and the Barbarian Conspiracy, an apparently concerted attack on Roman Britain by the Picts, Saxons, and Irish. There are fewer ancient instances of conspiracy theories in the usual modern sense—the assumption, in other words, that a secret organization is pulling strings behind the scenes.*

The affair of the herms in Classical Athens is one of the best-documented examples. Athens, famously, had a democratic government, in which a large part of the citizen body participated. In combination with a lively tradition of criticizing public figures, the immediacy of the democracy made the schemes and scandals of prominent politicians a popular conversation topic. The most talked-about of all Athenian politicians was the brilliant, charming, and utterly unscrupulous Alcibiades. A scion of the same aristocratic family that had produced Pericles, Alcibiades made his name by promoting an aggressive foreign policy against Sparta. He was admired

---

* Speculation about those in power, of course, is as old as civilization itself, and our sources reverberate with rumors about the undue influence of courtiers and relatives of rulers. After his death, for example, Claudius's dependence on his freedmen—who, it was rumored, were the real rulers of Rome—was skewered in Seneca's *Apocolocyntosis*, a bizarre satire in which the gods debate whether the emperor's soul is worthy of being deified. At the end, for no adequately explained reason, Caligula shows up, claims Claudius as his slave, and hands him over to Aeacus, one of the judges of the underworld, as a secretary.

for his compelling speeches before the Assembly,* and for such political stunts as entering seven chariots in the Olympic race. His dissolute private life, however, led many Athenians to distrust him, and set the stage for the affair of the herms.[1]

Herms were small statues placed at crossroads and beside doorways. They consisted of a simple stone pillar, topped by a god's head and garnished with a prominent erect phallus. In the spring of 415 BCE, just as the Athenian government, spurred by Alcibiades, was about to launch a vast armada to conquer Sicily, nearly all the herms in Athens had their noses and phalluses knocked off. While this might seem like a harmless prank, the mutilation of the herms threw Athens into a frenzy. Since herms represented the gods, any injury to them was sacrilege. That so many divine images had been damaged at the outset of the Sicilian expedition seemed a bad omen. A conspiracy theory arose that the herms had been broken by a secret cabal, which sought to destroy the government.[2]

A public investigation brought additional information to light: shortly before the herms were mutilated, a group of young men had broken other religious statues and mimicked the Eleusinian Mysteries, the most sacred Athenian ritual.† One of the participants, it was said, had been Alcibiades. It began to be whispered that Alcibiades had also been responsible for smashing the herms, and that his acts of sacrilege were part of a plot to overthrow the democracy.[3]

As one of the leaders of the Sicilian expedition, Alcibiades was forced to leave the city before he could clear his name. In his absence, the conspiracy theory continued to grow, connecting the mutilation of the herms and violation of the mysteries with an aristocratic scheme to replace the government. When a small Spartan force was reported in the vicinity, it was immediately assumed that they had been summoned by the conspirators. Arrests were made; armed

---

* He was very persuasive: during a short stay in Sparta, he managed—or so it was said—to seduce the king's wife.

† Profaning sacred rites was a serious charge in the classical world. Centuries after the affair of the herms, the Roman politician Clodius was accused of trying to infiltrate a ritual reserved for women (supposedly with the aim of seducing Julius Caesar's wife Pompeia). Although Clodius was acquitted in the subsequent trial, Caesar divorced Pompeia, commenting that any wife of his must be above suspicion.

A miniature bronze herm, now in the Metropolitan Museum of Art. *Public domain*

patrols were posted in the city center; and finally, Alcibiades himself was summoned back to Athens to be tried for his supposed crimes.

Although it's entirely plausible that Alcibiades mimicked the mysteries with his friends, and not impossible that he was associated with the men who mutilated the herms, there is no reason to think that he was plotting to overthrow the democracy. Aristocratic coups were a legitimate threat—there would be two within a decade of the Sicilian expedition*—but Alcibiades had little to gain from overthrowing a government that had just awarded him an important command. In this case, he seems to have been nothing more or less than the victim of a conspiracy theory.

To a degree that a democratic leader like Alcibiades could only envy, monarchs dominated both public discourse and popular suspicion in antiquity. The most familiar examples are the Roman emperors, whose plots, perversions, and peccadilloes pervade our sources.† Emperors were frequently implicated in conspiracy theories, especially—and understandably—when their predecessors perished under suspicious circumstances. Perhaps the most interesting conspiracy theory involving a classical ruler, however, centers on the death of Alexander the Great.[4]

Alexander died at Babylon on June 10, 323 BCE, aged thirty-two. According to his most reliable ancient biographers, he had fallen ill ten days before, during or shortly after a wine-soaked banquet. His illness began as a fever, mild enough—at first—for the king to ignore as he prepared to invade Arabia. Within a few days, however, he had become too weak to sit up or speak. Still burning with fever, he lapsed into a coma and never woke. An alternative tradition added dramatic details. At the fatal banquet, according to this version of events, Alexander was draining a goblet of wine when he cried out in pain. Collapsing, he was carried away by his friends, and lay in agony until the coma overtook him.[5]

---

* In 411 and again in 404 BCE, the Athenian democracy was overthrown and replaced by an aristocratic oligarchy. The second oligarchy, led by the so-called Thirty Tyrants, executed hundreds of political opponents before being driven from power.

† Claudius, for example, caused a scandal by marrying his niece. Later, with breathtaking indifference to irony, he executed his nephew for incest.

Almost as soon as Alexander died, it began to be rumored that he had been poisoned. The culprit was said to be Antipater, the king's regent in Europe, who had sent his young son Iollas to dose Alexander's cup with a potion prepared by Aristotle. Aristotle certainly had reason to resent Alexander. When the Persian campaign began, he had sent his nephew Callisthenes to accompany the Macedonian army and write a history of its conquests. Alexander, however, proceeded to execute Callisthenes on a trumped-up treason charge. As might be imagined, this did not improve his relationship with the young historian's uncle. According to the rumors that sprouted after Alexander's death, Aristotle had procured water from the bitter springs of the river Styx, whose deadly current would dissolve any container besides the hoof of a mule. With the connivance of Antipater, Antipater's son Cassander, and a very literal drug mule, the poison made its way to Babylon, and to the king's cup.[6]

The Styx water is legendary, and the involvement of Aristotle supremely unlikely. That Alexander was poisoned, however, is not beyond the realm of possibility. Alexander's mother Olympias believed—or claimed to believe—that Antipater was responsible for her son's death. She executed several men on charges of involvement in the plot, and dishonored the supposed poisoner Iollas by exhuming his body and scattering the bones. Antipater's son Cassander, Iollas's brother, returned the favor by executing Olympias and leaving her body to rot unburied. He also took vengeance on Hyperides, an Athenian orator who had dared to propose honoring Iollas for poisoning Alexander. After Hyperides was captured by a bounty hunter, his tongue was cut out, he was executed, and his body was left to be devoured by the birds and beasts.[7]

The dramatic sequence of accusations and murders that followed Alexander's death does not prove that the king was poisoned. Our most reliable ancient sources roundly reject the theory, which seems to be a product of popular suspicion and political maneuvering. Although we'll never know for certain, malaria—exacerbated by alcoholism and old battle wounds—is a far more likely culprit than poison for Alexander's death at Babylon.

Not far from Babylon, but more than half a millennium after the death of Alexander, a prophet named Mani began to preach a new religion. Mani's creed, which we call Manichaeism, proclaimed a universal conflict between the powers of light and darkness. To ensure the ultimate triumph of the light, a chosen few—the elect—were called upon to renounce all worldly possessions and devote their lives to rituals combating the darkness.* It was the duty of all other believers—the hearers—to support the elect with alms, and so gain a chance to be reborn as an elect, and finally escape the prison of the flesh.

With the personal support of the shah, Mani proselytized throughout the Persian Empire, proclaiming a religion that perfected and replaced the teachings of Zoroaster, the Buddha, and Jesus. Missionaries were sent to central Asia,† India, and the Roman Empire. Adda, one of Mani's chief disciples, led the first Roman mission, which established communities in the provinces of Syria and Egypt. Equipped with translations of Mani's scriptures and trained to engage philosophers and priests in theological debate, Manichaean preachers quickly gained converts, sowing cells of believers from Alexandria to Rome.

Traditionally, the Romans were tolerant of any religion that respected the established social and political order. Sects that seemed to encourage rebellion, however, were repressed. The most famous example is Christianity, but instances stretched back to the Roman Republic, which had crushed the cult of Bacchus for inciting immoral behavior. These precedents conditioned the imperial response to Manichaeism.

In 302, Diocletian was notified of disruptions caused by Manichaean preaching in the province of Africa. The more the emperor learned about the new religion, the more alarmed he became. Mani had been a friend of the Persian shah, archenemy of all things right

---

* Since the act of digesting and breathing forth the residue of fruits and vegetables was believed to strengthen the light, the daily routine of the elect involved ritualized vegetarian meals known as "soul services."

† Manichaeism spread widely through central Asia and China, where communities are attested as late as the sixteenth century.

and Roman. To Diocletian and his advisors, this seemed a clear indication that Manichaeism was nothing less than a Persian plot intended to overthrow the Roman Empire. In an imperial edict, Diocletian proclaimed that the Manichaeans were seeking to infect the "innocent, orderly, and tranquil Roman people" with the "damnable customs and perverse laws of the Persians, as with the poison of a malignant serpent." Any Roman who converted to Manichaeism would be executed; any official who supported the cult would be sent to the mines; and the Manichaean preachers themselves were to be burned alive atop piles of their scriptures.[8]

As the Great Persecution of the Christians would soon demonstrate, the provincial governors responsible for enforcing imperial edicts were not always enthusiastic about extreme measures, and most Manichaeans seem to have escaped punishment. Throughout the fourth century and beyond, however, emperors continued to issue edicts stripping Manichaeans of their civil rights, declaring them outlaws, and condemning them to death. As the Roman Empire became Christian, the Manichaeans were branded heretics and corrupters of the faith. Saint Augustine—a former convert to Manichaeism—was the most famous of the many Christian thinkers who attacked the so-called Persian heresy. Increasingly savage penalties drove the sect underground and eventually expelled it from the empire.

Manichaeism was never actually a Persian plot. Although Mani had indeed enjoyed the patronage of one shah, he had been imprisoned by that shah's successor, and his religion was being persecuted in its native land by the Zoroastrian priesthood long before Diocletian issued his edict. Yet the Roman crusade against the Manichaeans lasted, with interruptions, for more than two centuries. In keeping with the late imperial synthesis of church and state, it became an issue of both policy and belief. It had its origins, however, in the fatal simplicity of a conspiracy theory.

How Many Romans Were Stoics?

*J*ulian the Apostate was a skillful general, a tireless administrator, and an implacable opponent of Christianity. But in his own mind he was always, before all else, a scholar. He displayed his erudition to good effect in the *Caesars*, a satire imagining a banquet on Olympus attended by all the emperors of the past. In Julian's tale, Caesar enters first, followed by Augustus, Tiberius, and all the rest, from Nero— still strumming his lyre—to Diocletian and the tetrarchs, who enter holding hands. The gods hold a contest to determine which of the emperors is most worthy. Each candidate speaks on his own behalf. Caesar boasts of his conquests. Augustus describes his prudence. Trajan proclaims his clemency. But the prize goes to Marcus Aurelius,* who is judged worthy of joining the gods because of his dedication to philosophy.[1]

Despite a rich prehistory, the classical tradition of Greco-Roman philosophy began with Socrates, the man—to paraphrase Cicero—who called philosophy down from the heavens, and applied it to the questions of human existence. Socrates himself, who wrote nothing, is an elusive figure. But he inspired a series of profound inquiries into morality, justice, and truth through the dialogues of

---

* Even in Julian's time, nearly two hundred years after his death, Marcus Aurelius was remembered and revered as the emperor who had applied Stoic principles to rulership— the first and only example, according to a late antique biography, of a true philosopher-king. Though philosophically eclectic himself, Julian seems to have regarded Stoicism as a system suitable for emperors: in the *Caesars*, he has the gods send the soul of Augustus to learn wisdom from a Stoic philosopher.

his student Plato, who founded the Academy, the first philosophical school,* in a sacred grove just outside Athens.[2]

Aristotle, Plato's most brilliant pupil, eventually founded a school of his own at the Lyceum, an exercise yard a short distance beyond the city walls. Despite many disagreements—which became more acrimonious over time, as both sides fortified doctrines and sharpened polemics[†]—followers of Plato and Aristotle did not differ fundamentally with regard to practical ethics.[3] The two philosophical schools that emerged in the generation after Aristotle's death, however, proclaimed antithetical approaches to the virtuous life, and would be rivals for the rest of antiquity.[4]

The Epicurean school—the first philosophical system to emerge from the tumult of the Hellenistic world—contended that all matter consisted of atoms, invisible and indivisible particles adrift in an infinite void. Humans were composed of atoms, and dissolved into them, body and soul, when they died. The gods, also made of atoms, were indifferent to mankind. There was, therefore, no need to fear divine wrath or the terrors of an afterlife. It was wiser to seek pleasure—to retreat to a tranquil place, enjoy the company of like-minded friends, and avoid the storms and shocks of public life.[‡]

The Stoics—the other great Hellenistic school—imagined a universe infused with an all-encompassing principle variously identified as Nature, Reason, and Fate. This principle permeated all things, predetermining the course of history. Human decisions still mattered: it was imperative to act righteously and strive for the most moral end. But it was equally imperative to accept that some circumstances lay beyond one's control. Such acceptance—living in accord with Nature, Reason, and Fate—was the philosopher's part.

---

* A possible predecessor of Plato's Academy was the "school" of Pythagoras, a quasi-mythical figure said to have had a thigh of gold, strong opinions on the inadvisability of eating beans, and an abiding passion for triangles.

† Cicero mentions a Roman proconsul who tried to force the city's squabbling philosophers to resolve their quarrels. It didn't work.

‡ During the second century, Diogenes—a wealthy resident of Oenoanda, in what is now Turkey—had a detailed survey of the teachings of Epicurus inscribed on the walls of a portico. The inscription reproduced a series of key texts, praised the serenity of the Epicurean life, and looked forward to a world without slavery or injustice. The inscription is thought to have totaled more than twenty-five thousand words—about a third the length of this book.

Both Stoicism and Epicureanism came to Roman attention as the legions of the expanding Republic overran the Greek world.* Epicureanism won a number of wealthy Roman converts, as is attested both by Lucretius's *De Rerum Natura*—a Latin epic on the principles of Epicurean philosophy—and by the Epicurean library discovered in the Villa of the Papyri at Herculaneum. But Stoicism, with its acceptance of traditional morality and public life, was always the preferred philosophy of the Roman elite, especially in times of political turmoil. Cato the Younger—Caesar's most uncompromising opponent—was a dedicated Stoic, as was Caesar's assassin Brutus. A century later, a series of senators drew upon Stoicism in their opposition to the Flavian emperors, prompting the tyrannical emperor Domitian to briefly expel all philosophers from Rome.[5]

Stoicism's broad appeal to the aristocracy is encapsulated by the careers of the best-known Roman Stoics. Seneca, a wealthy senator from Spain, composed a series of philosophical treatises while serving as the tutor and advisor of Nero. Epictetus, though born a slave, attracted Hadrian and dozens of other notables to his lectures on the Stoic life. Marcus Aurelius, the philosopher-emperor, famously applied Stoic principles to the governance of the empire itself.

It remains unclear how widespread such convictions were outside the elite, since only the wealthiest Romans had the leisure for a philosophical education. At first glance, the evidence is not encouraging. In Petronius's *Satyricon*, the wealthy freedman Trimalchio tells his guests that he has ordered the phrase "He never listened to a philosopher" inscribed on his mausoleum. And at a bath in Ostia, Rome's port, portraits of the seven sages of ancient Greece were captioned with bathroom humor.[6]

There are, however, some signs that at least basic philosophical principles reached popular audiences. Philosophers harangued crowds at street corners, clashed in public disputations, and occasionally

---

* The Roman conquests changed the course of Greek philosophy. When Sulla besieged Athens in 87–86 BCE, for example, he destroyed the Academy and the Lyceum, spurring the decentralization of both schools. On a more positive note, he supposedly saved the scientific works of Aristotle from oblivion by bringing the original library of the Academy to Rome.

immolated themselves on pyres at festivals. Horace describes a slave haranguing his master with Stoic precepts. The absent-minded philosopher was familiar enough to appear in a late antique joke book and in a popular life of Aesop. Perhaps most tellingly, dozens of Greek and Latin epitaphs, some associated with quite modest tombs, reference philosophical themes.[7]

There is no way to quantify how widespread Stoic principles were in any given period or place. But it seems clear that—even if a profound knowledge of texts and tenets was largely confined to the elite—Stoic ethics became a buttress and burnishing of popular morality, available for ready reference and appeal. In this sense, as a recurring pattern in the kaleidoscope of Roman thought, Stoicism was as ubiquitous as fate.

How Many Roman Soldiers
Survived to Retirement?

$\mathscr{B}$eneath an orchard in southern Wales, not far from the legionary fortress at Caerleon, the ruins of a Roman mausoleum were discovered. Among the charred bones and broken urns were eight inscriptions, set up by the families who had shared the tomb. One of these, incised on a rough limestone slab, commemorated Julius Valens, a veteran of Legio II Augusta who had died at the overripe old age of one hundred.[1]

The professional Roman army of the imperial era demanded lengthy periods of service from recruits. By the second century, most legionaries, auxiliaries, and sailors served between twenty-three and twenty-eight years,* and some men—like the standard-bearer, known from an inscription, who died on active duty at the age of seventy-two—remained in the ranks considerably longer.[2]

These years of service were dangerous. Death in battle was always a possibility. Although disasters on the scale of the Teutoburg Forest—where three legions were lost—or the virtual annihilation of Legio XII Fulminata during the Jewish War were rare, any skirmish could be fatal: a tombstone found near Hadrian's Wall commemorates a centurion and his son, killed by raiders who had infiltrated their fort.[3]

The hazards of campaigning were not limited to battle. A strength report for a cohort stationed in the Balkans during the reign

---

* There were always variations in the standard period of service. Praetorian guards, for example, initially enlisted for only sixteen years, while their counterparts in the *equites singulares* served nearly thirty.

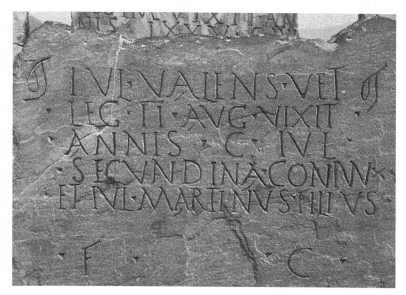

The inscription commemorating Julius Valens, now in the National Roman Legion Museum at Caerleon. *Author's photo*

of Trajan, for example, records losses from bandit ambushes and drownings at river crossings. Even the weather could be deadly. During the reign of Nero, when a Roman army was forced to winter in the frigid Armenian mountains, some soldiers died of hypothermia, and many more lost fingers and toes to frostbite. A few years later, another army, camped just outside Rome at the height of an Italian summer, was immobilized by heat exhaustion and fever.[4]

Discipline was brutal. Minor infractions were punished with beatings.* For a more serious offense, a soldier might have his hands hacked off or his legs broken. The death penalty was decreed for anyone who slept through their watch or deserted in battle. The most infamous of all military punishments was decimation, the execution of every tenth man in a unit deemed guilty of cowardice.

---

* The symbol of a centurion's authority was his vinewood cane, used to beat any soldier who stepped out of line. During the reign of Tiberius, a mutinous legion lynched a centurion nicknamed "Get Me Another" for his habit of breaking canes over soldiers' backs and calling for replacements.

Though rare, it was far from unheard of: in one notorious instance, Octavian—the future Augustus—decimated a cohort that fled from a band of Illyrian rebels, and had two of its centurions executed for good measure.[5]

The greatest threat to a Roman soldier's survival, however, was disease. Despite considerable investment in medical personnel and infrastructure—medics followed the troops into battle, and many camps were equipped with hospitals—the absence of anything resembling germ theory left soldiers vulnerable to a wide range of maladies. A probably typical strength report from an auxiliary cohort stationed along Hadrian's Wall lists more than 10 percent of the men there as unfit for duty on account of wounds, illness, or inflammation of the eyes. On the other side of the empire, an Egyptian legionary's letters to his father describe how—in addition to being injured while policing a riot at Alexandria—he had been laid low by a nasty case of food poisoning from bad fish.[6]

If a soldier survived to the end of his enlistment, he was formally discharged.* Every other year, on January 7, men whose terms had expired were mustered out and granted the rewards of their service to the state. Auxiliaries received Roman citizenship. Legionaries were given a massive bonus†—equivalent to more than a decade of pay—either in cash or in land.[7]

Although there is no way of calculating the odds that a Roman soldier in a given place or period would survive to enjoy his retirement benefits, a comprehensive survey of the tombstones belonging to soldiers of Legio III Augusta gives an average age at death of about forty-seven. Since most legionaries served about twenty-five years, and since the average age at enlistment was around twenty,

---

* Servius Sulpicius Similis, a centurion raised to high office under Trajan and Hadrian, spent the last seven years of his life in contented retirement on a farm. He wrote his own epitaph: "Here rests Similis, who existed for so many years, and truly lived for seven."

† Legionaries were paid about as well as skilled craftsmen: 225 denarii a year from the days of Caesar to the reign of Domitian, who raised the annual wage to 300 denarii. Augustus fixed the discharge bonus at 3,000 denarii; by the reign of Caracalla, this had risen to 5,000 denarii. Although the land offered to discharged legionaries was sometimes less than ideal, the standard plot seems to have been a substantial farm, worth considerably more—at least in settled areas—than the cash alternative.

most men were thus approaching their life expectancy by the time they were discharged.[8]

In the demographic regime of the ancient Mediterranean, we would expect roughly 78 percent of men who enlisted in the legions at age twenty to still be alive at age thirty-five. About 69 percent would be expected to reach forty, and 60 percent to attain the age of forty-five, roughly when most would be discharged. The actual percentage of men lasting to their discharge date would have been lower than this, thanks to violent death, disease, and early dismissal. In the light of these statistics, it would be reasonable to estimate that only about half of the soldiers who enlisted in the imperial Roman army survived to retirement.[9]

What Was the Life Expectancy
of a Roman Emperor?

*T*he fields were empty, and the roads creaked with dust. Beneath a burning summer sun, from the hazy peak of Vesuvius to the distant shimmer of the bay, all was stillness. At the epicenter of the quiet, in a villa ringed by guards, Augustus lay. He murmured a few words. He kissed his wife. Then the first Roman emperor received the quiet passing for which he had always hoped. The last Roman emperor met a less peaceful end. As Turks poured through a breach in the shattered walls of Constantinople, Constantine XI cast his crown aside, drew his sword, and plunged into the fighting. His body was never recovered.[1]

Between Augustus and Constantine XI, there were more than 150 Roman emperors.[2] Many succumbed to accidents. Theodosius II fell from his horse in the course of a placid ride.* Basil I managed to get his belt caught in the antlers of a stag he had just shot, and was dragged to his death when the panicked animal revived and bolted into the woods. Performing one's imperial duties could be equally hazardous: Valentinian I became so enraged by the insolence of some barbarian envoys that he suffered a cerebral hemorrhage. Even taking a nap might be perilous, as Jovian discovered when he was suffocated by smoky braziers in his campaign tent. Emperors were also subject

---

* Though an unprepossessing sovereign, Theodosius II was a talented calligrapher. Fittingly, a papyrus from Egypt bears his signature, the only extant example of a Roman emperor's handwriting.

to a dismaying array of fatal illnesses. Antoninus Pius, who perished after dining on alpine cheeses, may have fallen foul of food poisoning. Claudius Gothicus was carried off by a mysterious pestilence. Bubonic plague nearly killed Justinian; and although John VI survived the Black Death, the epidemic took one of his sons.[3]

About 40 percent of Roman emperors were assassinated or executed.[*] Although at least one emperor was killed by the husband of a woman he had seduced, violent ends tended to be politically motivated. Notorious cases include Caligula—set upon by a party of praetorians in a passageway under the Palatine—and Caracalla, stabbed in the back as he relieved himself by the roadside.[†] Assassins discovered the aptly named Michael the Drunkard lying unconscious after a party, and saw fit to hack his hands off before dispatching him. This was merciful in comparison with the fate of Andronicus I, who—caught trying to escape Constantinople with his wife and one of his mistresses—was literally torn to pieces by a mob.[4]

The Byzantines made a habit of blinding or mutilating deposed emperors. Though not necessarily fatal—Justinian II, for example, had his nose cut off, but returned to power a few years later with a golden proboscis and a thirst for vengeance—this could be an effective death sentence. After her son plotted against her, Empress Irene had his eyes put out so savagely that he died soon after.[‡] Two other emperors met similar fates. Although swords and daggers were the usual instruments of imperial demise, Claudius was poisoned by a dish of mushrooms.[§] Poison, however, was not always effective:

---

[*] Two factors made Roman emperors especially susceptible to assassination. First, since the Roman imperial system—thanks to its republican roots—never developed an unambiguous tradition of dynastic succession, transitions of power were always liable to disruption. Second, the close connection between imperial power and military success undermined the authority of any emperor who lost a battle, and threatened to make any victorious general look like an emperor-in-waiting.

[†] Marius, a short-lived emperor who had started life as a blacksmith, was reportedly executed with a sword that he had forged himself.

[‡] The Byzantines sometimes employed noninvasive methods of blinding, such as scalding eyes with hot vinegar or exposing them to the light of red-hot cups. But gouging (performed with a knife, candlestick, or tent stake) was the surest way.

[§] Shortly afterward, Nero poisoned Claudius's son Britannicus. Although he had the victim's body coated with gypsum to conceal the telltale signs, heavy rain washed away the powder during the funeral procession.

Commodus succumbed so unconscionably slowly to a dose given in his wine that it was found necessary to strangle him.[5]

A remarkable number of imperial personages met their ends in baths. Commodus was strangled in his bath, Constantine's wife Fausta was suffocated in a sealed bathhouse, Constans II was bludgeoned with a bucket in a sauna, and Romanus III was drowned on his wife's orders* as he lay soaking in a tub.[6]

There were quiet assassinations: John Tzimiskes crept into his predecessor's bedroom and dispatched him as he slept, and Numerian seems to have been suffocated so surreptitiously that nobody noticed until his closed litter began to reek of decay. Subtlety, however, was not necessarily desirable. The people of Rome stoned an emperor who tried to flee in advance of a barbarian invasion. Centuries later, the Crusaders hurled an emperor who had outlived his usefulness from the top of a tall column. Heraclius publicly executed his predecessor Phocas on the deck of his flagship.[7]

The teenaged Gordian III was the first emperor to die in battle, possibly at the hands of a disgruntled officer. Decius was cut down with his son and army in a Balkan swamp. Maxentius drowned in the Tiber during a retreat, Julian was felled by a Persian spear, and Valens burned in a hut on the field of Adrianople. After another disastrous defeat half a millennium later, the skull of Nicephorus I became a favorite drinking cup of the Bulgar Khan.[8]

Nero ended his own life in a villa just outside Rome, famously lamenting, "What an artist dies in me!" His successor Otho stabbed himself in the heart, rather than continue a civil war. The third case of imperial suicide is suspicious, since the emperor—Valentinian II, found hanged in his chamber—was involved in a furious dispute with a general who had both motive and opportunity to murder him. A few other imperial deaths are equally mysterious. Carus was apparently struck by lightning outside the Persian capital. And according to different authors, Valerian—the only emperor to perish in

---

* Although it is impossible, at a millennium's remove, to prove the empress's involvement conclusively, the fact that she married her lover a few hours after Romanus died is rather suggestive. The patriarch of Constantinople thought so too, and only agreed to bless the union after receiving fifty pounds of gold.

captivity*—was either flayed alive by the Persians, choked on molten gold, or died of natural causes.⁹

A few Roman emperors died in childhood,† but a surprising number—including John VI, who lived to be ninety-one—reached old age. Although imperial life expectancy varied considerably from period to period, with a noticeable trough in the assassination-prone third century, the average across the whole millennium and a half of imperial history was about fifty-one years. The "average" emperor reigned just under eleven years.‡ Leaving aside emperors who retired,§ combining that figure with our estimate for life expectancy gives an average age of about forty at accession. Most emperors, in other words, came to power well after they had passed the gauntlet of childhood diseases that killed half of all Romans in childhood. A life expectancy in the early fifties, in fact, is about what we would expect for any group of Roman men who had survived adolescence. Emperors were much more likely to be assassinated than the average Roman; but the average Roman wasn't likely to be much longer-lived.¹⁰

---

* It was rumored that Valerian's body was embalmed, stuffed, and displayed as a trophy in a Persian temple. Although this was probably unfounded, it's likely that troops captured with the emperor constructed the so-called Bridge of Valerian in what is now Iran, the easternmost product of Roman engineering.

† Leo II ruled briefly (with his father) at age seven. Diadumenian, the son of Macrinus, was murdered at age nine. Philip the Arab's son Philip may have briefly been sole emperor at age twelve before being killed. Alexius II Comnenus was assassinated at thirteen after a reign of three years.

‡ Leaving aside evanescent usurpers, the shortest reigns on record were those of the father-and-son team Gordian I and Gordian II, who lasted twenty-two days. Basil II, by contrast, reigned for sixty-five years—though since he became emperor when he was a toddler, only fifty of those years saw him ruling independently.

§ Diocletian, the first emperor to retire, spent his final years in a gargantuan fortified villa, where he took up gardening. Justin II, who suffered from bouts of insanity—during which, it was said, only organ music could soothe him—gave up the throne when his affliction became debilitating. Glycerius became the personal bishop of Julius Nepos, the man who had deposed him. Quite a few Byzantine emperors were forced to become monks after being evicted from the throne. Isaac I Comnenus ended his days as the doorman of a monastery in Constantinople. John VI spent the last three decades of his life as a monk and author, composing various theological works, a commentary on Aristotle's *Ethics*, and a history of his own reign.

· 32 ·

What Was It Like to Live through the Fall of the Roman Empire?

$\mathcal{O}$n August 24, 410, a band of Visigoths entered the Salarian Gate. Even before the other gates were taken and the whole horde streamed into the city, smoke started to rise above the manicured treetops of the emperor's gardens. Soon, the first screams were echoing down the canyon-like streets of the imperial city, as parties of barbarians smashed their way into proud mansions, looking for loot.* Rome had fallen. "With one city," wrote Saint Jerome, who heard the news in Bethlehem, "the whole world has died."[1]

By contrast, the event regarded by modern historians as the end of the Western Roman Empire—the overthrow of Romulus Augustulus, the last western emperor, in 476—seems to have been virtually unnoticed by contemporaries.† This is partly a consequence of the scantiness of our sources, and partly an acknowledgment that the western empire was little more than a political fiction by the time it fell. More generally, it reflects the fact that the fall of the Western Roman Empire was a process, not an event. Only in retrospect did its significance and permanence become clear.[2]

---

* Not long before the sack, the historian Ammianus Marcellinus described Rome as a city filled with billowy silk robes, professional gamblers, twenty-four-hour taverns, and legions of erotic dancers. The Visigoths, it would seem, had their work cut out for them.

† Odoacer, the Germanic general who deposed Romulus, treated the erstwhile emperor mercifully. To quote Gibbon: "The life of this inoffensive youth was spared by the generous clemency of Odoacer; who dismissed him, with his whole family, from the imperial palace, fixed his annual allowance at six thousand pieces of gold, and assigned the castle of Lucullus, in Campania, for the place of his exile or retirement."

The fall of the Western Roman Empire—in the sense of an end to effective imperial authority in a given region—was not always dramatic or even noticeable. Wars and invasions cost many Romans their property, their freedom, or their lives. But for many others, the fall of the empire represented nothing more or less than the gradual disappearance of familiar things, from Roman patrols on the roads to Roman pots in the kitchen.

The familiar things faded swiftest in Britain, the first part of the western empire to slip from imperial control. Over the subsequent decades, under the pressure of Germanic raids and the struggles of local warlords,* the social structure of the former province collapsed. Cities and villas were abandoned, the production of trade goods ceased, and standards of living sank to their lowest ebb in more than a millennium. A British monk, writing a century later, described the period in apocalyptic terms: "As flames roared and swords gleamed on every side, priests and people were hacked down together." A generation after the end of Roman rule in Britain, a Gallic bishop named Germanus crossed the English Channel to combat heresy. Although he met priests and soldiers still attuned to developments in the empire, he also encountered a marauding band of Saxon raiders. Undaunted, the good bishop rose to the occasion: appointing himself head of the local militia, he sallied forth against the barbarians, and put them to flight with a war cry of "Alleluia!"[3]

Although Britain's post-Roman trauma was exceptional, most of the frontier provinces were profoundly affected by the collapse of Roman authority. Besides the fact that they were the first regions to be overrun by invaders, their economies tended to be heavily dependent on their garrisons. Once the imperial government stopped paying its troops, the whole provincial economy frayed. Many frontier cities came to resemble the once-great legionary fortress of Naissus, which a visitor in the mid-fifth century† described as a ruin ringed by fields of bones.[4]

---

* One such warlord was the former commander of Birdoswald fort on Hadrian's Wall, whose successors dominated the surrounding region for decades after the Roman withdrawal.

† This visitor was Priscus, an emissary from the Eastern Roman emperor to Attila the Hun. In Attila's camp, Priscus encountered a Roman renegade who claimed that the huts of the Huns were infinitely preferable to the cities of the empire, where taxation was high, justice elusive, and war continual.

The most vivid account of the end of Roman rule on the frontier appears in an ancient biography of Saint Severinus, a holy man who lived in Noricum (modern Austria). By the time Severinus arrived in the mid-fifth century, the provincial administration had disintegrated, leaving each city to fend for itself. Although the border defenses were in ruins and the field armies long gone, a few garrisons held out along the old frontier. By Severinus's time, only one of these garrisons was still in contact with the imperial government. But since no official dared to enter Noricum, the garrison commander was forced to send soldiers over the Alps to retrieve pay from Italy. The last time this journey was attempted, the men were ambushed by barbarians. Their bodies, washed up on the banks of a local river, were the only news the garrison ever received of the disaster. As the last imperial troops melted away, Germanic tribes moved in to fill the power vacuum. Severinus did what he could to mediate between the invaders and the local inhabitants, convincing one king to free all the Romans his warriors had taken captive. But despite the saint's efforts, raiders continued to sack cities and enslave their inhabitants. After Severinus died, the situation deteriorated to the point that all the remaining Romans were evacuated from the province.[5]

The end of imperial authority tended to be less dramatic in the heartlands of the western empire. This was especially true of southern Gaul, whose powerful aristocrats struggled against, negotiated with, and finally served under the Germanic invaders with remarkable facility. The perspective and experiences of the Gallic aristocracy at the moment of transition from Roman rule are epitomized by the letters of Sidonius Apollinaris. After a distinguished political career at Rome, Sidonius became bishop of Clermont in his native Gaul, and fought to keep his city within the swiftly eroding empire. But eventually, after a siege that reduced them to eating grass, the citizens of Clermont opened their gates to the Goths. In a letter to a friend, Sidonius—who had urged continued resistance—despaired:* "Our

---

* Sidonius was not the only Gallic aristocrat to lament the passing of the old order. One of his contemporaries, a priest from Marseilles, exclaimed: "Once the Romans were feared, but now they live in fear; once the barbarians paid tribute to them, but now they are tributary to the barbarians . . . what could be more wretched?"

ancestors," he wrote, "will no longer glory in the name of Rome, if they have no [Roman] descendants." Sidonius praised those who fought the Goths, telling a man who had sallied out against the invaders that he had "made Romans of [his] fellow-citizens." In the end, however, like most members of his class, he accepted the demise of the empire, and resigned himself to the realities of living under the rule of the Goths, even commending one of his younger correspondents for combining "Burgundian eloquence with a Roman spirit" by learning German.[6]

Accommodation was also the strategy pursued by the great Roman magnates of Italy. Thanks to their willingness to cooperate with the new Germanic ruling class, the Italian elites preserved most of their wealth, lands, and prestige. The Senate continued to meet in Rome, consuls continued to be chosen, and games were still staged at the Colosseum and Circus Maximus, financed by men from the same families that had dominated politics in the last years of the western empire.[7]

One such man was Anicius Manlius Severinus Boethius. A scion of Rome's most distinguished clans, Boethius rose to literary distinction as a young man, composing learned treatises on a wide range of philosophical and theological subjects. He also achieved political success, becoming consul and master of offices under King Theodoric. Then, at the height of his power, he was accused of treachery and imprisoned. As he awaited judgment and execution, Boethius composed *The Consolation of Philosophy*, a dialogue exploring the nature of happiness and free will in brilliant prose interspersed with a series of poems. The final lines of one poem seem to summarize the experience of those who lived through the fall of the Western Roman Empire:

> This law no earthly thing transcends:
> All that has a beginning, ends[8]

IV

WHAT'S LEFT?

Why Are the Noses of
Ancient Statues Broken?

*O*ne warm summer evening, as sunset gilded the crosses and cupo-
las of Rome, I spent an hour exploring the Chiaramonti Museum.
The museum—part of the vast Vatican Museums complex—consists
of a single vaulted corridor, lined by hundreds of Roman statues.
Emperors stand with philosophers, merchants beside matrons, soldiers by freed slaves. Despite their variety, I noticed, virtually all of
these statues had one thing in common: their noses had been broken.

Statues were indispensable ornaments of the classical city. They
stood sentry over tombs, gazed down from the galleries of theaters,
and garnished the gardens and villas of the rich.* Each temple was
centered on a magnificent likeness of its indwelling deity; every
sanctuary shone with portraits of worshippers and gods. Busts of the
emperors presided in courtrooms, and petrified dignitaries crowded
the boulevards, their pedestals proclaiming services to city and state,
their ranks multiplying with the centuries. By late antiquity, the city
of Rome boasted nearly four thousand bronze statues, and as many
marble statues—it was said—as living men.[1]

Although classical sculptors employed many materials—some
temples sheltered images carved from wood or hewn from meteorites,

---

* From the late Republic onward, the townhouses and villas of Roman aristocrats were
expected to contain at least a few statues, often replicas of famous Greek masterpieces.
The huge assemblage of high-quality bronzes discovered in the House of the Papyri at
Herculaneum must have been mirrored in hundreds of mansions.

while others gloried in gods of gold and ivory*—most freestanding statues were made of bronze or marble. The tensile strength of bronze made possible both the dynamic poses favored by the greatest classical sculptors and the vast scale of the Colossus of Rhodes, which was roughly the size of the Statue of Liberty. But in most periods and places, the material of choice was marble. There were many varieties—translucent Parian, purple-veined Phrygian, stolid Luna†—which were quarried, by the Roman imperial era, on a proto-industrial scale that scattered marble statues from Britain to Syria.[2]

During late antiquity, the glittering ranks of statues began to be decimated. Bronze—used in everything from coins to cannonballs—was scavenged early and often, to the point that virtually every bronze statue above ground during the Middle Ages was melted down.‡ The survival rate for marble statues, fortunately, was higher; and although thousands were burned to produce lime, sheer quantity ensured that thousands more would survive to the Renaissance.

Most of these marble survivors—to return to our initial topic—are missing their original noses. In some cases, this reflects deliberate mutilation. During the fourth and fifth centuries, Christians

---

* Chryselephantine sculptures—made of ivory with golden details—were the most expensive and prestigious statues in the Greek world, despite the fact that their ivory skins tended to crack if they became too dry. Phidias's chryselephantine Athena in the Parthenon incorporated over a ton of gold, molded into plates that could be removed and melted down in the case of a financial emergency. The golden bust of Marcus Aurelius found at Aventicum (in modern Switzerland) is a rare extant example of the gilded statues that glowed in many Roman cities and sanctuaries.

† White marble statues were usually painted with natural hair and skin tones, though weathering and overly zealous cleaning have stripped the pigment from most of the examples displayed in museums. Their glass paste eyes have normally also fallen victim to the centuries.

‡ Throughout the Roman era, but especially during the second and first centuries BCE, huge quantities of sculpture were shipped from Greece and Asia Minor to Italy, to feed the Roman aristocracy's voracious appetite for all things Greek. Along the way, some of the ships transporting statues sank. One was discovered in 1926, when a fisherman near the Greek island of Euboea pulled up a bronze arm in his nets. Although he reported the find, nothing was done until two years later, when reports trickled into Athens of illegal salvagers working in the area. Lurching into action at last, the authorities caught men in the act of raising a bronze statue from the seabed. That statue proved to be the Artemision Bronze, a magnificent classical representation of Zeus or Poseidon. Two years later, divers brought up parts of a bronze equestrian statue. Once a fishing vessel discovered additional fragments, the sculpture was revealed to be a life-size representation of a jockey on a racehorse. Like the Artemision Bronze, it became a highlight of the National Archaeological Museum in Athens.

destroyed statues that represented the old gods. At Alexandria, a mob dismembered and burned a great statue of the god Serapis.* A bishop led a detachment of soldiers through the temples and palaces of Gaza, smashing every "idol" he found. An inscription discovered at Ephesus records how a statue of Artemis was broken and replaced with a cross, and the pediments of the Parthenon still bear the scars of statues torn down when the building was converted into a church.[3]

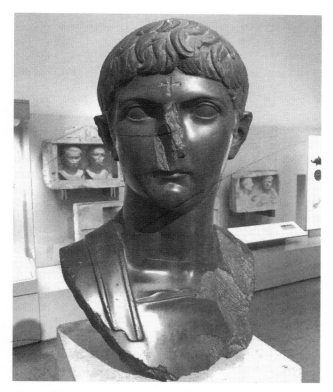

A bust of Germanicus with its nose knocked off and a cross cut into its forehead, now in the British Museum. *Public domain*

---

* The Alexandrian mob seems to have acquired a real taste for this sort of thing: in the late fifth century, twenty camel loads of statues from the Temple of Isis at Memphis were brought to Alexandria for public destruction.

Although such destruction was far from universal—usually, only the most prominent images of the old gods were targeted—ancient statues that survived into the Middle Ages tended to be seen as dangerous curiosities, prone to demonic possession and enchantment by magicians.* In an effort to neutralize their malignant power, crosses were sometimes cut into their foreheads and bodies. And in Roman Egypt, at least, their noses were broken. Since the pharaonic period, the Egyptians had regarded statues as receptacles for the essence of the gods and the spirits of the dead, and as the instruments through which gods and spirits could communicate with the living. Such communion, however, was predicated on the physical integrity of the statue. If its ears were broken, it could not hear; and if its nose were destroyed, the spirit within, unable to breathe, would die. Knowing this, Egyptian Christians sometimes "killed" ancient statues by smashing their noses.†

Outside Egypt, however, there is no evidence that noses were deliberately targeted. In most cases, a statue's nose seems to have simply broken when it fell—as statues almost always did, sooner or later. Most of the Mediterranean is prone to strong earthquakes, and these shocks have sent statues—including the Colossus of Rhodes, snapped at the knees by a tremor—tumbling since antiquity. Whether felled by earthquake, vandalism, or simple age, marble statues tended to shatter along a few points of vulnerability. The most obvious of these was the neck, but the limbs—especially if outstretched—were equally fragile. And if a statue fell forward or was struck in the face by rubble, its nose would break.

---

* These attitudes were especially visible in Byzantine Constantinople, whose magnificent collection of ancient statues survived largely intact until the Fourth Crusade. As early as the eighth century, knowledge of the statues' original identities had faded, displaced by a curious blend of half-remembered myths and popular superstition. It was said that a certain statue with four horns could detect unfaithful wives, that bronze figures of mosquitos and fleas kept those pests at bay, and that a bronze boar in the Hippodrome held the key to the emperor's soul. A statue with three heads was decapitated on the patriarch's orders, since it was believed that doing so would forestall the approach of a barbarian horde with three chieftains.

† The nose of the Great Sphinx at Giza appears to have survived until the fourteenth century, when it was chiseled off by a zealous Sufi.

This rule is disguised by the fact that, from the Renaissance until the nineteenth century, it was standard practice to restore the broken noses and limbs of ancient statues. Cellini, Bernini, and many other artists earned a substantial part of their income from restoration work, which sometimes extended to the point of creating entirely new works from ancient fragments.* Such reconstructions are on display in virtually every museum with a collection of classical sculpture. As I walked through the Chiaramonti Museum on that warm summer evening, I could see, on statue after statue, the hairline cracks that betray a replacement nose. But after a while, I stopped noticing. I was too entranced by that long gallery and its thousand portraits, which looked—I imagined—as the heart of Rome must once have looked, before the statues fell.

---

* In Renaissance Italy, for example, it became fashionable for wealthy families to display ancient busts of the twelve Caesars—that is, of Julius Caesar and the first Roman emperors—in their homes. But since authentic busts of short-lived emperors like Galba and Otho were rare, sculptors sometimes "restored" unrelated busts into portraits that suited their clients' demands.

Why Are Ancient Cities Buried?

$\mathcal{O}$ne October morning, a decade or so ago, I took a long walk on the roof of Detroit's Packard Plant.* A gargantuan complex—nearly three-quarters of a mile long, two city blocks wide, and up to ten stories tall—the plant has been mostly empty since 1958, and completely abandoned for about twenty years. Thanks to scrapping, vandalism, and a series of fires, whole sections have fallen into ruin, leaving holes in the roof that I was careful to skirt on my walk. As I picked my way along, I noticed plants growing from every crack and crevice: grasses, shrubs, and hundreds of saplings with rustling leaves. I was reminded of old engravings of the ruins of Rome, mantled and buried in shrouds of vegetation. Given another century or two, I remember thinking, the Packard Plant would look much the same.

The roof of the Packard Plant illustrates the beginnings of the processes that have left so many Greek and Roman cities deep underground. The best-preserved building in the Roman Forum, for example, is the Curia, or senate house, which was converted into a church during the Middle Ages. By the eleventh century, the ground level around the building had risen so much that a new door had to be cut through the front wall, ten feet higher than the original. The ground level continued to rise, and during the Renaissance another door had to be cut, this time more than twenty feet above the ancient pavement. By the time the area around the Curia was excavated in

---

* Don't do this. It was dangerous then, and it's even more dangerous now.

the late nineteenth century, even this door was recessed below the street. The difference between ancient and later ground levels is equally apparent at the nearby Temple of Antoninus and Faustina, where the entrance of the church that was built into the temple during the Renaissance is two stories above the Roman steps.

The processes that bury cities vary with factors ranging from climate to building material. In Mesopotamia, the sites of ancient cities are often marked by the artificial hills known as tells, which consist largely of melted mudbrick.* Unlike fired brick or stone, mudbrick cannot be reused. So when a mudbrick structure began to decay, it was simply leveled, and a replacement constructed on top. Multiplied by millennia, this practice created mounds up to 150 feet tall. By contrast, some Roman villages on the arid plateaus of Syria are still at ground level, since their stone houses, occupied for centuries, were repaired instead of being replaced.

Soil accumulates in and around abandoned buildings. Desert drifts of dust and sand can overwhelm whole settlements. Aurel Stein, for example, discovered a series of Silk Road caravan towns that had been engulfed by dunes. In temperate climates, seeds are carried along with windborne dust. Taking root in corners and along ledges, they sprout and die, contributing their organic matter to the soil deposits from which they grew. Although the classical world lacked the jungles that swallowed Angkor Wat and the Mayan cities of Central America, forests flourished in the ruined cities of Greece and Italy,† producing soil that built up slowly but steadily.

Waterborne sediment arrives more dramatically. Rome was prone to winter floods of the Tiber, which submerged the neighborhood around the Pantheon in up to fifteen feet of water. Each flood left a film of silt, gradually raising the ground level. Cities in hilly terrain had to contend with soil washing downslope. Parts of Sardis—in modern Turkey—have been covered by up to seventy feet of landslip

---

* In Egypt, decayed mudbrick—*sebakh*—has historically been used as a fertilizer, with catastrophic consequences for archaeological sites.

† A nineteenth-century botanist counted 420 species of plants growing in the Colosseum. These included flowers found nowhere else in Europe, whose ancestors may have been seeds stuck to the fur of exotic animals hunted in the arena.

An eighteenth-century engraving of the overgrown ruins of Hadrian's Villa.
Courtesy of the Minneapolis Institute of Art

debris.* The frescoes and bronze statues of a Roman temple in Brixia (modern Brescia) were preserved for posterity by a medieval mudslide, as were the spectacular mosaics of the Villa Romana del Casale in Sicily. On the edge of the Roman Forum, an earthquake-induced landslide entombed the church of Santa Maria Antiqua.†

Fire could bury a city as effectively as water. To judge from excavations near the Circus Maximus, for example, the ashes and debris left by the Great Fire in the reign of Nero raised the ground level by ten feet or more in parts of Rome. This effect was already obvious in antiquity, when one author observed that the hills of Rome were higher than they had once been, thanks to the rubble of many

---

* The acropolis of Sardis, on the hill overlooking the city, is gradually eroding away. The power of erosion is even more visible at Sillyon, another ancient Greek city in modern Turkey, where most of the theater has washed downhill over the past few centuries.

† A rarer phenomenon, subsidence, has left much of ancient Alexandria underwater. At Baiae, on the Bay of Naples, volcanic bradyseism has caused the ground level to fluctuate by as much as twenty feet, alternately submerging and uplifting the city's Roman ruins.

fires. In the Athenian Agora, fires started by a millennium of invaders, from the Persians to the Visigoths, repeatedly raised the ground level. The Syrian metropolis of Antioch, devastated many times by earthquake, invasion, and conflagration, lies beneath forty feet of its own debris.[1]

Most ancient cities, however, were buried largely by the people who lived in them. Sometimes, this took the form of deliberate dumping, such as the massive construction projects that filled the valley of the Colosseum and buried the necropolis beneath old St. Peter's Basilica.* But it was the unstructured habits of centuries—emptying chamber pots from a window, kicking broken pots into alleys, tossing trash in the closest convenient place—that ultimately had a greater impact. Refuse accumulated, and the ground level inched upward.

The process accelerated dramatically when buildings fell out of use and began to crumble. Take a typical Roman apartment building, three or four stories tall: the walls are brick-faced concrete and the roof is tiled, but the floors and partitions are plaster and wood. A few decades after the building is abandoned, the roof collapses, leaving a head-high heap of tiles and rotten wood inside the masonry shell. After a century or two of rain and frost have weakened the mortar, an earthquake or windstorm brings the walls crashing down. And where our apartment building once stood, there is now a mound, a story or so tall, spilling over the adjacent streets. Multiply that building by tens of thousands, and you have the situation in medieval Rome, where whole districts were submerged in rubble.

It is, in short, a combination of rubble, refuse, ash, and water- and windborne sediment that buries most ancient cities, often leaving only tantalizing traces on the surface. Once, while exploring a remote site in Turkey, I came upon a lone column in a field of dry grass, buried almost to its capital. For a moment, laying a hand on the sun-warmed stone, I imagined the invisible city beneath my feet. Then I went away with my thoughts, cicadas in the treetops humming their answer to the silent eloquence of ruins.

---

* At Dura-Europos, on Rome's Syrian frontier, a whole row of buildings—including a synagogue with vibrant frescoes—was preserved by being buried in an embankment meant to strengthen the adjacent city wall.

Are Any Ancient Buildings Still in Use?

*W*ind and rain, roots and frost, fires, earthquakes, gravity's pull, and people with urgent needs and short memories have ensured that the vast majority of ancient Greek and Roman buildings are gutted, gaping, or gone. A remarkable number, however, are not only intact, but still being used for their original purpose.

Although a number of subterranean residential complexes—from the Sassi of Matera to Cappadocian cave cities—have been used continuously since the Roman period, intact ancient houses are rare above ground.* A partial exception is hidden in plain sight a short walk from the Colosseum. During late antiquity, the Caelian Hill was crowned by one of Rome's most exclusive neighborhoods, where the mansions of senators and dignitaries peered superciliously over winding streets. One of the grandest houses belonged to the family of Gregorius, the senator's son who would become Pope Gregory the Great. In 575, a decade before his election to the papacy, Gregory converted his ancestral mansion into a monastery. A sprawling structure, already centuries old, the house seems to have had warrens of rooms ringing its central courtyard and reception halls. One reception hall became the monastery church, which still stands.†

---

* Beneath the Palazzo Comunale of Spoleto is a Roman mansion—possibly built by Vespasian's mother—that seems to have been continuously inhabited from antiquity to the late medieval period.

† The church—San Gregorio Magno al Celio—was reconstructed in the thirteenth century and has been renovated several times since. The only obviously ancient feature of the interior is a marble throne, said to have been used by Gregory himself. While we have no way of knowing whether this is true, the throne is certainly old enough to have come from the original house. The neighboring chapel of Santa Barbara preserves an ancient marble table at which Gregory is said to have served the poor of Rome.

Roman houses with living residents can be found in the Syrian Hauran, a dry but fertile region dotted with ancient cities and towns.* Thanks to an almost complete lack of wood, the walls, roofs, and even doors of local houses were fashioned from thick slabs of volcanic stone. All but impervious to the passage of time, these houses were simply reused in the modern period, when the Hauran was resettled after a long period of depopulation. A nineteenth-century traveler described an exceptionally impressive two-story mansion with a central courtyard, inhabited by a sheik who used the rooms of the ground floor as offices, housed his wives and children upstairs, and received guests in the same great hall where his Roman predecessor had staged banquets fifteen centuries before.[1]

The Tower of Hercules in A Coruña, Spain, is a working Roman lighthouse. The spectacular Segovia aqueduct, also in Spain, carried water until 1973 (albeit with a hiatus caused by damage from medieval warfare). The Aqueduct of Valens, still a prominent landmark in modern Istanbul, was repaired by both Byzantine emperors and Ottoman sultans, and only replaced when the city's modern water mains were installed. Rome's Aqua Virgo has remained in operation since the reign of Augustus, and still supplies the Trevi Fountain.

There are a handful of Roman baths still in operation. At Bath, England, the Romans channeled the waters of a hot spring into a bathing complex centered on a lead-lined pool. Though smothered with debris during the Middle Ages,† the pool was excavated and restored in the nineteenth century, and used by bathers until 1978. At Hierapolis, in what is now southwestern Turkey, a hot spring cascading over snow-white travertine terraces became the site of a Roman bath. A medieval earthquake caused a temple to collapse into the spring, but the sacred pool has changed little over the millennia, and teems with tourists today. In the forested hills of northeastern Algeria, another Roman bathing complex was erected around the twin pools of a hot spring. Although its porticoes and service buildings

---

* The so-called Dead Cities, a cluster of prosperous late antique villages on the limestone plateau of northwestern Syria, also contain remarkably well-preserved late Roman houses, some recently reinhabited.

† "The Ruin," an Old English poem lamenting the destruction of an ancient city, seems to have been inspired by the Roman remains of Bath.

have been restored several times, the bath—now known as Hammam Essalihine—has remained in use continuously since the first century.

Services are still held in quite a few early Christian churches. To focus on Rome, the Basilica of Santa Sabina looks much as it did when it was completed in 432, and even has its original wooden doors. The Papal Basilica of Santa Maria Maggiore, completed around the same time, has retained most of its ancient mosaics. Equally spectacular Roman mosaics are on display in Santa Costanza, built to serve as a mausoleum for one of Constantine's daughters. And at Santi Giovanni e Paolo, constructed shortly before Alaric's sack of Rome, visitors can view the frescoed rooms of a Roman mansion that was incorporated into the church's foundations.* Though exceptional in its wealth of early Christian architecture, Rome is far from unique: Milan, Ravenna, and Thessaloniki all have multiple ancient churches still in use.

Many classical temples were converted into churches. Well-known examples include the Maison Carrée in Nimes, the Temple of Augustus and Livia in Vienne, the Temple of Minerva in Assisi, and the Temple of Augustus in Pula. At Rome, two temples built during the second century BCE, originally dedicated to Hercules Victor and Portunus, served as churches until the late nineteenth century. The Pantheon, the best-preserved and most impressive of all Roman buildings, has been a church since the seventh century, and is still consecrated.† At Athens, the Parthenon and the Temple of Hephaestus in the Agora became churches in late antiquity, which had the incidental effect of keeping both buildings intact through the Middle Ages. The so-called Temple of Concordia at Agrigento was preserved by the same means.

Perhaps the most fascinating of all converted Greek temples is the Duomo of Syracuse. Originally a Temple of Athena built to commemorate a victory over Carthage in 480 BCE, it became the

---

* Unfortunately, Rome's greatest early Christian churches no longer exist. Old St. Peter's, begun by Constantine, was demolished to make way for the present church. The western half of the old basilica was torn down in 1506; the eastern half, a century later. (During deconstruction of the roof, incidentally, the huge oak rafters were found to be so solid that several were reused in the Borghese Palace.) The other great loss is St. Paul Outside the Walls, a vast fourth-century basilica that was almost perfectly preserved until 1823, when a fire started by a careless workman consumed most of the building.

† Another church in Rome, Santa Maria degli Angeli, has occupied the gargantuan frigidarium of the Baths of Diocletian since the sixteenth century.

The Temple of Hephaestus in the Athenian Agora, converted into a church during late antiquity. *Author's photo*

city's cathedral a millennium later. Made a mosque by the conquering Muslims in 878, it was reconverted to Christianity two centuries later and remains a working church today. One summer afternoon, I sat outside a café opposite the Duomo's north side, and passed the better part of an hour tracing the centuries up and down its patchwork masonry, where ancient columns jut from medieval walls.

On another summer afternoon, I drove across one of the hundreds of working Roman bridges scattered across the territory of the former empire. This particular example—over the Eurymedon River near Selge, Turkey—was relatively modest, spanning a canyon only twenty-five feet wide. But as I crept across in my rental car, I was reminded of a line from an inscription commemorating an architect on the other side* of the Roman world: "He built this bridge to last forever."[2]

---

* The inscription celebrates Gaius Julius Lacer, architect of the famous Alcántara Bridge in Spain.

· 36 ·

What Happened to the Treasures of the Roman Emperors?

$\mathcal{T}$he palaces, villas, and storehouses of the Roman emperors held the accumulated riches and curiosities of the known world. The imperial collections included such gewgaws as the skeletons of giants, the tusks of the mythical Caledonian Boar, and a stuffed centaur from the Arabian Desert. In the palace cellars, amphorae filled with fine wines—some centuries old—stood beside stores of precious cinnamon, iron chests of gemstones, and heaps of golden crowns.* The rooms above held such relics as a book in the hand of Pythagoras, bronzes from the ruins of Corinth, and paintings by the great Greek masters.† The palace banquet halls, with their Persian couch covers, priceless alabaster goblets, and acres of silver plate, were especially spectacular.[1]

The imperial collections waxed and waned over time. Although emperors received a steady stream of gifts from embassies (and sometimes confiscated objects that struck their fancy), treasures continually flowed out of the palace, given or auctioned away. To raise money for the Marcomannic Wars, for example, Marcus Aurelius

---

* Provincial cities customarily sent the emperors golden crowns to commemorate victories and imperial anniversaries. An embassy of Gauls once presented Augustus with a gargantuan golden torque weighing a hundred pounds.

† Many of the artistic treasures owned by emperors were displayed in public places. To judge from the ancient inventory number still visible on its abdomen, the life-size bronze statue known as the Hellenistic Prince, now at Rome's Palazzo Massimo Museum, originated in one of these "galleries." Other masterpieces were reserved for the emperors' private pleasure, like the bronze Amazon that accompanied Nero wherever he traveled.

sold furniture, garments, goblets, and gems. The outflow became a flood in late antiquity, as the imperial system contracted and the contents of the palaces were dispersed.[2]

Over the centuries, a few spectacular troves from the imperial treasuries have come to light. In 1544, two caskets filled with golden vessels and gemstones were discovered in the tomb of Maria, wife of the fifth-century emperor Honorius, under old St. Peter's Basilica. During the eighteenth century, a beautiful bronze vase—now in the Capitoline Museums—was found among the ruins of Nero's Villa at Antium. A series of Renaissance princes cherished a Roman ring, engraved with a sphinx, supposedly taken from the tomb of Augustus.* In 2005, the scepter of Maxentius, the rival of Constantine, was discovered at the base of the Palatine Hill.

Some of the finest imperial treasures were brought to Constantinople in late antiquity, and remained there until the soldiers of the Fourth Crusade captured and sacked the city in 1204. The artifacts they seized from the Great Palace gradually found their way into the courts and churches of western Europe, where a remarkable number can still be seen today.

The Farnese Cup, an elaborate dish carved from a single piece of agate, was in Constantinople for centuries. Donated—presumably by an emperor—to one of the city's churches, it was taken by the crusaders and sold to Holy Roman Emperor Frederick II, an enthusiastic collector of Roman artifacts. Two centuries later, it was sent as a diplomatic present to Timur, a ruthless central Asian warlord who divided his time between patronizing the arts and building pyramids from the skulls of his enemies. Returning to Italy after Timur's death, the cup was purchased by Alfonso of Aragon, confiscated by Pope Paul II, and served as the centerpiece of Lorenzo de' Medici's famous

---

* A spectacular ring, carved from a sapphire and apparently bearing the likeness of Empress Caesonia, was recently auctioned as the ring of Caligula. But the only extant ring that can confidently be associated with an eminent Roman belonged to Scipio Barbatus, a consul and general in the early third century BCE. Discovered with its owner's bones in 1780, Scipio's ring was granted by the pope to a French scholar, and eventually incorporated into the collection of the Dukes of Northumberland.

The Farnese Cup. *Wikimedia Commons*

collection of ancient gems. After inspiring Botticelli, the cup passed to the Farnese family, and finally to the Bourbon kings of Naples. It remains in the Naples Archeological Museum today.*

Another agate cup from Constantinople, likely carved at a palace workshop in late antiquity, became famous for the veins in its stone, which seem to spell the name of Christ in Greek. After it was pilfered by the Crusaders, the cup became one of the most cherished possessions of the Habsburg dynasty, and was hailed as the

---

* In 1925, a disgruntled museum guard attacked the cup with his umbrella, smashing the right side. Fortunately, the damage was quickly repaired.

Holy Grail, the cup Christ used at the Last Supper.* Holy Roman Emperor Ferdinand I declared it an inalienable treasure of the House of Austria, too precious to ever be sold. It never was, and can still be visited in the Imperial Treasury at Vienna's Hofburg Palace.

The so-called Rubens Vase was carved in Constantinople around the end of the fourth century, almost certainly for a member of the imperial family. Taken by the Crusaders, it was sold to the Dukes of Anjou, and eventually reached the collections of the French kings. After being stolen from a royal villa by a band of rebels, it was purchased by Peter Paul Rubens, who sketched it at least once. Rubens sold the vase in 1626, and it seems to have reached Mughal India before returning to Europe in time to be bought by William Beckford, an immensely wealthy English magnate. For a few years, the vase was displayed at Fonthill Abbey, Beckford's colossal faux-Gothic manor. Then Beckford sold the vase, not long before his house's three-hundred-foot tower collapsed, destroying many of his remaining treasures. The vase passed through a series of aristocratic English hands before being purchased by the American art collector Henry Walters. It now resides in Baltimore's Walters Art Museum.

Storied through the careers of the Rubens Vase and Farnese Cup were, no former treasure of the Roman emperors can match the tragic tale of the Great Cameo of Constantine, a carved slab of agate that depicts Constantine and his family in a triumphal chariot.[3] Commissioned by the Roman Senate, the cameo was probably presented to Constantine in 315, three years after his victory at the Milvian Bridge. It was brought to Constantinople and remained there, likely in the imperial treasury, until the Crusaders came. After

---

* Several other Roman cups have been hailed as the Grail over the centuries. The Santo Caliz of Valencia, for example, is an ancient cup of red agate that was transformed into a chalice with the additions of a golden base and handles. Another vessel, the so-called Chalice of Antioch, was discovered in Syria around the beginning of the twentieth century. For years, it occupied a safety-deposit box in Manhattan, from which it was marketed to prospective buyers as the Holy Grail. It was displayed with great fanfare at the 1933 World's Fair in Chicago, and inspired *The Silver Chalice*, a novel turned into a Hollywood blockbuster starring Paul Newman. Eventually, the chalice was sold to the Metropolitan Museum of Art, where it can be viewed today.

centuries in France, the cameo was purchased—like the Baltimore vase—by Peter Paul Rubens. A few years later, Rubens sold it to an Amsterdam jeweler, who devised a plan to sell it to Jahangir, the Mughal emperor of India. Along with ten chests of silver and many other treasures, the cameo was loaded into the hold of the *Batavia*, the flagship of the Dutch East India Company.

The voyage turned disastrous on June 4, 1629, when the *Batavia* struck a reef in the uncharted waters off the western Australian coast. As the ship sank, most of the passengers managed to escape onto two tiny islands. The commander and senior officers set out in the ship's boat in a desperate bid to reach the Dutch colony on Java. Within a few days of their departure, the rest of the survivors chose Jeronimus Cornelisz, a disgraced former merchant, as their leader. Jeronimus moved the treasures of the *Batavia* into his tent and displayed the Great Cameo of Constantine to the ship's soldiers, proclaiming this was only the beginning of the wealth that could be theirs if they joined his cause. Over the next few weeks, he ruthlessly consolidated his power, urging his followers to kill anyone who opposed his authority. By the time the ship's commander returned with a rescue vessel, more than one hundred passengers had been murdered.

Jeronimus and his gang were hanged for their crimes, and the treasures of the *Batavia*—including the Great Cameo of Constantine—were carried to Indonesia. The cameo was then brought to India, where attempts were made to sell it to the Mughal court. When these failed, it was marketed to the shah of Persia and various princes in India and Indonesia. None were willing to pay the asking price. And so, in 1656, the Great Cameo of Constantine returned to the Netherlands. Purchased by the Dutch king after two centuries in the hands of private collectors, it is now displayed in the National Museum of Antiquities at Leiden.

The treasury of St. Mark's Basilica in Venice holds dozens of objects from the palaces and churches of Constantinople. On one shelf stand two spectacular chalices, both fashioned from sardonyx bowls by a tenth-century emperor. The bowls are ancient, perhaps a millennium older than their gold and enamel Byzantine settings. Both likely originated in the imperial treasury. They were carried, along with so many other antiquities, to St. Mark's.* And despite a devastating medieval fire, a daring theft attempt, and the depredations of Napoleon's lieutenants, they remain in the treasury today, lapped by floodwaters and tides of tourists, eight centuries and half a world from the ashes of Constantinople.

---

* St. Mark's contains many bits and pieces pilfered from Constantinople, from the porphyry tetrarchs embedded in the Piazzetta facade to the famous bronze horses long displayed on the loggia. I especially like "Carmagnola," a porphyry head (probably of Justinian) stuck onto a corner of the loggia's balustrade.

How Much Roman Gold
Still Exists Today?

Gold was everywhere in ancient Rome. It shone on every noble hand,* flickered from the greatest temples' roofs, clinked in coins,† plated the walls of mansions, wrapped the horns of sacrificial oxen, dusted the manes of lions at the Colosseum, and trailed in slender chains from the fins of favored pet fish.[1]

Much of this gold had originated in the Hellenistic world. Although gold coins from Lydia and Persia circulated in Classical Athens, and the great statue of Athena in the Parthenon shone with more than a metric ton of gold, silver was the predominant precious metal in Greece until the fourth century BCE, when Philip II of Macedon opened productive gold mines in Thrace. Philip's son Alexander took vast quantities of gold—by one estimate, more than three hundred tons—from the Persians, fueling a flood of gold coins, jewelry, and plate. Alexander himself was buried in a golden coffin. The western Mediterranean was also rich in gold. Even before the fabulously productive mines of Spain were opened, gold coins were circulating in Gaul, and the Roman general Caepio could seize a

---

* Roman satirists describe men with six golden rings on each finger, and rings so massive that they were uncomfortable to wear in the heat of summer.

† After its introduction by Julius Caesar, the aureus—a gold piece worth 25 silver denarii—was the Roman Empire's highest-value coin, used by individuals to store and transfer large sums, and by the government to pay soldiers and officials. Buried hoards showcase the scale of the gold coinage. In 1993, for example, a bronze pot containing more than 2,600 aurei came to light in a foundation hole at Trier. The lost Brescello hoard, the most valuable Roman treasure ever discovered, consisted of some 80,000 aurei.

spectacular golden treasure from a sanctuary at Tolosa.* Much of the gold struck into Caesar's first aurei came from looted Gallic cities and temples.[2]

Although the pace of plunder slowed under the emperors, both Titus's sack of Jerusalem and Trajan's Dacian Wars brought vast influxes of bullion. The treasury of the Dacian king, recovered from its hiding place beneath the bed of a rushing river, reportedly contained hundreds of tons of gold. Even more gold entered the economy from the vast mining enterprises of the imperial era. The tortured landscape of Las Médulas in northwestern Spain attests to the scope of these efforts, as does the massive spike in atmospheric lead—generated by Roman smelters—that can still be detected in cores from the Greenland ice cap.[†]

Gold was always leaving the Roman economy, both from the steady attrition of wear and hoarding and from payments made to foreign merchants and external enemies. Pliny the Elder claimed that 100,000,000 sestertii in gold and silver were lost every year, traded for eastern luxuries. During late antiquity, subsidies and tribute payments to Persia and northern barbarians became a serious drain on the gold supply. Starting in 424, for example, the Romans gave the Huns 350 pounds of gold each year to prevent raids. The payment was doubled when Attila came to power, and finally increased to 2,100 pounds. During his first siege of Rome, Alaric extorted 5,000 pounds of gold from the city.[3]

The amount of gold in the Roman Empire at any given time is difficult to assess. The Romans may have mined as much as five hundred tons of gold, and likely pilfered at least as much during their conquests. One scholar has estimated that four hundred tons of aurei were in circulation during the reign of Hadrian. We have no way of knowing how accurate this estimate is, or the proportion of the gold

---

* The treasure included an estimated 15,000 talents of gold and silver. Since only a tiny fraction of that ever reached Rome, it was rumored that the treasure had been stolen in transit, perhaps with the connivance of Caepio himself.

† Lead levels peaked during the early imperial era, then fell in tandem with the exhaustion of Roman mines in Spain and the general inanition of the Roman economy. Emissions only returned to Roman levels during the early modern period.

above ground that those coins represented. It seems likely, however, that something on the order of one thousand tons of gold circulated through the Roman world over the course of the imperial era.[4]

After the fall of the Roman Empire, the gold supply shrank, falling to its lowest ebb during the Great Bullion Famine of the late Middle Ages. By 1500, all the gold in Europe could have been compressed into a cube little more than six feet on each side. The gold supply increased dramatically during the nineteenth century, spurred by the institution of an international gold standard and fed by finds from Siberia to South Africa. By 1910, all the gold above ground would have made a cube with thirty-three-foot sides. The twentieth century witnessed enormous leaps in production, to the point that roughly two-thirds of all the gold above ground today has been mined since 1950. The world gold supply is now slightly over two hundred thousand metric tons, enough to make a cube seventy-one feet to a side.*

Since gold is a noble metal, impervious to corrosion, virtually all the gold ever discovered still exists. And since gold has been valued throughout human history, it has been constantly recycled—including, over the past few decades, into the circuitry of computers, smartphones, and other electronic devices. If my estimate of the Roman gold supply is roughly correct, something like 1/200th (0.5 percent) of the gold currently above ground was mined or plundered by the Romans. So if you're using an e-reader or listening to this book on your smartphone, there may be a few glittering motes of ancient Rome behind your screen.

---

* In 2021, by way of contrast, nearly two billion metric tons of steel were produced. All the gold mined over the course of human history could fit easily on a single modern oil tanker or container ship.

· 38 ·

How Much Did the Byzantines Know about Roman History?

$\mathcal{O}$n May 11, 330, Constantine, resplendent in golden robes and jeweled diadem, dedicated the city of Constantinople. Over the six years since he had proclaimed the foundation of his second Rome, a dazzling imperial capital had come into being, complete with a senate and seven hills. At its heart lay a newly constructed forum, centered on a porphyry column that bore a statue of the emperor as Apollo, with the radiate crown of the rising sun. But in keeping with Constantine's vision of a Christian empire, each of the crown's seven rays contained a sliver from the nails of the True Cross.[1]

For more than a thousand years, Constantinople would be the center of the Eastern Roman Empire. Although that empire never ceased to be Roman, it evolved into a polity profoundly different from the classical Roman Empire—the state and society we call Byzantium. This is a misnomer, in the sense that the Byzantines always called themselves Romans* and remained keenly aware that their emperors were the heirs of Caesar and Augustus. The distinction between "Roman" and "Byzantine" remains useful, however, to the degree that it reflects the profound transformations that marked the end of antiquity.

---

* The western European habit of referring to the Byzantines as Greeks caused more than one furious diplomatic incident. The Byzantines' eastern neighbors, by contrast, always referred to them as Romans: the first Turkish state founded on former Byzantine territory was known as the Sultanate of Rum (Rome).

The Column of Constantine. The emperor's statue was toppled by a medieval windstorm. *Author's photo*

The chronological division between "Roman" and "Byzantine" is usually placed in the seventh century, when generations of almost continuous warfare with the Persians, Slavs, and Arabs reduced the Eastern Roman Empire to an impoverished fragment of its former self. Through the crisis, the intellectual heritage of the classical world remained alive in schools and monasteries. But at least on the popular level, much knowledge was lost. The identities of the ancient statues that loomed over the public places of Constantinople, for example, were forgotten, and the statues themselves came to be regarded as magical talismans. Ancient ruins and temples were dreaded as the homes of demons. And at every level of Byzantine society, knowledge of Latin became rare* outside a few legal circles.[2]

Knowledge of the Greek classics, by contrast, remained very much alive. Although the pronunciation and grammar of spoken Byzantine Greek differed substantially from their ancient antecedents, Byzantine education was founded on the interpretation and imitation of classical texts—the same texts, in many cases, that had shaped the Greek curriculum since the Hellenistic era. The eleventh-century princess Anna Comnena, for example, quotes Sophocles and Homer, and mentions studying the works of Plato and Aristotle. Byzantine students often read the historian Xenophon—who was admired for the clarity of his Greek—and were likely to acquire at least a vague sense of Classical Athenian history from reading so many Classical Athenian authors. But works of Roman history were not normally studied.

---

* Constantinople had been a Latin-speaking enclave for much of late antiquity: the University of Constantinople, founded by Theodosius II in 425, originally had almost equal numbers of professors for Latin and Greek rhetoric, and the great Latin grammar of Priscian was composed there. Justinian, likewise, issued his famous code in Latin from Constantinople. But by the late sixth century, only a few decades after Justinian's death, it had become hard to find competent Latinists in the city. Emperor Heraclius's decision to begin calling himself by the Greek title "Basileus" (rather than by the Latin—or by Greek translations of—"Imperator" and "Augustus") in 629 was emblematic of Latin's eclipse. Although closer contacts with western Europe encouraged a modest revival in Latin learning from the eleventh century onward, few Byzantines of that era read Latin texts for pleasure. There were, however, a few exceptions. John Tzetzes, writing in the twelfth century, inserted a few lines of rather ungrammatical Latin into one of his poems. A century later, Maximus Planudes translated the poems of Ovid, Cicero's orations, and other Latin classics into Greek for the benefit of Byzantines interested in Roman literature. There is little evidence, however, that his translations were greeted with widespread enthusiasm.

Histories of the classical Roman Empire, however, could still be found at Constantinople, and were still being read by a few intellectuals. During the ninth century, for example, the scholar (and sometime patriarch) Photius produced summaries of nearly four hundred obscure works, about half of them pre-Christian, which he had read. His list included a number of Roman historians, most notably Appian, chronicler of the civil wars that ended the Republic. Although the breadth of Photius's reading was exceptional, the essentials of Roman history were accessible to every literate Byzantine via the chronicles that comprised the most popular and enduring form of Byzantine historiography. These works, pioneered by Eusebius of Caesarea and other patristic authors, were essentially religious in character, focused on salvation history and the growth of the church. They made reference, however, to the chronological framework of the Roman monarchy, Republic, and Empire. A more substantial, if diffuse, account of Roman history was available in the sprawling tenth-century encyclopedia known as the *Suda*. Although most of the historical entries in this very popular work dealt with late antiquity, about a third explored such topics as the institutions of the Roman Republic, biographies of early Roman emperors, and Trajan's wars of conquest.[3]

Perhaps the most intriguing middle Byzantine survey of Roman history is Michael Psellus's *Historia Syntomos*, written for the benefit of his pupil, the future emperor Michael VII. Beginning with Romulus and the kings of Rome, Psellus covers the foundation of the Roman Republic, and then skips ahead to Caesar, Augustus, and their successors, providing a brief moralizing biography of each emperor. The fall of the Western Roman Empire is ignored, and the string of imperial lives extended to Basil II, who died in 1025—only a generation before Psellus was writing. Although there are plenty of mistakes—Nerva is "Gerva," Carus is "Marus," and Trajan is described as a Celtic barbarian—the most striking aspect of Psellus's work is its unremitting emphasis on the emperors and their foibles. This reflects both the *Historia*'s princely audience and the fact that the Byzantines only remembered—or rather, only took pains to preserve—aspects of Roman history that seemed relevant to their own state and society.

Historical texts that lacked such immediacy were likely to disappear, whether from simple neglect or in one of the conflagrations that periodically swept Constantinople. Yet despite the attrition of ancient texts, educated Byzantines never forgot their Roman roots.* A Byzantine prince who visited the ruins of Pergamum in the thirteenth century remarked that the huge Roman buildings reminded him of the greatness of his ancestors. Later, in the twilight of Byzantine history, Emperor Manuel II marveled at the remains of a city founded by Pompey the Great. On seeing a deserted plain nearby, he reflected:

> This place must have had a name, when it was fortunate enough to be ruled and peopled by Romans. But when I ask what that name was . . . no one can tell me. Most of the cities are in ruins . . . and when I ask what they were called, I receive the reply "men destroyed those cities, but time took their names."[4]

This Byzantine emperor, at least, knew how fragile history can be.

---

* Late Byzantine scholars, in fact, were responsible for forging new connections between Constantinople and Rome. Manuel Chrysoloras, who taught Greek to a rising generation of Renaissance humanists in Florence, wrote a learned comparison of the old and new Rome. Later, Cardinal Bessarion (a Byzantine monk who became a Roman prelate) assembled a library of precious Greek manuscripts, which he gave to the Republic of Venice.

How Much Was Lost When the Library of Alexandria Burned?

$\mathcal{N}$obody knows how many books the Library of Alexandria contained. One ancient author claims that there were two hundred thousand; another, that there were four hundred thousand. A Byzantine scholar specifies that were 400,000 books containing multiple works, 90,000 devoted to a single work, and an additional 42,800 outside the main complex—a total of 532,800. Two Roman texts record that no fewer than seven hundred thousand volumes were lost when the library burned. However many there were, they were organized by genre into eleven sections, ranging from epic poetry to law, and stored in labeled book boxes arrayed on shelves.[1]

The books in the Library of Alexandria were scrolls made from papyrus, a reed native to the Nile delta. The average height of a scroll was about ten inches. The length ranged from ten to more than eighty feet—enough for one Greek tragedy or a single book of a prose author like Thucydides. The scroll was often wrapped around a wooden or ivory rod, to which an identifying tag might be tied. The text was written as a continuous string of capital letters,* with only cursory attempts at punctuation. Scientific works were illustrated,† as were deluxe editions of literary classics.[2]

---

* Books were copied by professional scribes, who could work—according to one estimate—at the brisk pace of 250 lines (of poetry) an hour. Although a few works were copied and distributed by their authors, most were only "published" by booksellers, who had no obligation to seek an author's permission or pay him royalties.

† The Vienna Dioscurides, a late antique manuscript of a Roman work on medicinal plants, contains more than four hundred illustrations. A few other ancient manuscripts, such as the Vatican Virgil and Ambrosian Iliad, are illustrated almost as lavishly. The Roman author Varro composed a work that included no fewer than seven hundred portraits of famous men, each captioned with an epigram.

In the centuries after Aristotle assembled antiquity's first library at his school in Athens, kings, emperors, and local benefactors followed his example, establishing libraries in every corner of the classical world. By late antiquity, Rome had no fewer than twenty-eight major public libraries.* The north Italian town of Como could boast a library worth a million sestertii; the library of Timgad, on the edge of the Sahara, contained thousands of volumes. Some private libraries were even larger: one third-century scholar reportedly owned more than sixty thousand books.[3]

Established by Ptolemy I, the first Greek king of Egypt, the Library of Alexandria reached its apogee under his son and grandson—Ptolemy II and Ptolemy III—who made Egypt the richest and

The Library of Celsus at Ephesus, which held an estimated twelve thousand books. *Author's photo*

---

* Books were usually forbidden to leave ancient libraries. Aulus Gellius, however, describes one of his companions borrowing a volume of Aristotle from the local library, and Marcus Aurelius mentions bringing a few scrolls from a library in Rome with him on vacation.

most powerful of the kingdoms born from the wreckage of Alexander's empire. The library was part of the Museion, a sort of proto-university where scholars conducted research, took meals together, and—like academics of every era—bickered over points of pedantry, a habit that earned the Museion the nickname "birdcage of the Muses." It was in the Museion that the circumference of the earth was first calculated, that the standard texts of the Homeric poems were established, and—appropriately—that the first library catalog was devised. Like this research, the library was a royal prestige project, intended to burnish the reputation of the Ptolemaic regime and the young metropolis of Alexandria. Ptolemy II and Ptolemy III sent agents to scour the markets of the Greek world for manuscripts, and even compelled ships arriving in Alexandria to surrender all the books on board for copying.[4]

Under the later rulers of the Ptolemaic dynasty, however, the library began to decline. Disaster struck when Julius Caesar—who had involved himself in a civil war between Cleopatra and her brother—burned a fleet moored in Alexandria's harbor. Flames spread from the docks to the adjacent palace quarter, reaching the library. Some authors claim that only a small part of the collection was destroyed; others, that the entire library went up in flames. The fact that Mark Antony gave Cleopatra two hundred thousand books from Pergamum a few years later, presumably to replace books lost in the fire, suggests that the damage was extensive.[5]

The library's collections were apparently still substantial in the Roman imperial era: when Domitian decided to replenish the Greek libraries of Rome, he commissioned scribes to copy texts from Alexandria. The Museion, now subsidized by the Romans, continued to house and feed scholars. Claudius sponsored an expansion of the complex, and asked in return that his twenty-book history of the Etruscans be read aloud to the resident scholars once a year. During the third and fourth centuries, however, Alexandria experienced a massacre, an invasion, a civil war, and a tsunami, any of which might have destroyed the library. By the end of the fourth century, if not before, the palace quarter, in which the main library was located, was mostly abandoned.[6]

Ptolemy II had established a branch of the library, accessible to the public, in the marble porticoes surrounding the Temple of Serapis. But in 391, amid savage street warfare between Christian and pagan mobs, the temple was demolished. Although the stoas that had sheltered the library survived, we hear nothing more about the books kept there. A medieval legend attributed the final act of destruction to Caliph Omar, who supposedly ordered the scrolls to be fed into the furnaces of Alexandria's bathhouses. There were so many books, the story goes, that it took six months to burn them all.

Tragic though the destruction of the Library of Alexandria was, it should be seen in perspective. The Roman world was, by premodern standards, rich in books.* The loss of all but a tiny fraction of ancient literature during the Middle Ages was not brought about by the disappearance of a single library. It was, instead, a consequence of the basic fragility of texts before the advent of printing. Although papyrus scrolls were durable,† they had to be recopied every century or so. With the collapse of the Roman Empire, the elites who had traditionally commissioned new copies all but vanished. Far fewer manuscripts were produced, and those that were tended to serve the particular purposes of religion (Bibles, patristic texts), education (a narrow selection of classics), and the technical disciplines (philosophy and applied science). Authors who wrote in unfamiliar dialects (e.g., Sappho), on topics repugnant to the church (such as the sex manual of Philaenis), or at inordinate length (like many historians) were not recopied, and faded into oblivion.[7]

Another barrier to survival was the invention of the codex, the prototype of the modern book. From the first century onward, the

---

* In the preface of his encyclopedia, Pliny the Elder claims that he consulted two thousand works (from which he extracted some twenty thousand interesting facts). A learned guest at a second-century dinner party claimed to have read more than eight hundred Greek comedies. Individual authors might be heroically prolific: the Alexandrian scholar Didymus—nicknamed "Bronze Guts" for his inhuman work ethic—reportedly produced four thousand books. Nero's fawning courtiers urged him to indite a four-hundred-book poem.

† Pliny the Elder mentions scrolls that remained well preserved for centuries. Some of the scrolls found in the Villa of the Papyri at Herculaneum were more than three hundred years old when Vesuvius carbonized them. Alcuin of York—writing at the end of the eighth century—saw papyrus scrolls at Tours that must have been at least half a millennium old. In the humid climates of western Europe, however, few papyri were so durable.

Romans used notebooks with parchment* leaves to keep personal records and accounts. The format soon began to be employed for certain literary genres, and was adopted by the growing Christian community, which preferred codices for the ease of referencing scripture. Over the course of the third and fourth centuries, codices definitively displaced scrolls. Any text not copied to a codex by the end of antiquity was unlikely to survive the Middle Ages. Another "technological" change occurred over the course of the ninth century when, in both Greek and Latin, cumbersome ancient scripts were replaced by cursive hands that facilitated copying and reading. Texts not reproduced in the new minuscule scripts were forgotten.[8]

Since the population of manuscripts was so much smaller during the Middle Ages than it had been in antiquity,[†] a single fire could be devastating. The Crusader sack of Constantinople in 1204, for example, seems to have destroyed the last copies of dozens of ancient works that had survived to that point.[‡] The Ottoman sack of Constantinople in 1453 only claimed fewer literary victims because Byzantine scholars had already transmitted many texts to Italy. The Renaissance humanists who received, copied, and eventually printed those manuscripts determined the modern canon of classical literature.[§]

Returning to Alexandria, there can be no doubt that some rare works perished with the library. But it was only because the library's downfall coincided with a broader decline—because, in other words,

---

* Parchment was usually made from the tanned skins of sheep, goats, or cattle. A library in Constantinople contained an edition of the *Iliad* and *Odyssey* inscribed on a single snakeskin reputed to be 120 feet long. On the opposite end of the scale, incidentally, a miniature *Iliad* was once written on tiny pages and enclosed in a nutshell.

† To focus on Latin classics, five books of Livy were preserved only in a single thousand-year-old manuscript discovered at a German abbey during the sixteenth century. One eleventh-century manuscript at Monte Cassino is responsible for our knowledge of Tacitus's *Histories* and the later books of the *Annals*. The first six books of the *Annals* existed only in a manuscript found at the monastery of Corvey.

‡ Of 386 rare books read and reviewed by the Byzantine scholar Photius in the ninth century, no fewer than 211 are now partially or completely lost. Most of those losses probably occurred during the sack of 1204 and the terrible fire that preceded it.

§ The Renaissance enthusiasm for ancient texts was so great that a few were invented. At the age of twenty, Leon Battista Alberti wrote a Latin comedy that circulated for centuries as a genuine Roman work. Annius of Viterbo fabricated a whole series of "rediscovered" classical texts to support his eccentric vision of ancient history.

all the ancient world's libraries fell into decay during late antiquity—
that so much of the knowledge it once contained has been lost. The
scrolls in the Library of Alexandria did not contain the bases, as
is sometimes claimed, for great technological advances. Although
there were many scientific works in the library, the most important
of these were widely disseminated. What vanished with the library
were abstruse monographs and cumbersome commentaries, unread
epics and dead philosophies, the knowing nods and navel gazing
of a sophisticated literary culture. These works would be a treasure
beyond price for scholars of the classics, but they were not the substance of a foreclosed modernity.

How Much Do We Know about the Ancient Greeks and Romans?

$\mathcal{N}$inety-nine percent of the literature written in ancient Greek and Latin has vanished. We have 7 of the 120 tragedies written by Sophocles, 1 of Menander's 108 comedies, and none of the four thousand books scribbled by the prolific Alexandrian scholar Didymus. Yet despite such dramatic losses, a remarkable number of classical texts survive. Besides the familiar works still featured on school curriculums, we have descriptions of steam-driven machinery, a dream interpretation manual, grimoires, obscene poetry, proto–science fiction, and much more. There are about 550 novel-sized volumes in the Loeb Classical Library, which assembles the best-known works of Greek and Latin literature. Migne's *Patrologia*, the most comprehensive collection of early Christian literature, includes some 160 huge volumes of works written before 600 CE. The extant works of Galen alone contain more than three million words.*

Although the oldest copy of most ancient works is a medieval manuscript, a remarkable number of physical texts date back to antiquity. There are nearly two thousand extant Latin manuscripts written before the year 800. The core collection of the Vatican Library, which may date back to the fourth century, contains such treasures as the Vatican Virgil, an illustrated late antique edition of the greatest Roman poet. The oldest known Latin manuscript, a

---

* The word count for all extant Greek literature written before 200 CE is about nineteen million. For Greek literature of late antiquity—the third to the seventh centuries—the number is over seventy million.

A page from the Vatican Virgil, with an illustration depicting the death of Laocoön. *Wikimedia Commons*

fragment from the Augustan era, contains the verses of a poet* who was probably still alive when it was written.[1]

Egypt's arid climate has preserved vast numbers of papyri, containing texts of every conceivable kind. In addition to literary works ranging from apocryphal Gospels to the poems of Sappho, we have

---

* A papyrus dated to the fourth century BCE preserves part of a tragedy written by Timotheus of Miletus only a few decades earlier. As might be expected, there are more autograph manuscripts from the Byzantine period; the original of Eustathius's great commentary on Homer's *Odyssey*, for example, can be found at the Bibliotheca Marciana in Venice. Intriguingly, there was a brisk ancient trade in first editions. Lucian mentions the sale of a (probably spurious) autograph copy of a famous work on rhetoric. Scrolls artificially "aged" by being buried in grain were sometimes offered on the Roman market as genuine antiques.

letters and petitions, contracts and wills, disputes between landlords and tenants, tax receipts, and even the minutes of trials.* About 650 volumes of transcribed and translated papyri have been published over the past century, but these represent only a tiny fraction of the total. Between 1896 and 1907, for example, a British team recovered more than a half a million papyri, most in tiny fragments, from ancient dumps around the town of Oxyrhynchus. Although eighty-six thick volumes have been published,† 98 percent of these papyri remain in their boxes at Oxford, waiting to be edited.[2]

An even more tantalizing source of new texts came to light in 1752, when diggers tunneling through the remains of a Roman mansion just outside Herculaneum began to encounter lumps of what appeared to be charcoal. Only gradually, and after several had been burned as fuel, were the lumps identified as scrolls, carbonized by the eruption of Vesuvius. In the Villa of the Papyri—as the mansion came to be called—some scrolls were discovered in the charred remains of a cabinet, and others in three carrying cases. But the vast majority were found in a small room lined with wooden shelves.‡ Although there were a few fragmentary Latin texts, the majority

---

* Theft is the most common crime reported in papyri. One man went away to a funeral and returned to find his house stripped bare. Another, at home when he was robbed, was beaten by the burglars when he tried to stop them. Yet another man identified the thieves who ransacked his house as his ex-wife and mother-in-law. Thieves entered one dwelling by carefully drawing nails from the door. A less subtle pair used a log to batter down a bricked-up window. A (probably fictional) fourth-century papyrus describes the murder of a prostitute by a powerful member of the Alexandrian city council. Despite the efforts of his cronies, the councilman is arrested and brought to trial. He has a dramatic confrontation with the prostitute's elderly mother, confesses to the crime, and is sentenced to death by beheading.

† Literary highlights include Aristotle's *Constitution of Athens*, the sole surviving comedy of Menander, a satyr play by Sophocles, and the mysterious Oxyrhynchus historian.

‡ Initial efforts to open the scrolls involved chopping them in half lengthwise and peeling back layers from the inside. As might be imagined, this succeeded only in destroying many of them. Fortunately, after a few years of butchery, the scrolls were entrusted to Father Antonio Piaggio, a scholar from the Vatican Library who devised an ingenious machine that unrolled the scrolls using weights on strings. Though effective, the process was painfully slow: over forty-four years of work, Piaggio managed to unroll only seventeen papyri. After Piaggio's death, his machine was used to at least partially unroll (if not necessarily decipher) more than two hundred of the best-preserved scrolls. Other papyri were doused in chemicals, blasted with gases, sliced, diced, and pulverized in various attempts to read them. Efforts are currently underway to "virtually unwrap" the scrolls using modern imaging technology and software.

of the scrolls proved to be Greek philosophical treatises, almost all associated with the Epicurean school. A remarkable number were works of Philodemus of Gadara—so many, that scholars now believe the room in which most of the scrolls were found to have been the working library of Philodemus himself. The villa's main library, containing a much wider range of Greek and Latin literature, may still await discovery.

Inscriptions provide another major category of evidence. Despite a literacy rate that hovered around 10 percent, writing was everywhere in classical cities—tombstones, milestones, monuments, stele, and graffiti. The epigraphic habit reached its apogee in the Roman imperial era, when it produced texts as diverse as a twenty-five-thousand-word summary of Epicurean philosophy and a 110-line epitaph for a 110-year-old man. Although only about 5 percent of the inscriptions carved during the Roman era still exist, the surviving numbers are impressive. The largest collection of Roman inscriptions, the *Corpus Inscriptionum Latinarum*, includes about 180,000 examples. But this is far from a complete count. It has been estimated that more than three hundred thousand Latin inscriptions have been discovered since the Renaissance, including nearly one hundred thousand from the city of Rome alone. To these must be added something like four hundred thousand Greek inscriptions from the eastern provinces.[3]

Even the number of inscriptions, however, pales beside the awesome quantity of the numismatic evidence.* Although the survival ratio for ancient coins has been estimated at between 1/1000 and 1/5000, huge numbers are still extant. The Reka Devnia Hoard included more than one hundred thousand denarii. An incredible three hundred thousand third-century Roman coins were uncovered near the Croatian village of Komin. Afghanistan's Mir Zakah Hoard contained an estimated five hundred thousand Greek, Greco-Bactrian, and Indo-Greek coins. As many as ten million coins from the ancient Greek world may still exist. The number of extant Roman coins is in the hundreds of millions.

---

* Coins tell us a great deal about classical history. Their legends and iconography proclaim political policies, their metal content tracks fiscal health, and their distribution in hoards provides invaluable information about the operations of the ancient economy.

Manuscripts, papyri, inscriptions, and coins represent only part of our evidence for the classical world. Add the dozens of shipwrecks discovered in recent years, the hundreds of excavations currently in progress, and the hundreds of thousands of artifacts already in museums and private collections, and it becomes clear that, while there are many things that we do not know about the ancient Greeks and Romans, and many things that we will never know, we know more now than ever before—and we're learning more all the time.

Notes

A NOTE ABOUT THE NOTES

*W*henever possible, I've cited primary sources. Thanks to the magic of the internet, the works of every major classical author are only a few keystrokes away, often in good English translations. Do yourself the favor of exploring them.

The citations are couched in the arcane abbreviations beloved of classicists. But fear not! Wherever possible, they follow the conventions of the Oxford Classical Dictionary, which are helpfully listed online: https://oxfordre.com/classics/page/abbreviation-list/#1.

PREFACE

1. Plutarch: *Quaest. Rom.* 6 (*Mor.* 265B–E). Hercules: *NA* 1.1.

CHAPTER 1

1. Homer's heroes: e.g., *Od.* 10.358–63. Hundreds of baths: Plin., *HN* 36.121; the Regionaries enumerate nearly nine hundred baths in Rome.
2. Hours for the sick: SHA, *Hadr.* 22.7. Wounded should avoid the pools: Celsus, *Med.* 5.26.28. Commodus: SHA, *Comm.* 11.5. Retinue of slaves: e.g., Amm. Marc. 28.4.19. Entry fee: e.g., Sen., *Ep.* 86.9.

3. Water from the Dead Sea: Galen, *De Simp. Medicament. Facultatibus* 4.20.
4. Villa on the Tiber: Cic., *Cael.* 36. Naked Greeks: e.g., Cic., *Tusc.* 4.70. Aristocratic Roman lady: Gell., *NA* 10.3. Cato: Plut., *Cato Mai.* 20.5. Women bathing with men: e.g., Plin., *HN* 33.153. Repeatedly banned: SHA, *Hadr.* 18, *Marc.* 23, *Alex. Sev.* 24. Justinian: *Cod. Iust.* 5.15, 11.2.
5. Garments in the baths: Mart. 3.87. Girlfriend: ibid. 3.51. Leather girdles: ibid. 7.35. Bathing costume: SHA, *Alex. Sev.* 42.1. Curse tablet: *Tab. Sulis* 32. Abundant literary references: e.g., Mart. 7.35; Plin., *HN* 29.26.

CHAPTER 2

1. Bacchus as god of all intoxication: Diod. Sic. 3.73, 4.2. Barbarians deprived of his blessings: Julius Africanus, *Cesti* 1.19. Angry Pannonians: Cass. Dio 49.36.
2. Armenian beer: Xen., *An.* 4.5.27. German beer: Tac., *Germ.* 23. Beer foam good for the skin: Plin., *HN* 22.164. Aristotle: Ath. 10.447. Dioscorides: 5.87–88. Julian: *Anth. Pal.* 9.365.
3. Beer in Gaul: e.g., Dion. Hal., *Ant. Rom.* 13.10; Plin., *HN* 14.149. Aurochs horns: Caes., *BGall.* 6.28. Fill me with beer: *CIL* XIII 10012. Beer in Egypt: e.g., Hdt. 2.77; Diod. Sic. 1.34. Alexandrian diet: Gal., *Hipp. Aph.* 2.20.
4. While I lived, I drank: *ILS* 2238. Letter: *Tab. Vindol.* III.628. Retired soldiers as brewers: e.g., *AE* 1928.183.
5. Price Edict: II.11–12. Drinker of beer: Amm. Marc. 26.8.2. Slave for a wine jar: Diod. Sic. 5.26. Gallic vineyards: e.g., Auson., *Mos.* 161–68.
6. Anthimus, *De observatione ciborum ad Theodoricum regem Francorum epistula*, 15.

CHAPTER 3

1. Sweat lodges: Hdt. 4.73–75; cf. 1.202.
2. Helen's opium: Hom., *Od.* 4.219–29. Poppies widely grown: e.g., Plin., *HN* 18.61. Preparations of opium: e.g., Plin., *HN* 20.200. Marcus Aurelius: Gal., *Ant.* 1.1, 2.9; Cass. Dio 71.6. Opium fatal: Dioscorides 4.64. Euthanasia: Plin., *HN* 20.199.
3. Sensation of warmth: Oribasius, *Coll. med.* 4.20, 4.31. Diminished sex drive: Dioscorides 3.148; Gal. 12.8 K; cf. Plin., *HN* 20.259.
4. Laughter: Plin., *HN* 24.164. Hempseed at banquets: Gal. 6.54 K.

CHAPTER 4

1. Dream interpretation: Artem. 1.79. Hippias's lament: Hdt. 6.107.
2. Augustus: Suet., *Aug.* 79.2. Nero: Suet., *Vesp.* 5.5. Agathocles: Diod. Sic. 21.16.4. Henbane: Scr. Largus 54. Sweet figs and rotten teeth: [Arist.], *Problemata* 22.14. Corrosive humors: Gal., *Comp. Med. Loc.* 5. Vulture and porcupine quills: Plin., *HN* 30.27. Mastic wood: Mart. 6.74, 14.22. Toothpicks as gifts: e.g., Mart. 7.53.
3. Pumice: Plin., *HN* 36.156. Messalina: Scr. Largus 60. Sheep sweat: Plin., *HN* 29.38. Wolf head: Plin., *HN* 28.178. Urine as mouthwash: Strabo 3.4.16; Diod. Sic. 5.33.5; Catull. 39.17–21. Bad breath: e.g., Mart. 3.28, 6.93. Honey-soaked wool: Plin., *HN* 29.31. Mouse ash: ibid. 30.27. Unmixed wine: ibid. 28.56. Mankind prone to bad breath: ibid. 11.277. Mad dogs: ibid. 30.21. Horns of snails: ibid. 30.24. Boiled frogs: ibid. 32.80.
4. Dentistry in Classical Greece: e.g., [Hippoc.], *Art.* 32. Filing teeth: Paulus Aegineta 6.28. Lancing gums: Oribasius, *Coll. Med.* 17.1. Risks of extraction: e.g., Celsus, *Med.* 7.12. Spring in Susa: Vitr. 8.3.23. Earthworm: Plin., *HN* 30.23. Rejuvenated teeth: Plin., *HN* 11.167. Tooth doctors: e.g., Mart. 10.56. Extraction process: e.g., Celsus, *Med.* 7.12. Teeth in Roman Forum: M. J. Becker, "Dentistry in Ancient Rome," *International Journal of Anthropology* 29 (2014): 209–26.
5. Gold wire: e.g., Celsus, *Med.* 7.12. Law against burying gold: Cic., *Leg.* 2.24. Roman dentures: e.g., Hor., *Sat.* 1.847–50; Mart. 1.72, 2.41, 9.38. Personified tooth powder: Mart. 14.56.
6. Skeletons at Herculaneum: Estelle Lazer, *Resurrecting Pompeii* (New York: Routledge, 2009), 168–79. Children brushing their teeth: *C. Gloss. Lat.* III, 379, 74f.

CHAPTER 5

1. Tattoos of Thracian women: e.g., Hdt. 5.6.2. Tattoos in Roman Egypt: Sext. Emp., *Pyr.* 3.202. Xenophon: *Anab.* 5.4.32. Syrian worshippers: e.g., Luc., *Syr. D.* 59. Israelites: *Lev.* 19.28.
2. Alexander: Curt. 5.5.6. Thebans: Hdt. 7.233. Hellespont: Hdt. 7.35.
3. Plato's Laws: 854D. Slave lover: Herod. 5.65–67, 77–79. Whore of Babylon: *Rev.* 17.5. Horse of Syracuse: Plut., *Nic.* 29.2; cf. *Per.* 26.4. Artemisia: Vitr. 2.8.15.
4. Caligula: Suet., *Calig.* 27.3. Fake tattoos: Petron. 103.1–5, 105.11–106.1. Constantine: *Cod. Theod.* 9.40.2. Theophilus: Zonaras 3.409.

5. Tattooing recruits: Veg., *Mil* 1.8, 2.5. Workers in arms factories: *Cod. Theod.* 10.22.4. Medical treatise: Aetius 8.12.

6. Epidaurus: *IG* IV² 1.121.48–54. Removing tattoos: e.g., Plin., *HN* 25.173; Scr. Largus 231; Aetius 8.12. Covering tattoos: e.g., Mart. 2.29.9–10; Lib. 25.21.

7. Carpocratians: Irenaeus, *Her.* 1.25.6; Epip., *Pan.* 27.5. Epimenides: *Suda*, s.v. Epimenides. Ptolemy IV: Plut., *De ad. et am.* 56E. Christian tattoos: e.g., Procop., *Comm. In Isaiam* 44.5. Heretical monk: Victor Vit. 2.2. Macrina: Greg. Nyss., *V. Macr.* 992A–C.

8. Maurice and the Turks: Theoph. Sim., 5.10.13–15. Images of Alexander: e.g., Joh. Chrys., *Hom.* 26.

CHAPTER 6

1. Pompeii graffiti: *CIL* IV 10529, 4966, 4342, 8356.

2. Divorce cases: Sen., *Ben.* 3.16. Nero's Amphitheater: Tac., *Ann.* 3.31.

3. Rain of dirt: Plin., *HN* 8.61. Dog: ibid. 7.53. Brawl: ibid. 2.57. Architect: Cass. Dio 57.21.

4. Parody: Petron. 53.

5. Wounded at heart: Quint., *Inst.* 9.4.17.

6. The gazette in your ear: Sen., *Controv.* 2.1.35. Olus Granius: *ILS* 1932.

7. The gazette in the provinces: e.g., Tac., *Ann.* 16.22. Overnight messenger: Cic., *Rosc. Am.* 19. Death of Nero: *OGIS* 669. No place on earth: *Sull.* 43.

CHAPTER 7

1. Storm at sea: Ath. 8.338B.

2. Exciting pipes: e.g., Philostr., *VA* 5.21.

3. Nero: Suet., *Ner.* 41.2. Titus: Suet., *Tit.* 3. Hadrian: SHA, *Hadr.* 14.

4. Pipe strike: Livy 9.30. Slave musicians in Roman houses: Cic., *Rosc. Am.* 45, 134; Gell., *NA* 19.9.3–5; Sen., *Prov.* 3.10. Orchestral performances: Sen., *Ep.* 84.9; Ath. V 205F; SHA, *Carin.* 19.

5. Refusing to play for Augustus: Hor., *Sat.* 1.3.1–8. Theater of Pompey: Mart. 14.166. Professional applauders: Mart. 4.5.8.

6. Slabs of lead: Suet., *Ner.* 20, 25. Tall harp: Ath. IV 183E. Connoisseurs: Cic., *Acad. Pr.* 2.7.20.

7. Princeps: Phaedrus 5.7. Mesomedes's "Hymn to Nemesis" is especially well known; you can find recordings online.

8. Expulsion of the pantomimes: Cass. Dio 57.21; cf. Tac., *Ann.* 4.4.

CHAPTER 8

1. *ILS* 5177; cf. *CIL* VI 18324, 21846, 33929.

2. Augustus: Suet., *Aug.* 85. Claudius: Suet., *Claud.* 42. Hadrian: SHA, *Hadr.* 25.9–10. Philosopher: Diog. Laert. 2.115. Spirits: [Pl.], *Ax.* 371c–d.

3. School for palace slaves: e.g., *ILS* 1825–36. Free schools: e.g., *Syll.*³ 577, 578; *ILS* 2927. Municipal teachers: e.g., August., *Conf.* 6.7. Busts of authors: Juv. 7.226–27. Wall maps: Pan. Lat. 4.20.

4. Teacher who drafted wills: *ILS* 7763. Teachers exempt from taxes: *Dig.* 50.4.18, 27.1.6. Dionysius: Cic., *Tusc.* 3.27. Disgraced senators: Suet., *Gramm.* 28; Plin., *Ep.* 4.11. Demonstration of skills: *Cod. Theod.* 13.3.5. Sheep teeth: Gell., *NA* 16.6.1.

5. Harsh discipline: e.g., Mart. 10.62.8–10; Auson., *Protr.* 12–34. Roman summer vacation: Mart. 10.62.

6. Early Greek education: e.g., Ar., *Nub.* 961–83. Learning the alphabet: Quint. 1.1.24. Models of the letters: ibid. 1.1.26. Herodes and his twenty-four slaves: Philostr., VS 558.

7. Our two languages: *Carm.* 3.8.5. Greek nannies: Quint. 1.1.12–14. Augustine: *Conf.* 1.14, 23. Theology of numbers: Phot., *Bib.* 187.

8. Homer as educator of Greece: Pl., *Resp.* 10.606. Memorizing Homer: e.g., Xen, *Symp.* 3.5. Recitations: *Syll.*³ 959, 960. Criticizing Homer: Pl., *Resp.* 377a–92b. Alcibiades: Plut., *Alc.* 7. The grammarian's task: Quint. 1.4.2.

9. Moralizing Homer: e.g., Plut., *De aud. poet.* 18 F.

10. Second homes, papyrus: Philostr., *VS* 603. Artificial islands: ibid. 606. Polemon: ibid. 532–44.

11. Suasoriae: Sen., *Suas.* 3, 1, 6. Controversiae: Sen., *Controv.* 1.3.

12. Endowed professorships: Suet., *Vesp.* 18; Cass. Dio 72.31. University of Constantinople: *Cod. Theod.* 14.9.3. Rowdy at the races: Lib., *Or.* 1.37–38; *Dig.* 3.1.5. Pranks: Lib., *Or.* 58. Hazing: Greg. Naz., *Or.* 43.16. Wild parties: e.g., *Cod. Theod.* 14.9.1.

13. Gal., *Lib. Prop.* 11–18.

14. Traditional legal education: e.g., Cic., *Brut.* 306. Beirut curriculum: Justinian, *Omnem reipublicae* 2–6.

15. Athens and Jerusalem: Tert., *Praescr.* 7; cf. Jer., *Ep.* 22, 30. Julian's ban: *Cod. Theod.* 13.3.5. Reworking the Bible: Soc., *HE* 3.16. Basil: *Hom.* 22.

CHAPTER 9

1. *Hou Hanshu* 88, 12.

2. Frogs around a pond: *Phd.* 109a–b. Knowledge of the world in classical Greece: e.g., Hdt. 3.106–16.

3. Spherical earth recognized: e.g., Pl., *Phd.* 108e–109a, Arist., *Mete.* 296b–97b. Sailing around the globe: Arist., *Mete.* 362b. Earth's shadow: Arist., *Cael.* 297b. Christian scholars: e.g., Lactant., *Div. inst.* 3.24; Cosmas Indikopleustes 2.

4. Flying snakes: Hdt. 3.106f. Roman campaign: Strabo 16.4.22–24; Plin., *HN* 6.160–62.

5. Mountains of the Moon: Ptol., *Geog.* 4.8.2. Roman army in Nubia: Plin., *HN* 6.181–82. Nero's expedition: Sen., *QNat.* 6.8.3–5; Plin., *HN* 6.181, 184–86.

6. Crossing the Atlas: Plin., *HN* 5.14–15. Roman merchant: Ptol., *Geog.* 1.8.4, 4.9.2. Heads in their chests: Plin., *HN* 5.46. Dog king: Ael., *NA* 7.40.

7. Polybius: Plin., *HN* 5.9. Volcano: *Peripl. Han.* 16. Gorillas: *Peripl. Han.* 18; cf. Plin., *HN* 6.200.

8. Canary Islands: Plin., *HN* 6.202–5. Madeira: Plut., *Sert.* 8. Continent in the west: e.g., Arist., *Mete.* 354a.

9. Demetrius: Plut., *De def. or.* 18. Circumnavigation: Tac., *Agr.* 10.

10. Pytheas on Thule: e.g., Strabo 2.4.1–2, 4.5.5. Procopius on Thule: *Goth.* 6.15.4–13. Incredible tales: Phot., *Bib.* 166.

11. Pytheas: e.g., Plin., *HN* 37.35. Roman fleet: Plin., *HN* 2.167. Amber for Nero: Plin., *HN* 37.45. East of the Baltic: Tac., *Germ.* 46.

12. Herodotus: 4.1ff. Anacharsis: e.g., Hdt. 4.76–77. Troops in northern Iran: Tac., *Hist.* 1.6.

13. Soldiers of Crassus: Plin., *HN* 6.47. Shape of the Caspian: Ptol., *Geog.* 5.8.6–7 (though misconceptions endured—see Plin., *HN* 6.15). Hyperboreans: e.g., Plin., *HN* 4.89. Ice: Plin., *HN* 4.104; Tac., *Germ.* 45.

14. Eudoxus: Strabo 2.3.4. Monsoon winds: *Peripl. M. Eux.* 57. 120 ships: Strabo 2.5.12. The temple of Augustus is marked on the Peutinger Map. Roman knowledge of Indochina: Ptol., *Geog.* 7.2.

15. Fair-haired Chinese: Plin., *HN* 6.24. Syrian merchant: Ptol., *Geog.* 1.12.7–8. Merchant with escort: *Liang-shu*, 48.

16. Acrobats: *Shiji*, 123. The Xian Stele is the most vivid evidence for Nestorians in China. The name of the artist at Miran was actually "Tita," the Sanskrit transliteration of Titus. Aurel Stein—the archaeologist who discovered the fresco and inscription—could only guess at the circumstances that brought a man with a Roman name to the deserts of western China.

CHAPTER 10

1. Menander: Strabo 11.11.1; Plut., *Mor.* 821d.
2. Pliny's complaint: *HN* 12.84.
3. Greek comedy set in India: *POxy.* 413. Indians in Alexandria: Ptol., *Geog.* 1.17. Buddhist ascetic: Dio Chrys., *Or.* 32.40.
4. First mention of the Buddha: Clem. Al., Strom. 1.15. Founder of a sect of gymnosophists: Jer., *Adv. Iovinian.* 1.42. Pyrrho of Elis: Diog. Laert. 9.61; cf. Paus. 4.32.4; Ael., *VH* 4.20.

CHAPTER 11

1. Suet., *Iul.* 88.
2. Heliocentric speculation: Archim., *Aren.* 4–5. For a defense of the geocentric system, see Ptol., *Alm.* 1.1–8. Aristotle on the sun: e.g., *Mete.* 340a–41a.
3. Characteristics of the planets: e.g., Ptol., *Tetr.* 1.4–7. Characteristics of the signs of the Zodiac: e.g., Manil. 2.270–432.
4. Influence of the stars: e.g., Ptol., *Tetr.* 1.2. Critiques of astrology: e.g., Gell., *NA* 14.1. Astrology as applied astronomy: Ptol., *Tetr.* 1.1–3; cf. Plin., *HN* 7.50. Thrasyllus: Suet., *Tib.* 14.4. Balbillus: Suet., *Ner.* 36.1. Augustus: Suet., *Aug.* 94.12; Cass. Dio 56.25. Hadrian: SHA, *Hadr.* 16.7. Septimius Severus: SHA, *Sev.* 3.9.
5. Firm. Mat. 8.25, 28.
6. Gong: Sext. Emp., *Math.* 5.27.
7. Expulsions of philosophers: e.g., Tac., *Ann.* 2.32, 12.52; Cass. Dio 66.9.2. Christian opposition: e.g., August., *De civ. D.* 5.1–7.

CHAPTER 12

1. Amm. Marc. 17.4.
2. Mycenae: Paus. 2.15.4–2.16.7. Tiryns: Paus. 2.25.8. Pelasgians: e.g., Hdt. 6.137.
3. Theseus: Plut., *Cim.* 8; Thes. 36. Numa: Plut., *Num.* 22.4–5. Vespasian's vases: Suet., *Vesp.* 7.3. Agesilaus: Plut., *Mor.* 577A–78A.
4. Criticism of Egyptian gods: e.g., Juv. 15. Criticism of Egyptians: e.g., Amm. Marc. 22.16.23. A land filled with wonders: Hdt. 2.35.

5. Criticism of Pyramids: Plin., *HN* 36.75, 78. Watching villagers: Plin. *HN* 36.76. Achievements of a Roman governor: Cass. Dio 53.23.

6. Egyptian monarchy—Herodotus: 2.142. Diodorus: 1.44.1. Pliny the Elder: 7.193. Age of the Pyramids—Herodotus: 2.112f, 2.145. Diodorus: 1.62.1, 1.63.5. Rhodopis: Diod. Sic. 1.64.11; Strabo 17.33; Plin., *HN* 36.82. (Herodotus knew better: 2.134.)

7. Symbolic hieroglyphs: e.g., Tac., *Ann.* 11.14. Fantastic tale: Tac., *Ann.* 2.60.

CHAPTER 13

1. Seneca on the world's end: *QNat.* 3.27–30. Nature's secrets: *QNat.* 7.25.4–5; 7.30.5.

2. Hes., *Op.* 109–201; among many other imitations, see Ov., *Met.* 1.89–150.

3. Polyb. 6.4–9; compare Pl., *Leg.* 677A–81D. Heraclitus: Diog. Laert. 9.7–9. Empedocles: Diog. Laert. 8.76. Stoics: e.g., Nemesius, *De nat. hom.* 38.

4. List of inventions: Plin., *HN* 7.191–215; compare Lucr. 5.925–1357, 1448–57.

5. For descriptions of the golden age, or age of Saturn, see e.g., Verg., *Aen.* 8.314–27; Tib. 1.3.35–52. The most famous evocation of the new golden age is Verg., *Ecl.* 4.

6. Rejected precise predictions: August., *De civ. D* 20. Prophecy: *Dan.* 2:31–45. Justinian as the Antichrist: Procop., *Anec.* 12.14–32.

CHAPTER 14

1. Agath. 5.7–8.

2. Carthaginian handbook: Plin., *HN* 18.22; cf. Varro, *Rust.* 1.18.8. Cicero: *Tusc.* 1.1.2. Vallus: Plin., *HN* 18.296; Palladius, *De re rust.* 7.2.1–4.

3. Rio Tinto: J. G. Landels, *Engineering in the Ancient World* (Berkeley: University of California Press, 2000), 69–70. Spanish silver mine: Plin., *HN* 33.97.

4. Early mentions of mills: Vitr. 10.5; Strabo 12.556.

5. Aeolipile: Heron, *Pneum.* 2.11.

6. Impracticality of the aeolipile: Landels, *Engineering in the Ancient World*, 29. Philo of Byzantium explicitly refers to the discovery of formulae

governing the power and range of artillery discovered by repeated experiments financed by the Ptolemies (*Belopoeica* 50.3). Cf. invention of the catapult (Diod. Sic. 14.41–42). Compare Hero and Archimedes (Plut., Marc. 14–19).

7. Banausic: e. g. Arist., *Pol.* 1337b. Seneca's disdain: *Ep.* 90.25–26; cf. Plut., *Marc.* 17.3–5; Cic., *Off.* 1.150–51. Tiberius: Plin., *HN* 36.195; cf. Petron. 51; Cass. Dio 57.21. Vespasian: Suet., *Vesp.* 18.

CHAPTER 15

1. First Nero: Tac., *Hist.* 2.8–9. Second Nero: Cass. Dio 66.19.3. Third Nero: Suet., *Ner.* 57.2.

2. Two slaves: Plin., *Ep.* 10.29. Escaped slave: Plin., *Ep.* 10.74. Cicero's slave: Cic., *Fam.* 5.9, 5.10a, 13.77.3. Workhouses: e.g., Quint., *Inst.* 7.4.14. Tattooed steward: Scr. Largus 231.

3. Penalty for pretending to be a citizen: e.g., Suet., *Claud.* 25.3. Records of Christ's birth: Justin, *Apol.* 1.34. Vaults under the Hippodrome: Lydus, *Mag.* 160–63.

4. Papyrus: *POxy* 1022. Tattoos: Veg., *Mil.* 1.8, 2.5.

5. Saint Paul: *Acts* 22.25–29. Claudius: Suet., *Claud.* 16.2.

6. Petronia Iusta: the evidence is recorded in the eighteen *Tabulae Herculanenses* discovered in the peristyle of the House of the Bicentenary. Cf. the case of Sempronia Gemella: *P. Mich.* III.169.

7. Archias: Cic., *Arch.*, esp. 4, 11. Titus Flavius Longus: *CPL* 102.

8. Distinguishing free man from slave: *Dig.* 18.1.5. I am a Roman citizen: Cic., *II Verr.* 5.147.

CHAPTER 16

1. Rich freedman: Plin., *HN* 33.135. Crassus: Plin., *HN* 33.134; Plut., *Crass.* 2.2–6.

2. Using bankers to transfer money: e.g., Cic., *Fam.* 2.17.4, *Att.* 7.18.4. Safes were discovered in the House of the Vettii and the House of Obellius Firmus at Pompeii. Million sestertii: Suet., *Galb.* 8.1 (probably in the form of 10,000 aurei). In a letter to Atticus, Cicero mentions that he has 600,000 sestertii at home, though this presumably refers to a combination of cash and easily salable assets (*Att.* 12.25.1). Caesar's laws: Cass. Dio 41.37.3.

3. Melania: Pall., *Hist. Laus.* 61.5. 3 million sestertii: Mart. 4.37 (this figure included rents from both urban and rural properties). Cicero the slumlord: Cic., *Att.* 14.9.1. Adding heated baths: Plin., *HN* 26.16. Freedman: *CIL* VI 29791.

4. Risk of fire: Gell., *NA* 15.1. Estate worth 5 million: Cic., *Rosc. Am.* 2.6. Caesar's housing crash: Cic., *Att.* 7.17, 10.8.

5. Cato: Plut., *Cat. Mai.* 21.6. 7 million sestertii: *PVindob.* G40822.

6. Brutus: Cic., *Att.* 5.21, 6.1–3. Seneca: Cass. Dio 62.21; cf. Val. Max. 4.8.3.

7. Credit crisis under Tiberius: Tac., *Ann.* 6.16. Domitian: Suet., *Dom.* 7.2.

CHAPTER 18

1. Twisting and tangled: Tac., *Ann.* 15.38; cf. Livy 40.5. Blaming the Gauls: Livy 5.55. Eight feet wide: Varro, *Ling.* 7.15; cf. *Cod. Iust.* 8.10.12 (the streets were, however, often blocked with stalls: Mart. 7.61).

2. Rome's slippery and muddy streets: e.g., Juv. 3.247; Mart. 3.36, 5.22, 7.61. Nero's sunny streets: Tac., *Ann.* 15.43. Caligula: Suet., *Vesp.* 5.3. Juvenal walking in Rome: 3.244–48.

3. Heavy carts rattling the sewers: Plin., *HN* 36.106. Caesar's law: *CIL* I 593.56–67. Rental cabs: e.g., *CIL* X 1064, 4660. Ban on riding horses: Suet., *Claud.* 25.2; cf. SHA, *Marc.* 23.8. Heaviest carts: SHA, *Hadr.* 22.6. Carriages of the elite: e.g., Cass. Dio 76.4; SHA, *Alex. Sev.* 43.1; Amm. Marc. 14.6.

4. Traffic kept to the right: Eric Poehler, *The Traffic Systems of Pompeii* (New York: Oxford University Press, 2017), 220f. Traffic tickets: *CIL* I 594.104; cf. *Dig.* 18.6.13–14. Turn at the big fig: Ter., *Ad.* 573–84. Venus Lane: *CIL* IV 8356.

5. Slipping: e.g., Tac., *Hist.* 2.88; Mart. 5.22, 8.75. Wagons: *Dig.* 9.2.52.2. Crushed to death: Suet., *Iul.* 39.

6. Roar of traffic: e.g., Plin., *Ep.* 1.9.7, 3.5.14. Stray pig: Hor., *Epod.* 2.2.75. Funeral: Hor., *Sat.* 1.6.42–44. Noise at night: e.g., Plin., *HN* 26.111; Juv. 3.232.

CHAPTER 19

1. Private bath: Fronto, *Ep.* 263.41. Large public bath: *CIL* XIV 98. Aqueduct in Nicomedia: Plin., *Ep.* 10.37. Aqua Marcia: Frontin., *Aq.* 7.

Anio Novus and Claudia: Plin., *HN* 36.122. Aqueduct sources: Vitr. 8.1. Subiaco dams: Front., *Aq.* 94.

2. The Romans understood the siphon principle: Vitr. 8.6–7; Plin., *HN* 31.57. Disoriented tunnelers: *CIL* VIII 2728.

3. Danger of lead pipes: Vitr. 8.6.10–11.

4. Cirta nymphaeum: *ILS* 4921b.

5. Calix regulations: Frontin., *Aq.* 105–7.

6. Maintenance staff: Frontin., *Aq.* 116–17, 121.

7. The scale of Rome's aqueducts: Frontin., *Aq.* 16; Plin., *HN* 36.123. Fountains connected to multiple aqueducts: Frontin., *Aq.* 87. Marcia and Alsietina: Frontin., *Aq.* 7,11, 92. Nero in the springs: Tac., *Ann.* 14.22.

CHAPTER 20

1. Apollinaris: *CIL* IV 10619.

2. Vile sponge: Sen., *Ep.* 70.20; cf. Mart. 12.48.7.

3. Latrine demon: *Acta Pauli et Theclae* 7.

CHAPTER 21

1. Ancient comments on greatness of Roman roads: Plin., *HN* 36.75; Strabo 5.3.8.

2. A first-century poet (Stat., *Silv.* 4.3.40–49; cf. Procop., *Goth.* 14.6–11) describes the construction of the Via Domitiana, a shortcut along the Appia between Sinuessa and Puteoli. Causeway in swamp: e.g., Tac., *Ann.* 1.63. Roads unpaved outside cities: noted by Livy 41.27.5.

3. Galen's praise of Trajan's road building: *MM* 9.8.

4. Repair costs: *ILS* 5875. Replacing limestone with basalt: *CIL* X 6854.

CHAPTER 22

1. Poppaea: Tac., *Ann.* 16.6. The Christian rejection of cremation: e.g., Min. Fel., *Oct.* 11.

2. Regulations on burial within the city: Plut., *Quaest. Rom* 79; *Dig.* 47.12.3.5.

CHAPTER 23

1. Plato's earring: Sext. Emp., *Math* 1.258. The trial and death of Socrates are immortalized in Plato's *Apology* and *Phaedo*.
2. *Ti.* 20d–25e.
3. *Criti.* 108c–121c.
4. Strabo reports the comment (2.3.6), which he later attributes to Aristotle (13.1.36), that Atlantis was destroyed by its creator—i.e., Plato. Late antique commentary: Procl., *In Ti.* 75.26ff.
5. In the dialogue *Gorgias*, Plato has Socrates repeatedly describe a contrived myth about the judgment of souls as "true" (523a, 524b).
6. John V. Luce, *The End of Atlantis* (London: Thames & Hudson, 1969). Sacrificial bulls: *Criti.* 119d–e.
7. Atalante: Thuc. 3.89. Helike: Strabo 8.7.2; Paus. 7.24.6–13. Cycles of destruction are a recurring motif in Plato's dialogues. See, for example, *Leg.* 677a, a passage that closely resembles the Egyptian priest's comment about how the Athenians have forgotten their own ancient history (*Ti.* 24d–e).

CHAPTER 24

1. For Schliemann's own (self-serving and at least partially fabricated) account, see Heinrich Schliemann, *Troy and Its Remains* (London: J. Murray, 1875), 323–40. "Priam's Treasure" as it was later displayed almost certainly combined finds from several hoards scattered around the site.
2. Missing Helen: Hdt. 2.112–18. No Helen: Thuc. 1.9–11. Strabo argued at length that Troy had actually been located near, but not at, Ilion (13.1.24–27).
3. Xerxes: Hdt. 7.43. Alexander: Arr., *Anab.* 1.11–12. Caesar: Suet., *Caes.* 79.3. Caracalla: Hdn. 4.8.4–5. Roman visitor: Boston MFA Acc. No. 63.2644. Julian's tour: Julian, *Ep.* 19.
4. Unsettling grin: Heinrich Schliemann, *Mycenae: A Narrative of Researches and Discoveries at Mycenae and Tiryns* (New York: Scribner, 1880), 297 (fig. 454).
5. For the definitive statement of Parry's ideas, see Albert Lord, *The Singer of Tales* (Cambridge, MA: Harvard University Press, 1960).
6. There is only one reference to writing in the *Iliad* (6.168–70).
7. The letters referred to are, respectively, the Manapa-Tarhunta Letter (*CTH* 191) and the so-called Tawagalawa Letter (*CTH* 181).

8. A few of the *Iliad*'s echoes of the Bronze Age are particularly famous: the tower shield of Ajax (7.219–23), the boar's tusk helmet of Odysseus (10.261–65), and Nestor's Cup (11.632f).

CHAPTER 25

1. Agis, Cleomenes, Agesilaus: Plut., *Mor.* 215D, 224B, 210E. Shade: ibid. 225B (cf. Hdt. 7.226). Come and take them: ibid. 225D.

2. Sparta's outsized influence: e.g., Xen., *Lac.* 1.1; cf. Thuc. 1.10. Spartan stability: e.g., Thuc. 1.18.1. Government as expression of citizen qualities: e.g., Xen., *Lac.* 8; Arist., *Pol.* 1337a.

3. Ancient descriptions of the so-called *Agoge* may be found in Xen., *Lac.* 2–3 and Plut., *Lyc.* 16–18. Exercise at Thermopylae: Hdt. 7.208.

4. Dance: e.g., Ar., *Lys.* 81–82. Spartan wedding: Plut., *Lyc.* 15. Polyandry: Xen., *Lac.* 1.8–9.

5. Forcing helots to drink: Plut., *Lyc.* 28.8–9. Krypteia: Plut., *Lyc.* 28.1–4. Executed in cold blood: Thuc. 4.80. Declaration of war: Plut., *Lyc.* 28.4.

6. Pig blood soup: Plut., *Lyc.* 12.7. Spartan luxury: e.g., Arist., *Pol.* 1269b. Combing hair at Thermopylae: Hdt. 7.208. Signet ring for a comb: Plut., *Artax.* 18. Chariot racing: e.g., Paus. 6.1.7–2.1.

7. Early defeats: e.g., Hdt. 1.66–67. Surrender: Thuc. 4.38. Spartans unable to replace losses: e.g., Arist., *Pol.* 1270a.

8. Contrast with Athens: e.g., Thuc. 2.37–39.

9. Festival: *IG* V.1.18–19. Contingents of soldiers: *IG* V.1.116, 816, 818. Endurance contest: Plut., *Lyc.* 18.

CHAPTER 26

1. Caligula's bridge: Suet., *Calig.* 19; Cass. Dio 59.17; Joseph. *AJ* 19.5–6.

2. I can do what I want: Suet., *Calig.* 29.1. Senators: ibid. 26.2. Living god: ibid. 22.2. Caligula's extravagance: e.g., ibid. 37.1–2.

3. Prisoners to the beasts: Suet., *Calig.* 27.1. Executions: ibid. 27.4. Tiny cuts: ibid. 30.1. Chest of poison: ibid. 49.3; cf. Orosius 7.5.10–11.

4. Caligula's outfits: ibid. 52.1. Moon goddess: ibid. 22.4. Caligula's dance: ibid. 54.2.

5. Fever: Philo, *Leg.* 14–22. Love potion: Joseph., *AJ* 19.193. Character flaws: Cass. Dio 59.3–4.

6. Drusilla: Suet., *Calig.* 24.1–2; Joseph., *AJ* 19.204; Cass. Dio 59.3.6. Incitatus: Suet., *Calig.* 55.2–3; Cass. Dio 59.14.7.

7. Suet., *Calig.* 46; Cass. Dio 59.25; Aur. Vict., *Caes.* 3.11–12.

8. Suet., *Calig.* 19; Cass. Dio 59.17; Joseph., *AJ* 19.5–6.

CHAPTER 27

1. Spartacus: Frontin., *Str.* 1.5.21; cf. Plut., *Crass.* 9, Vell. Pat. 2.30.5. Forest gone: Strabo 5.4.8. Similarities to Etna: Diod. Sic. 4.21.5; Vitr. 2.6.2; Strabo 5.4.8. Typhoeus: e.g., Pind., *Pyth.* 1.16–28. Vulcan: e.g., Thuc. 3.88. Subterranean winds: Lucr. 6.662–69; Sen., *Ep.* 79.2–7; Plin., *HN* 2.236–38.

2. Plin., *Ep.* 6.16, 6.20.

CHAPTER 28

1. Seducing the king's wife: Plut., *Lys.* 22.3–4. Seven chariots: Thuc. 6.16.2.

2. On the affair of the herms, see Thuc. 6.27–30; Andoc., *Or.* 1.

3. Profaning the Eleusinian Mysteries: Thuc. 6.53, 61. Clodius: e.g., Plut., *Caes.* 9–10.

4. Claudius: Tac., *Ann.* 12.5–7; Suet., *Claud.* 26, 39.

5. Death of Alexander: Arr., *Anab.* 7.25–26; Plut., *Alex.* 76. Alternative tradition: e.g., Diod. Sic. 17.117.

6. The death of Callisthenes: e.g., Arr., *Anab.* 4.14. Aristotle: Plut., *Alex.* 77.3; Arr., *Anab.* 7.27. Styx water: Plut., *Alex.* 77.4; on the properties of the water, see Plin., *HN* 30.53.

7. Olympias: Plut., *Alex.* 77.2. Onesicritus, a historian who had accompanied Alexander on campaign, may have openly alleged that the king was poisoned (*FGrH* 134 F 37). Cassander and Olympias: e.g., Diod. Sic. 17.118. Hyperides: [Plut.], *Mor.* 849C, F.

8. Roman skepticism about new religions: e.g., Cass. Dio 52.36. Cult of Bacchus: Livy 39.8–19; *SC de Bacchanalibus*. Diocletian's edict: *Mosaicarum et romanarum legum collatio*, 15.3.4–7 (trans. M. Hyamson).

CHAPTER 29

1. Julian., *Caes.* 308Dff. Marcus Aurelius as philosopher-king: SHA, *Marc.* 27.6–7. Soul of Augustus: Julian, *Caes.* 309A–C.

2. Cicero on Socrates: *Tusc.* 5.10–11.

3. There were differences, of course; Aristotle, for example, rejected the Platonic theory of ideas, and thus saw no connection between practical ethics and the study of such "higher" sciences as mathematics. Yet the treatment of ethics in Plato's *Laws*—his most obviously "practical" work—has important commonalities with the discussions in Aristotle's ethical treatises.

4. Proconsul: Cic., *Leg.* 1.53.

5. Sulla and Aristotle: Strabo 13.1.4; Plut., *Sull.* 26.

6. Never listened to a philosopher: Petr. 71.

7. Harangued audiences: Luc., *Fug.* 16. Immolated themselves: Luc., *De mort. Peregr.* Horace: Sat. 2.7.83f. Joke book: *Philogelos.* Epitaphs: e.g., *CIL* VI 11252.12–13.

CHAPTER 30

1. Julius Valens: *RIB* 363 (my thanks to Gareth Harney for showing me this inscription). Compare Tiberius Julius Xanthus—a naval officer who reached the age of ninety (*ILS* 2816)—and Lucius Tonneius Martialis, a legionary scribe who died at ninety-three (*ILS* 2426).

2. Standard-bearer: *ILS* 2338.

3. Teutoburg Forest: e.g., *ILS* 2244. Legio XII Fulminata: Joseph., *BJ* 2.555. Raiders: *RIB* 3218.

4. Hypothermia: Tac., *Ann.* 13.35. Malaria: Tac., *Hist.* 2.93. Strength report: *PLondon* 2851.

5. Get Me Another: Tac., *Ann.* 1.23. Hands hacked off: SHA, *Avid. Cass.* 4.4–6. Octavian's decimation: App., *Ill.* 26.

6. Strength report: *Tab. Vindol.* 154. Egyptian legionary: *PMich.* 478.

7. Discharge bonus: Cass. Dio 55.23, 78.36. Land less than ideal: Tac., *Ann.* 1.17. Here lies Similis: Cass. Dio 69.19.

8. Yann Le Bohec, "Peut-on computer le mort des soldats de la IIIe Legion Auguste," *Colloque de Caen* 1987, 53–64.

9. Walter Scheidel, "Marriage, Families, and Survival: Demographic Aspects," in *A Companion to the Roman Army*, ed. Paul Erdkamp (Malden, MA: Blackwell, 2007), 426–27.

CHAPTER 31

1. Death of Augustus: Suet., *Aug.* 99; cf. Cass. Dio 56.30. Death of Constantine XI: Phrantzes, *Chron. Maius* 280–87, 290–1.

2. I've only counted emperors who were either recognized by the Senate (as long as that body had any authority) or were regarded as legitimate sovereign by the aristocracy of the capital. I have not included usurpers, the sovereigns of the splinter empires that formed after the sack of Constantinople in 1204, or imperial heirs who never reigned independently.

3. Theodosius II: Theodore Lector 2.64. Papyrus: *P. Leid.* II.Z. Basil I: e.g., *V. Euthymii* 1. Valentinian I: Amm. Marc. 30.6.3; Zos. 4.17.2. Jovian: Amm. Marc. 25.10.13. Antoninus Pius: SHA, *Ant. Pius* 12. Claudius Gothicus: SHA, *Claud.* 12. Justinian: Procop., *Goth.* 2.23.20.

4. Carinus: Aur. Vict., *Caes.* 39.11. Caligula: Joseph., *AJ* 19.1.14. Caracalla: Herodian 4.13.4–5. Marius: SHA, *Tyr. Trig.* 8. Michael III: Theophanes Cont. 130–31. Andronicus I: Niketas Choniates, *Chron.* 348–51.

5. Justinian II: Theophanes 369; Agnellus, *Lib.* 367. Irene: Theophanes 472. Other blinded emperors: Michael V (Psellus, *Chron.* 5.48–50) and Romanus IV (Attaleiates, *Hist.* 178). Claudius: Suet., *Claud.* 44.2–3. Claudius's son: Suet., *Ner.* 33.2–3; Cass. Dio 61.7. Commodus: Hdn. 1.17.8–11.

6. Commodus: Cass. Dio 73.22. Fausta: Zos. 2.29.2. Constans II: Theophanes 351. Romanus III: Skylitzes 390–1; Psellus, *Chron.* 3.26.

7. John: Skylitzes 280. Numerian: SHA, *Car.* 12. Stoned emperor: Prosper, *Epit. Chron.* 753–54; Jord., *Get.* 235. Column: Robert de Clari, *La Conquête de Constantinople* 103–4. Heraclius: Nicephorus, *Op. Hist.* 4.25–27; cf. Diocletian's execution of Aper (Aur. Vict., *Caes.* 39; Eutr. 9.20).

8. Gordian III: Eutr. 9.2.3; SHA, *Gord. Tres* 30. Decius: Aur. Vict., *Caes.* 29.5; Jord., *Get.* 18. Maxentius: Zos. 2.16.4. Julian: Amm. Marc. 25.3. Valens: Amm. Marc. 31.13.12–16. Nicephorus: Theophanes 490–1.

9. Nero: Suet., *Ner.* 48–49. Otho: Suet., *Otho* 11; Tac., *Hist.* 2.47–49. Valentinian II: Philostorgius 9.1. Carus: e.g., SHA, *Car.* 8. Valerian: e.g., Lactant., *De mort. pers.* 5.

10. Diocletian: Aur. Vict., *Caes.* 39.6. Justin II: Joh. Eph., *VE* 3.2–3. Isaac I: Skyzlitzes Cont. 109.

CHAPTER 32

1. Ammianus: 14.6. Jerome: *Comm. in Ezech* I, Pref. Episodes from the sack: Jerome, *Ep.* 127.12; Orosius 7.39–41; Soz. 9.8.9.

2. Events of 476: Anon. Val. 37–38; Procop., *Goth.* 1.1.1–8; Jord., *Get.* 242–43. Edward Gibbon, *The History of the Decline and Fall of the Roman Empire*, ed. J. B. Bury (N.p., 1909), 4:56.

3. British monk: Gildas, *De exc. Brit.* 24. Saxons: *V. Germ.* 17–18.

4. Priscus 8.

5. Ambushed by barbarians: Eugippius, *V. Severin.*, 20. Freeing Romans: ibid. 19. Raiders: ibid. 24, 27. Evacuation: ibid. 44.

6. Sidonius despaired: Sid. Apoll., *Epist.* 7.7.5. A priest from Marseilles: Salv., *Gub. Dei* 6.18. Making Romans: Sid. Apoll., *Epist.* 3.3.3. Burgundian eloquence: ibid. 5.5.3.

7. On the modus vivendi under Theodoric, see e.g., *Anon. Val.* 57–72; Cassiod., *Var.* 3.3–4.

8. *Consol.* 2.6.17–18.

CHAPTER 33

1. The estimate for the number of bronze statues in Rome comes from the Regionaries. Marble statues: Cassiod., *Var.* 7.15.

2. Parthenon Athena: according to Philochorus (*FHG* 328, F 121), the amount of gold used was 44 talents.

3. Serapis: Ruf., *HE* 11.23. Memphis: Zach. Rhet., *V. Sev.* (*PO* II, 27f). Gaza: Mar. Diac., *V. Porph.* 64–71. Artemis: *IvE* 1351.

CHAPTER 34

1. Hills of Rome higher: Frontin., *Aq.* 18.

CHAPTER 35

1. Melchior de Vogüé, *Syrie Centrale: Architecture civile et religieuse du Ier au VIIe siècle* (1865), 52–53.

2. Bridge inscription: *CIL* II 761.9–10.

CHAPTER 36

1. Giants: Plin., *HN* 7.74–75. Tusks: Paus. 8.46. Centaur: Plin., *HN* 7.35; Phlegon (*FGrH* F36). Chests of gems: Cass. Dio 78.6. Gauls: Quint., *Inst.* 6.3.79. Pythagoras: Philostr., *VA* 8.20. Couch covers: Plin., *HN* 8.196. Nero's Amazon: Plin., *HN* 34.82.

2. Marcus's auction: SHA, *Marc.* 17.4–5.

3. I'd like to thank Gareth Harney for bringing the story of this artifact to my attention.

CHAPTER 37

1. Rings: Mart. 11.59; Juv. 1.28. Gilded walls: Ludwig Friedländer, *Roman Life and Manners under the Early Empire* (New York: Routledge, 1913), 2:134. Fish: e.g., Ael., *NA* VIII.4.

2. Three hundred tons: Gary Reger, "Hellenistic Greece and Western Asia Minor," in *The Cambridge Economic History of the Greco-Roman World*, ed. Walter Scheidel, Ian Morris, and Richard P. Saller (Cambridge: Cambridge University Press, 2007), 471.

3. Pliny the Elder: *HN* 12.84.

4. I'd like to thank Dr. George Green for his estimate (hedged about with all due caution) of 350–550 tons for the total gold mine production of the imperial Roman world. Four hundred tons: Richard Duncan-Jones, *Money and Government in the Roman Empire* (Cambridge: Cambridge University Press, 1994), 168.

CHAPTER 38

1. *Scriptores originum Constantinopolitanarum* (ed. Preger) I, 17, 56–57; II, 177–78; Zonaras 13.3.

2. Statues of Constantinople: *Scriptores orig. Const.* I, 20f. Latin rare by the late sixth century: Greg., *Ep.* 7.27.

3. Anna Comnena: *Alex.*, pref. 1–2. Appian: Photius, *Bibl.* 57.

4. Pergamum: *Theodori Ducae Lascaris Epistulae CCXVII* (ed. Festa), Ep. 32. Manuel II: *Letters of Manuel II* (ed. Dennis), no. 16.22–32.

CHAPTER 39

1. Two hundred thousand: Joseph., *AJ* 12.2.1. Four hundred thousand: Orosius 6.15.31f. 532,800: Joh. Tzetzes, *Proleg. Comm.* 20. Seven hundred thousand: Gell., *NA* 7.17.3; Amm. Marc. 22.16.12. Most modern scholars believe that these numbers are exaggerated by an order of magnitude.

2. Authors copying their own work: Plin., *Ep.* 4.7.

3. Como: Plin., *Ep.* 1.8.2. Gellius: *NA* 19.5.5. Marcus Aurelius: Fronto, *Ep.* 4.5.2. Sixty thousand books: SHA, *Gord. Tres* 18.2.

4. Birdcage of the Muses: Ath. 1.22D. Ships surrendering books: Gal., *Hipp. Epid.* III 17.1 (601 K).

5. Small part of the collection destroyed: Sen., *Tranq.* 9.5; Cass. Dio 42.38.2; Orosius 6.15.31–32. Entire library destroyed: Plut., *Caes.* 49.6; Gell., *NA* 7.17.3; Amm. Marc. 22.16.13. Two hundred thousand books: Plut., *Ant.* 58.5.

6. Domitian: Suet., *Dom.* 20. Museion funded by Rome: Strabo 17.1.8. Feeding scholars: Philostr., *VS* 524. Claudius: Suet., *Claud.* 42.2. Destruction of the Serapeum: Ruf., *HE* 11.22–30.

7. Encyclopedia: Plin., *HN* Praef. 17. Didymus: Quint., *Inst.* 1.8.20; Sen., *Ep.* 10.88.37. On the difficulty of finding noncanonical texts in antiquity, see Gell., *NA* 16.8.2, 19.14.2. Nero's courtiers: Cass. Dio 62.29. Pliny: *HN* 26.83. Sex manual: some fragments have been discovered, but nothing explicit. Cf. Suet., *Tib.* 43.

8. Snakeskin Homer: Zonaras 14.2. Nutshell Iliad: Plin., *HN* 7.85. Codex used for literature: Mart. 1.2. Transfer from scroll to codex: Jerome, *De viris illustr.* 113.

CHAPTER 40

1. Autograph copy of rhetorical work: Luc., *Pseudol.* 30. Faked antique books: Dio Chrys., *Or.* 21.12; Gell., *NA* 5.4.

2. Funeral: *P. Teb.* 332. Beaten: *P. Teb.* 331. Ex-wife: *POxy.* 282, 315, 324. Bricked-up window: *POxy.* 69.

3. The twenty-five-thousand-word Epicurean inscription set up by Diogenes of Oenoanda is preserved only in fragments, which are still being recovered and edited. 110-line epitaph: *CIL* VIII 212–13.

Index